The Best War Ever

The American Moment

Stanley I. Kutler

SERIES EDITOR

The Best War Ever

America and World War II

Michael C. C. Adams

The Johns Hopkins University Press

Baltimore and London

6 8 9 7

The Johns Hopkins University Press
2715 North Charles Street
Baltimore, Maryland 21218-4363
www.press.jhu.edu

Library of Congress Cataloging-in-Publication Data
Adams, Michael C. C., 1945–
The best war ever : America and World War II / Michael C.C. Adams.
p.   cm. — (The American moment)
Includes bibliographical references (p.) and index.
ISBN 0-8018-4696-X (hard : acid-free paper). — ISBN 0-8018-4697-8
(pbk. : acid-free paper)
1. World War, 1939–1945—United States.   2. United States—History—1933–1945.
I. Title.   II. Series.
D769.A56   1994
940.53'73—dc20   93-4364

A catalog record for this book is available
from the British Library.

IN MEMORY OF

Charles Corringham Adams

British Royal Air Force

Fighter Command

WHO WAS KILLED

IN WORLD WAR II

Contents

	List of Illustrations and Maps	ix
	Editor's Foreword	xi
	Preface	xiii
	Acknowledgments	xvii
one	Mythmaking and the War	1
two	No Easy Answers	20
three	The Patterns of War, 1939–1945	43
four	The American War Machine	69
five	Overseas	91
six	Home Front Change	114
seven	A New World	136
	Afterword	156
	Bibliographical Essay	161
	Index	185

Illustrations and Maps

Illustrations

1. "Giving 'Em Hell from a 'Goldfish Bowl'"   18
2. The Abbey of Monte Cassino   52
3. The anguish of combat   99
4. A jeep squashes the torso of a dead enemy   106
5. FDR, George Bush, and B-17 bombers   116
6. The police arresting Hispanics during the zoot suit riots,
   June 1943   121
7. "Mother, when will you stay home again?"   133

Maps

1. Mediterranean Operations   50
2. The Cross-Channel Invasion   56
3. The Pacific War   59

Editor's Foreword

FOR GENERATIONS of Americans, World War II is the reference point that transformed and defined the rest of their lives. It *was* the "Good War"—"The Best War Ever," as Michael C. C. Adams has described it—fought against incalculable German evil and boundless Japanese military aggression. The enemies were very real and presented immediate threats to American values and security. The antiwar, almost isolationist, attitudes that spread across American society during and after the Vietnam War—especially in the liberal community—contrast sharply with the notion that the United States rightly and nobly committed its people and resources between 1941 and 1945.

We did not seek the war, so we believed; instead, we responded to the duty and challenge of a great power. We fought the war to preserve democracy; yet, we also envisioned a larger responsibility for protecting humanity. The end of the war decisively fulfilled the war's aims. German fascism and Japanese militarism were utterly crushed and discredited, and after the war American beneficence lifted those nations from the ashes of defeat, reshaped them in our image of democracy, contributed to their prosperity, and encouraged them to resume roles of world responsibility.

Meanwhile, at home, the war galvanized American patriotism and unity. Twelve million Americans served in the military; on the home front, the war propelled the nation out of the morass of the Great Depression and kindled a wave of prosperity. Americans moved south and west, pursuing the new jobs fueled by the war; women and blacks found employment opportunities; and birth rates accelerated. America, in short, prospered at home as it rose to the status of the world's greatest power.

And yet, the war had other dimensions, less celebratory, darker, and more sordid. Adams provocatively challenges the oversimplified and overglamorized prevailing image of the war. Combat laid a heavy toll on soldiers, both physical and psychological. Yet unlike the "living room war" in Vietnam, Americans hardly realized the carnage and brutality of the war, which censorship or celebratory Hollywood epics largely obscured. However noble the war's purposes, atrocities and cruelties on all sides were not very ennobling. At home, racial and ethnic prejudice pervaded the society, just as it had before the war. War inevitably causes social dislocations; the rising incidence of juvenile delinquency and divorce in the early 1940s are two apparent indicators. The war can still be memorialized as the nation's "Great Crusade," as General Dwight Eisenhower called it, one that destroyed menacing, evil regimes. Yet to know the war in all its dimensions is to better understand what we were and are as a society, both in the war and since.

STANLEY I. KUTLER
THE UNIVERSITY OF WISCONSIN

Preface

I T IS GENERALLY agreed that World War II was a necessary war. International aggression in Europe and Asia, carried out by nations claiming to be have-nots and trying to get what they thought they needed through conquest, brought untold misery to their victims and instability to the entire world. In Europe, Nazi aggression came to include a deliberate policy of genocide against those declared unfit to live under the Third Reich. This aggression had to be stopped. The Allied victory, demonstrating that systems based on parliamentary democracy and free enterprise, could win a struggle with authoritarianism and militarism, which were then deemed more efficient in organizing society for the pursuit of national goals, was an untold blessing for the future of humankind.

Over time, in the United States, this necessary war has been transformed into a good war, the Good War, the best war the country ever had. That this belief should have grown is understandable: America had suffered deeply in the Great Depression of the 1930s, and some people even began to despair of the ability of capitalism and democracy to solve such overriding economic problems. But then in World War II, the United States fought around the globe, contributed enormously to the Allied victory, and far from being depleted by this effort, emerged at war's end as the leader of the free world and the richest nation in human history. America shared this wealth generously with friend and former enemy alike, contributing immensely to their recovery. There was much for America to be proud of.

Since then, as America's economic predominance has been challenged and as problems at home and abroad have become less tractable, the war years have come to seem a golden age, an idyllic period when everything was simpler and a can-do generation of Americans solved the world's problems. In this mythic time of the Good War, everyone was united: there were no racial or gender tensions, no class conflicts. Things worked better, from kitchen gadgets to public schools. Families were well adjusted; kids read a lot and respected their elders; parents didn't divorce.

But the reality of combat in World War II has been mythologized.

Preface

Although we know that many Vietnam War veterans suffer post-traumatic stress disorder, it is commonly believed that nearly all World War II veterans adjusted quickly and easily. After all, they fought the Good War. Vietnam was the bad war, in which American troops, caught in an ugly situation, committed acts that later disturbed them.

In fact, combat in World War II was a horrible experience and left lasting physical and mental scars on many combatants. Because this fact does not fit the legend of the Good War, and because some scholars believe that combat is terrible only in a bad war, it was felt necessary to cite in text the sources for the descriptions of battle included in this book, descriptions by such WWII veterans as Norman Mailer, James Jones, and Paul Fussell. Other stereotypes, such as that all German officers were heel-clicking martinets and American generals were all rough and ready democratic improvisers, also die hard.

A powerful myth, when it reaches the proportions of an undisputed reality, can be destructive. By setting up a golden age when everything was better, we inevitably undercut our own efforts because we know that we do not live in perfect times and that not all our solutions work. By definition, we become lesser people than our ancestors. Thus a false sense of the past compromises the hope that we might entertain for the present and the future.

The goal of this book is to subject the major aspects of the Good War myth to fresh analysis in the hope of presenting a more realistic picture, one that does not demean the achievement of the United States and of liberal democracy but that at the same time does not diminish the stress, suffering, problems, and failures inevitably faced by a society at war. The nature of the task has dictated the scope of the work. This is not a chronological narrative, and some aspects of the war experience, those most subject to mythmaking, get more exposure than others. In addition, I discuss at length some facets of the wartime experience that usually receive little coverage. One example is the development of the teen culture, with its pervasive antiintellectualism and pursuit of pleasure, a phenomenon of American life that critics usually assume appeared at a much later date.

This book does not claim to be a definitive study of the war. I doubt that any work could claim that distinction, because our knowledge and our sense of what is relevant or appropriate to study is constantly changing. Today, it is even proper to include the treatment of homosexuals in a chapter on armed forces recruitment.

What I hope to do is provoke the reader to have fresh thoughts and new questions about the experience of World War II, about the nature of war in general, and about this particular period in history. Most of all, I want to convey the idea that we do both past and present a disservice when we simplify into mythology the complex patterns of human experience.

Acknowledgments

I AM GRATEFUL to Stanley I. Kutler, editor of the American Moment Series, who asked me to write this volume. His encouragement and constructive criticism were invaluable. I am also indebted to Henry Y. K. Tom, executive editor of the Johns Hopkins University Press, for his firm support of the project. Darryl G. Poole, former dean of arts and sciences at Northern Kentucky University, helped through grants of reassigned time from teaching. The Faculty Senate and the former provost of the university, David L. Jorns, made writing the book manageable by awarding me a sabbatical leave for the fall 1991 semester.

Elizabeth Merten, NKU media specialist in graphics, drew the three fine maps and supervised preparation of the illustrations. The interlibrary loan staff of the W. Frank Steely Library showed their customary efficiency in locating difficult-to-obtain literature. Marcus Cunliffe, my graduate school mentor, died before I could consult him about my concept of the work, but his style and approach continue to be an inspiration.

Richard Polenberg read the manuscript and made valuable suggestions for improvement. And my wife and colleague, Susan S. Kissel, advised me to write the book, encouraged me throughout the creative process, and read and commented upon the manuscript at each stage of development.

one

Mythmaking and
the War

ALL SOCIETIES to some degree reinvent their pasts. This is not intended, not a pattern of deliberate lying; but too much has happened for it all to be retained in popular memory. Therefore, to make our understanding of history manageable, we try to retrieve from the huge clutter of the past only those events that seem to be particularly useful, interesting, or exciting. Usable historical events appear to offer helpful insights into how people of the past confronted problems or situations similar to our own.

Examples of functional and engaging past happenings are dramatic disasters, such as the sinking of the Titanic, which serve as warnings, or great triumphs, such as World War II. We tend to dwell on the victories because they make us feel good about ourselves. We see them as events that showcase our national strength, collective courage, idealism, and other desirable traits.

Sometimes we conjure up the past in such a way that it appears better than it really was. We forget ugly things we did and magnify the good things. This is wishful thinking, the desire to retell our past not as it was but as we would like it to have been. If the past is remolded too drastically, it ceases to be real history. It becomes what we call myth, or folklore, instead. One task of the historian is to try to keep our knowledge of the past as complete and accurate as possible so that our popular version does not depart too far from reality. If history becomes too mythologized, it may lose its value as a tool for understanding our course as a society. Adolf Hitler presented a deeply distorted view of Germany's history and role in the twentieth century. When this was accepted by his people, they embarked on a course leading to national disaster.

The influence of historians is, however, limited. Because they must be comprehensive in their treatment of the past and cannot simply choose to highlight the exciting and dramatic, their work often strikes people as boring and tedious. It cannot compete with modern vehicles of folklore history: film and television. In addition, historians, too, are victims of the immenseness of the past: they can never read, digest, and describe all there is to know about an event or character (there are one million documents in the Lyndon Baines Johnson Library alone). They must be highly selective in what they choose to present to us, so their picture is incomplete, a distortion to some degree. And as they are creatures of their time and place, members of the society as well as professional observers of it, their retelling of history will be molded partly by the same biases and constraints that shape the popular view. Then, through repetition, people come to believe that this partial portrait is the whole landscape of history, and what is forgotten will be thought never to have existed.

Such a process happened with World War II, which has been converted over time from a complex, problematic event, full of nuance and debatable meaning, to a simple, shining legend of the Good War. For many, including a majority of survivors from the era, the war years have become America's golden age, a peak in the life of society when everything worked out and the good guys definitely got a happy ending. It was a great war. For Americans it was the best war ever.

This was the film age, and the script could have been written in Hollywood. The original villains were the Nazis and the Fascists, many of whom obligingly dressed in black. They bullied the weak-willed democratic politicians who tried to buy them off, which gave us the word *appeasement* as a catchall term of contempt for anyone who suggests a diplomatic solution to potential international aggression. The bad guys then took the first rounds, driving opponent after opponent out of the fighting. The Americans gave material aid to their cousins, the British, who finally fought pluckily with their backs to the wall, until the United States was brought into the fighting by the treacherous Japanese, who crippled the Pacific fleet at Pearl Harbor.

For a while, it looked grim all over, but then the Allies fought back, their victories culminating in the unconditional surrender of all enemy nations, who were then made over in our image. America emerged from the war strong, united, prosperous, and the unrivaled and admired leader of the free world.

In the search for a usable past, Americans increasingly return to this best war ever. Its image, as a time of glorious success, sparkles in the imagination. "Recapture the glory" urges the Franklin Mint: "Bring the full power and glory of the American spirit into your home" by buying a bronze miniature of the Iwo Jima memorial. There is a fetish for memorabilia of the period. The October 1988 issue of the journal *Military History* carried twelve separate advertisements for WWII films, uniforms and decorations, weapons, and books. Clothing catalogs like the *Cockpit* are devoted to reproductions of WWII gear. As American economic power, world prestige, and self-confidence have waned in the last decades, the Good War as a time when everything worked well has become hallowed, almost above criticism. Thus the *Time-Life* pictorial history of the war devoted a full page to "A tank that could swim, "the dual-drive fighting vehicles that were supposed to motor ashore atop the waves during the 1944 Normandy landings. We are not told that twenty-seven tanks, upon being lowered consecutively into the water, sank with their crews, and that nobody in authority thought to stop the horror.

As the world has become more complex, the solutions less certain, and the villains less obvious, the war era has taken on the aspect of a simpler time when issues were clear and everyone knew where they stood. President Lyndon B. Johnson talked nostalgically of this earlier age, when people didn't wake up with Vietnam or have the problems of Santo Domingo with lunch and those of the Congo with dinner. Part of the popular appeal of George Bush, a WWII veteran, according to *Newsweek* (April 15, 1991), was that he had "a sense of moral certainty" peculiar to his generation and, by implication, lacking among later Americans.

Newsweek cast another regretful glance at this supposedly more positive time during the week of March 19, 1990, when it discussed the shrinking of America's military commitment to NATO (North Atlantic Treaty Organization). More was at stake here than a mere cutback, said the article: "As America pulls back from the European theater it entered on D-Day, it will mean loosening ties with the last battlefield where U.S. military might was a symbol of unalloyed good, free of the moral and political ambiguities of Vietnam, Grenada, Lebanon or Panama."

Unlike some soldiers in later conflicts, particularly Vietnam, who were anguished and bewildered, WWII soldiers are seen as determined, sure of their cause, and united. A review (in the *Northerner*, a weekly campus newspaper, November 28, 1990) of the 1990 film *Memphis Belle*, a remake of *The Memphis Belle of 1943*, said that it was full of "true heroism, and good, old-fashioned patriotism." Matthew Modine, star of the new film, said that the willingness of the airmen to step up and be counted was "a kind of value that doesn't exist today. Today there's a lot of shirking of responsibility" (*Cincinnati Enquirer*, October 14, 1990). On a similar note, Tim McEnroe, an editorial writer for the same paper, said that so little social responsibility currently exists in the country "that we couldn't fight and win something as important as World War II today" (December 27, 1987).

The era has become a benchmark of excellence, not only in things military but in all areas of life. We think that products were made better and lasted longer. Kids were supposedly better behaved and learned more. Listening to some contemporary critics of education, one is led to believe that college students of the thirties and forties walked daily with Plato and Thomas Jefferson. And families loved each other more; in a recent biography of President Bush, Joe Hyams asserted that "Bush's generation seems to have had more respect for their marriage vows than young people today" (169). Bush was a naval pilot, and Hyams would also have us believe that all the airmen on his carrier were happy warriors who, despite having flown over fifty missions, "were always vying with one another to see who could get in the most" (5).

In creating a usable past, we seek formulas to apply in solving today's problems. Americans believe that World War II proved one rule above all others. It goes like this. By 1938 at the latest it was clear that Hitler was a bully bent on world domination. Britain and France should have stood up to him at the Munich conference (September 1938), when he demanded parts of Czechoslovakia as the price for peace. By their failure, World War II was made bloodier than it might have been. Conclusion: it is usually better to fight than to talk.

The political commentator Andy Rooney said that perhaps Hitler's worst crime was to convince Americans that international opponents are invariably bullies who must be met with military force. Admiral Gene LaRocque, like Rooney a veteran and a dissenter from the mainstream, said that "World War Two has warped our view of how we look at things today. We see things in terms of that war, which in a sense was a good war. But the twisted memory of it encourages the men of my generation to be willing, almost eager, to use military force anywhere in the world" (Terkel, 189).

Undoubtedly, the memory of Munich was partly responsible for the decision to use force rather than continued sanctions in the Persian Gulf crisis of 1990–91. President Bush took along a history of World War II as his reading material on Air Force One. He compared Saddam Hussein to Hitler, the Iraqi occupation of Kuwait to a German SS operation, and the UN alliance to a new world order, a phrase popular with both sides in World War II. Newspapers and readers' columns were full of warnings about appeasement. A typical comment from a member of the WWII generation, Victor H. Laws of Salisbury, Maryland, ran: "My generation learned the hard way—a bitter lesson: appeasement quickly leads to disaster because aggression feeds on appeasement" (*Newsweek*, November 19, 1990). An October 4, 1990, editorial by Mike McMurray in *East Side*, a midwestern local newspaper, said: "In 1939 [*sic*], Britain's appeasement to [sic] Hitler didn't work! Appeasement has never worked with a dictator. Appeasement will get us all killed."

In 1990–91 we came close to believing that we could wish upon a war: if we applied the magic formula of an allied war effort against an aggressive dictator, we could again have national unanimity of purpose, renewed world prestige, and a return of the leaping prosperity that was a hallmark of American life during the best war ever. Some people wanted to turn the clock back badly enough to believe the *World*'s claim that a very old Hitler (he would have been 111 years of age in 1990) had been captured by U.S. forces on his way to Iraq. *TV Guide*'s Lisa Stein thought General Norman Schwarzkopf, allied commander in the Gulf, was America's most visible hero since Dwight D. Eisenhower commanded Allied forces in Europe during World War II. Bob McKeown, who covered the Gulf for CBS News, said "He was John Wayne taking on the Iraqis." Wayne, of course, was the film star who came to be most associated with WWII hero roles. It was even said that Schwarzkopf's press briefings had the resonance of British Prime Minister Winston Churchill's pugnacious WWII speeches.

Early 1991 could be an exciting time if you believed deeply in the mythic view of World War II. An enthusiastic prowar student on the Kent State University Campus in Ohio, one of 60 percent of students polled there (during the first week of February 1991) who favored war, said in the student newspaper, "I feel like my generation is turning back to the World War II idea that it's honorable to fight for your country." The Gulf War was won in a remarkably one-sided victory, but not everything that had been expected followed. The much-looked-for prosperity did not occur: the prevailing economic recession only deepened. After an initial burst of flag-waving, political, social, and ethnic divisions quickly reappeared. Pursuit of a new world order proved elusive, as the United Nations balked at active military involvements in the civil wars of Yugoslavia and Somalia. The problem is that we may learn from the past but we cannot live in it. History cannot be repeated, particularly when our version of it is heavily mythical.

The idea that World War II was the best war America had is not entirely off the mark; like any enduring myth, it rests on a solid core of credible argument. America cemented its final rise to world power with relatively light losses: about 300,000 Americans died; a further 1 million were wounded, of whom 500,000 were seriously disabled. Tragic as these figures are, they are dwarfed by those for other belligerents. The Japanese lost 2.3 million, Germany about 5.6 million, China perhaps as many as 10 million, and the Soviet Union a staggering 20 million. Put another way, the death rate in the American Civil War of 1861–65 was 182 per ten thousand population. For World War II, the proportion of Americans killed was 30 per ten thousand.

Of the major belligerents, the United States was alone in enjoying a higher standard of living as a result of the war. Following the lean Depression years, the gross national product for 1940 was $97 billion. By 1944 it had reached $190 billion. The average gross weekly wage rose from $25.20 in 1940 to $43.39 in 1945, an increase of 72 percent. The United States was unique among the principal combatants in being neither invaded nor bombed, and most people, in or out of uniform, never saw a fighting front. As a result, the war was for many a prosperous, exciting, even safe change from the "ruined and colorless landscape of the Depression," as Russell Baker, a writer who grew up in the 1930s, termed the decade. "It was," he remembered, "a season of bread lines, soup kitchens, hobo jungles, bandits riding the highways." The Depression had been a lonely time; people struggled in isolation for survival, and some committed suicide. There was, said Baker, a felt loss of love and security (Baker, 30, 105, 115). World War II for a time gave Americans a sense of belonging, of community, as they were caught up in the war fever.

Most of us still agree that nazism was an evil so monstrous that the war in Europe had to be fought. "Unlike Vietnam—the war that dominated our children's lives," said 1940s veteran Roger Hilsman, "World War II was a 'good' war. Hitler was a maniacal monster, and young as we were, we saw this and understood its implications" (Hilsman, 1). Hilsman was correct about the need to fight. Yet he was writing with the benefit of hindsight. This is problematic, and it gives us a window through which to begin exploring what is wrong with the myth.

At the time, many Americans didn't fully understand the threat of Hitler; they wanted to beat the Japanese first because they hated them more (a 1942 poll showed 66 percent of Americans wanting the Pacific war to have priority). The Pacific campaigns were fought with a mutual ferocity that culminated in the Japanese kamikaze attacks and the Allied incendiary and atomic bombings of Japan's major cities. Many Americans of the war generation like to divorce the atom bombings from the conflict, seeing them as the curtain raiser on the nuclear age rather than the last act of our best war. But they were in fact the final destructive episode in a fight that, as historian John Ellis said, was won and lost by brute force.

Here is the point. To make World War II into the best war ever, we must leave out the area bombings and other questionable aspects while exaggerating the good things. The war myth is distorted not so much in what it says as in what it doesn't say. Combat in World War II was rarely glamorous. It was so bad that the breakdown rate for men consistently in action for twenty-eight days ran as high as 90 percent. Soldiers of all nations performed deeds of courage, but they also shot prisoners, machine-gunned defenseless enemies in the water or in parachutes, and raped women, including their own military personnel. And they had nightmares afterward about what they had seen and done. About 25 percent of the men still in the hospital from the war are psychiatric cases.

Posttraumatic stress disorder no more originated with Vietnam than did napalm. This terrible weapon, a jellied gasoline that burns its victims, was invented by American scientists during World War II and used in all major combat zones, along with phosphorous, another flesh-searing load for bombs and shells. On all battlefronts where there were perceived ethnic differences, the war was fought without many rules. Russians and Germans butchered each other indiscriminately. The Japanese abused Allied prisoners and were in turn often seen as subhuman "gooks."

Contrary to the popular myth that dumps all negatives on Vietnam, the worst war we had, there was significant discrimination in the armed forces during World War II. Many soldiers didn't know what the war was about, and some resented their war-long terms of service, feeling they were doing everybody's fighting. The majority of returning soldiers got no parades. James Jones, a veteran, noted that wounded men repatriated to the United States were treated as though diseased, and people rushed to wash their hands after greeting them (*WWII*, 150). Civilians feared that the GIs would think the country owed them a living, while veterans felt that "when you come back they treat you just like scum." Said this anonymous soldier: "If you ever get the boys all together they will probably kill all the civilians" (Holmes, 402).

America's industrial output to sustain the war was prodigious. As indicators, 86,000 tanks, 296,000 planes, and 71,000 warships were produced. Many of these were of sound design and quality. Others were not. For economy and swiftness, many American aircraft carriers had unarmored flight decks, which made them vulnerable to airborne attacks. American torpedoes were of poor quality initially, until Axis designs were copied. The "mulberries," floating artificial harbors used to assist the British-American Normandy landings, functioned poorly, and the American one at Omaha Beach was wrecked by high seas. Although Joe DeChick, a local talk-show host, recently called the B-17 Flying Fortress a "lean, mean fighting machine" that "was virtually invincible," it suffered heavy losses in raids over Germany until it could be protected by new, long-range fighter planes.

After the initial post–Pearl Harbor burst of unity and willing sacrifice, Americans showed the average amount of selfishness and cupidity. Politics became politics again. The administration collected gossip about General Douglas MacArthur's sex life to use if he ran for president on the Republican ticket (Schaller, 79). And innuendos about homosexuality helped to force Sumner Welles out of the State Department when it was decided he was too pro-Soviet (see Edward M. Bennett, *Franklin D. Roosevelt and the Search for Victory* [1990], 94). Labor-management disputes continued. Merchant seamen, taking badly needed supplies to the troops on Guadalcanal, turned back when they were refused extra pay (Manchester, 167). An elderly gentleman on a bus in Viola, Kentucky, home of a munitions plant, hit a female passenger with his umbrella when she said she hoped the war wouldn't end until she had worked long enough to buy a refrigerator.

The war massively altered the face of American society. Small farmers and storeowners went under, while big businesses became great corporations. Fed by the emergency, the federal bureaucracy mushroomed from 1 million to 3.8 million. Most people paid income tax for the first time. Millions of Americans moved, usually to the cities, which experienced considerable racial tension and some violence as ethnic groups were thrown together. The stress of social change also showed up in a record number of hospital admissions for patients suffering from psychoses. Family dislocation came to be a concern: with fathers in the armed forces and mothers working, kids seemed to go wild, and people worried about juvenile delinquency. In a 1946 opinion poll, a majority of adults said adolescent behavior had degenerated during the war; only 9 percent thought it had improved. And people may now think that marriages were more sacred back then, but marital strain led to a record high 600,000 divorces in 1946.

Americans may have been better educated then, too, but a 1942 poll showed that 59 percent of them couldn't locate China, a major ally, on the map. In the same year, Philip Wylie, a disillusioned federal official, published *Generation of Vipers*, a book cataloguing America's ills. The list is startlingly modern. Young people, he said, could no longer think because education failed to challenge them—and nobody flunked.

They listened to radio and watched movies instead of reading books. Teachers who were intellectually demanding got fired. Consumerism and uncritical boosterism were pervasive, making discussion of social issues like pollution, urban congestion, drug addiction, and materialism impossible. Many of Wylie's strictures were ignored at the time and have been forgotten since.

The selective process by which only positive aspects of the war received mainstream attention began during the conflict itself—one of the most censored events in modern history. Every nation rigorously edited the news. No Japanese or American newspaper, for example, carried a single report of atrocities by their own military, though there were in fact many. The beating and even killing of African-American soldiers by other U.S. service personnel also went undisclosed. Canadian correspondent Charles Lynch spoke for the whole international press corps when he said of the reporters: "We were cheerleaders." Perhaps, he thought, this was necessary for national survival in a total war. But "it wasn't good journalism. It wasn't journalism at all" (Knightley, 332–33).

The U.S. military censored all reports from the front, and those who broke the rules were sent home. In America, the Office of Censorship vetted public and private communications, while the Office of Facts and Figures, and later the Office of War Information, published propaganda in support of the war effort. The result was a cleaned-up, cosmetically-enhanced version of reality. The war, said writer Fletcher Pratt, was reported like a polite social function. "The official censors pretty well succeeded in putting over the legend that the war was won without a single mistake by a command consisting exclusively of geniuses" (Knightley, 276, 296). When Walter Cronkite filed a report that the Eighth Air Force had blindly bombed Germany through solid cloud cover, challenging the myth that all American bombing was pinpoint accurate and hit only military targets, his copy was held up. A combat photographer who recorded the murder of SS soldiers by their American guards was told the film couldn't be screened because of technical difficulties (Terkel, 379–80). And when Eric Sevareid tried to broadcast descriptions of faceless, limbless boys in military hospitals, the censors told him to write about new miracle drugs and medical instruments instead.

But the news wasn't manipulated only by the censors. John Steinbeck, a tough-minded writer who exposed human misery during the Depression, admitted that as a war reporter he deliberately slanted his stories to omit anything that might shock civilians. He didn't report on the rotten conditions suffered by the infantry or on homosexual activity in the military.

Censorship in the interests of military security, even protection of civilian morale, has its purpose. But the image-making went beyond this. Generals, even whole branches of the service like the paratroops and the Marine Corps, employed platoons of public relations officers and advertising agencies to make sure they looked good. General Douglas MacArthur was a notorious publicity hound. During the first months of 1942, when the Japanese were smashing his defenses in the Philippines, he still found time to publish 140 press releases. Manufacturing an enemy body count is usually associated with Vietnam, but for one two-year period in the Pacific war, MacArthur reported 200,000 Japanese killed for 122 Allied losses. After he was driven from the Philippines, the general became famous for the line, "I shall return." But this sound bite was manufactured from his speeches by staffers. When he did return, the dramatic scenes of him wading ashore were filmed several times on different beaches to get the right effect (Schaller, 62, 73; Knightley, 280).

Similarly, when Eisenhower and his generals went ashore in Normandy after the D-Day landings, fifty cameramen were on hand and were told which profiles to shoot (Fussell, *Wartime*, 160; Terkel, 379). Eisenhower saw reporters as part of the army and expected them to report the news as loyal soldiers and subordinates, not as independent observers. "Public opinion wins wars," he said. "I have always considered as quasi-staff officers, correspondents accredited to my headquarters" (Knightley, 315). Generals Mark Clark and George Patton were among the most image-conscious in the European theater. When the Allies liberated Rome, Clark took all the credit for his Fifth Army. The delicate, dangerous work of flushing out pockets of resistance had to be hurried, increasing the risk to the troops, because he had a photo opportunity arranged in the center of the city (Gervasi, 515; Sevareid, 411). Patton's seemingly spontaneous, emotionally charged speeches to the troops were often carefully rehearsed, as was the obligatory footage of him wading ashore in Sicily. Always aware of appearances, he advised senior officers to visit the dangerous front lines in a jeep for maximum visibility to the men and return to the safety of headquarters in a plane.

The public lapped up the images. This was a media generation; it had come of age with talking pictures and radio. By 1940 radio was a billion-dollar industry, and twenty-eight-million families owned sets. Commercials, with their snappy pace and upbeat messages, already dominated format and programming. The public's concentration span and ability to tolerate any but optimistic messages were being eroded. To meet this challenge the print media responded with glossy magazines and the *Reader's Digest*, whose circulation jumped in the 1930s from a quarter of a million to seven million. The *Digest*, like the commercials, offered short, easily digested concepts, laced with a philosophy of optimism. Gloomy endings, skepticism, and complexity were out. The media age also spawned comic books, whose superheroes further simplified the issues and made them black or white. By 1942, twelve million comic books a month were sold, one-third to people over eighteen. They were the favorite reading of the private soldier.

Towering above all other popular entertainments were the movies. They had allowed audiences a fantasy release from the Depression, and now they glamorized the war for them. Movie attendance, around sixty million per week in the 1930s, rose to an all-time peak of ninety million during the war. Hollywood made more than 300 feature films, over 40 percent of them musicals—like Irving Berlin's *This Is the Army* and Danny Kaye in *Up in Arms*. Movies like these offered a winning combination of escapism and toe-tapping patriotism. Hollywood, more than any other agency, made this into the best war ever. Daffy Duck got drafted, Donald Duck told filmgoers how saving would beat the Axis, and Bugs Bunny sold war bonds.

The censors hardly needed to tell the film producers that war movies should showcase American heroism and patriotism and that the enemy must be cruel, devious, and unprincipled. The infantry platoon became America's melting pot, where an Irish boy from Brooklyn, a Texas sharecropper, a fresh-faced midwesterner, a Chicago Italian, and even an intellectual all found their Americanism. When an American was killed, it was quick and painless (except for blacks or Hispanics, who might die in a more ghastly way). Wounds were clean and healed well. Grisly endings or lingering deaths were usually saved for the enemy. *Bataan*, a 1943 movie about the defense of the Philippines, starring Robert Taylor, set the tone for this genre. Most Americans never saw a battle zone (only 27 percent of the military actually endured combat), and many shied away from any realistic portrait of what it might be like; they preferred the film version.

One of the most popular mantel ornaments of the 1940s was a set of three brass monkeys, one covering its eyes, another its ears, a third its mouth. Called See No Evil, Hear No Evil, and Speak No Evil, they represented a quite common approach to life. When the Pentagon released candid photographs of American corpses after the battle for Tarawa in the Pacific, it received piles of abusive mail demanding that such obscene disclosures be stopped (Manchester, 242). After disfigured soldiers from the plastic surgery hospital in Pasadena, California, were allowed to go downtown, the local paper got letters asking, "Why can't they be kept on their own grounds and off the streets?" (Terkel, 130). An army survey of GI sexual practices overseas, including statistics on pregnancies caused, was kept secret for forty years after the war out of fear about public reaction (Costello, 99).

People liked to believe Bing Crosby's version of what their sons at war were like. Back from an armed forces show, he said clothes got smarter and salutes snappier the closer you got to the front. Actually, combat troops were filthy, as they had no way to bathe, and they never saluted superiors, because officers became targets for snipers once identified in this way.

So magical was the media image of war that even those at the front went to it for the "authentic" version of what they were experiencing. John Steinbeck noted that women in the British Royal Air Force who spent the day operating antiaircraft batteries against German bombers crowded into cinemas nightly to watch a pencil-mustached Hollywood hero "who through pure handsomeness, cleverness, bravery, and hokum defeats every resource of the Third Reich" (Steinbeck, 44). In the movie age, nothing was real until it was on film; to these women, this was the war as it ought to have been and as it finally became (in memory). Steinbeck had no problem with this blurring of image and reality. He wrote the stories for two blatantly propagandist films, *Lifeboat* (1944) and *The Moon Is Down* (1943). And he thought that Bob Hope, a noncombatant comedian, was the ultimate symbol of the war: "There's a man for you—there is really a man" (62–64).

Ernie Pyle, arguably one of America's top war reporters, admitted that at the front he lost focus on the war: amid the muck and death, the bits and pieces didn't add up to a grand, proud whole. He had to read the magazines from America to get the "true" picture, to recapture the glamor and excitement. "Only in the magazine from America could I catch the *real* spirit of the war" (Pyle, *Your War*, 101–2; italics added). For much of his time as a war reporter, Pyle tried to impose the cheerful, sanitized media version of war upon reality. In his reports from North Africa and Sicily, all the infantry were gung ho, especially the wounded, who "were anxious to return to their outfits" at the front. (Actually, American wounded were rarely returned to their original units but were funneled into other formations as needed, where they were treated as rookies, which was deeply demoralizing to these veteran soldiers.)

Even the doctors and nurses who tried to put back together the shattered bodies of combat soldiers were, in Pyle's stories, eager for more.

"Gosh, I hope I'm not stuck in a base hospital," said one doctor. "I want to get on to the front." A nurse "was so steamed up" at the Axis that "she could hardly wait for the next battle." Following the unwritten code, an Arab (i.e., "colored") woman had her arm blown off; and there were "pieces of Germans." But all wounds to white Americans were clean, and bodies remained whole. The GIs were happy warriors, "full of laughter," giving their rations to the local kids and grieving for animals hit by fire. There were no blunders by the great American war machine. The exact amount of everything needed by the frontline troops was delivered to them efficiently and promptly (Pyle, *Your War*, 24–25, 47, 65, 72–76, 81).

Yet try as he might, Pyle could not avoid the actuality of misery and death in war, which eventually became sickeningly real for him. Tired and demoralized, he tried to go home. But he was too popular. Reassigned to the Pacific war, his reports became more bitter, more honest. He no longer got on well with the troops, whom he thought were being brutalized by the slaughter of the Japanese. Finally, an unhappy and disillusioned man, he was killed by a sniper.

Pyle had the integrity to ultimately confront the full nature of war, but most Americans didn't have to. Like Walter Mitty, the protagonist of James Thurber's 1941 story about a hen-pecked husband who makes life tolerable by fantasizing that he is a hero, they could still dream large dreams about the glamour of war without ever having to challenge their assumptions.

The imposition of the media construct upon reality continued after the war. The year 1958 saw the musical *South Pacific*, loosely based on James A. Michener's 1947 war memoir, *Tales of the South Pacific*. Michener was not the most candid war writer, but he tried to deal with the whole picture. Sex-starved GIs tried to rape an army nurse. "From then on nurses rarely went out at night unless their dates carried loaded revolvers." The Pacific jungle was a hideous environment, hot, wet, bug-ridden, "oppressive and foreboding." "Prickly heat," a rash from excessive sweating, ate out the flesh of armpits and crotches, and a man lost three toes to foot fungus (Michener, 75, 95–96, 119–21). In the film, all this was cleaned up. The bleak environment became an island paradise. The nurses were glamorous but brainless sex objects in short shorts who acted and talked like little girls (Hollywood has failed consistently to take service women seriously). A captain explained that since they were on the defensive and losing daily in two hemispheres, they should put on a great Thanksgiving Day show to cheer up the men. The only reference to real war was the death of an American officer. But he died gallantly offscreen—and it was better for him this way, because he was about to marry a native girl.

The star most associated with World War II is John Wayne. Through many film roles he has come to epitomize the Hollywood version of the American fighting man, even though he was never a combat soldier. *Sands of Iwo Jima*, made in 1949, was perhaps the best of the genre. The movie had the integrity to suggest that Wayne's character, Sergeant Stryker, was not a perfect man. His devotion to the military cost him his marriage, and he could not communicate with his son. But the film continued the erosion of reality about the nature of combat. Stryker was a man's man who molded boys into marines: in battle, they became seasoned veterans and mature adults who knew what they were fighting for and had an infinite strength denied to their devious yellow enemy.

There were dissonant voices. The film *A Walk in the Sun* (1946) tried to show the confusion and random butchery of combat. *Let There Be Light* (1946) was a documentary dealing with psychologically damaged veterans. But these films did not have wide audiences. Veterans like Norman Mailer in *The Naked and the Dead* (1948) and James Jones in *The Thin Red Line* (1962) wrote starkly of the war, its brutality, confusion, insensitivity, the political ambitions of generals, and the sexual undertones inherent in the killing process. But their novels were not read by the mainstream, and the authors tended to be written off as the intellectual fringe, if not actually psychotics and sex perverts. Many would not read their works because they contained "bad language," even though it is an unfortunate truth of military life that the most important noun, adjective, and verb is *fuck*.

By 1962 at the latest, when Hollywood produced *The Longest Day*, its epic tribute to the D-Day landings, the movie replica had completely displaced the original. Films copied earlier films to get the "authentic" period look. For example, the film *December 7th*, made in 1943, used studio sets to recreate aspects of the attack on Pearl Harbor. But when *Winds of War* was made in 1983, the earlier film was assumed to be actual combat footage, and so the substitute reality was studiously copied. People went to the cinema to see what the war had been like, and the stars became synonymous with the generals they played. George C. Scott *was* George Patton. A real-life hero such as Audie Murphy, America's most decorated soldier in World War II, when he couldn't make the transition to the screen as a film hero, was remembered largely as a failed movie actor. The war had become a part of American folklore, captured forever in a manageable format and with a message acceptable to the public. As an advertisement for a John

Wayne reproduction army pistol put it, "from *Sands of Iwo Jima* to *The Green Berets* to *The Longest Day*, he captured our essence. Our Strength. Our values" (*USA Weekend*, March 25, 1988).

No group believed more fervently that this was the best war ever than the young men who enthusiastically left for Vietnam believing they were following in the footsteps of their WWII film fathers. A blue-collar veteran from Boston said he went to "kill a Commie for Jesus Christ and John Wayne" (McCloud, 87). Ron Kovic, a soldier who became partially paralyzed in Vietnam, said in his memoir *Born on the Fourth of July* that *Sands of Iwo Jima* so moved him as a youth that he cried each time he heard the music from it. Wayne "became one of my heroes" (Kovic, 53–55). Some Vietnam veterans realized that in Vietnam they had discovered the reality of war and that, on a day-to-day basis, it was not much different from what their fathers' generation had endured in the Pacific during World War II. They understood that the movies had misled them about what war would be like. Others continued to think of the films as the way war really was in the 1940s and blamed themselves for having fought a "bad war" in Vietnam. They forgot that media coverage of Vietnam was more candid and that therefore our view of the war was inevitably more realistic, less cosmetic.

Most Americans want to see Vietnam as a bad dream, a nightmare to be erased, so that they can return to the glory of the Good War. This is partly what the Gulf War was about. The magic was back. For example, a young American soldier, deeply depressed by her experience as a prisoner of war in Iraq, was given a hug by General Schwarzkopf "and then everything was fine," said a TV news reporter. No lingering post-traumatic stress disorder here.

Two recent public figures most closely represent the aura of the Good War era: George Bush, a WWII combat veteran, and Ronald Reagan, a film actor who came to embody America's good feelings about the golden years of the 1940s. Reagan's immense popularity as president rested partly on his remarkable talent to create a partial reality based on wishful thinking. This engagement with image-making began early in Reagan's radio career, when he made up the play-by-play for baseball games neither he nor the audience could see. His exciting illusions proved more popular than the real games. Though he saw no combat in World War II, and indeed was only out of the country once before he became president, Reagan later seemed to believe that he was a veteran who had been present at the U.S. opening of a Nazi concentration camp and that he did top secret work on the atom bomb project (all he actually did was work in Hollywood on the voice-over

for a film made to help pilots locate their bombing targets in Japan).
He told anecdotes about combat situations in the war that he believed
were real, yet all of these scenarios were from films he had either
worked on or had seen.

He is the ultimate symbol of the movie version becoming the reality. Thus, Reagan related the story of the bomber pilot on a doomed
plane who refused to parachute because a young wounded gunner
couldn't evacuate the ship. The pilot went down cradling the young-
ster's head in his lap until the very end. The story is obviously from a
film, because, since all the men on the plane died, we cannot know
what they did at the very end; the only witnesses are those who have
seen the movie. Yet Reagan refused to accept that the story was a fiction. Because he had seen WWII films in which black and white soldiers fought side by side, Reagan insisted that the WWII armed forces
were racially integrated. In fact, they were rigidly segregated; it was
only in 1948, three years after the war ended, that President Truman
ordered racial mixing in military units to begin.

Even Reagan's Star Wars project, the strategic defense initiative
aimed at putting weapons in space to knock out incoming hostile missiles, was inspired partly by a film he acted in during World War II;
Murder in the Air, made in 1940, used an "inertia projector," a primitive Star Wars device, to strike enemy planes from the skies. Not un-
expectedly, SDI as projected is not considered feasible by most experts
because it is not rooted in reality.

Reagan's deep belief in the legitimacy of the movie version of American history made him a living symbol for many Americans of their
best war ever and the magic formula for success that they thought was
the special possession of the 1940s generation. He was the final em-
bodiment of the movie star as war hero. "He's a real, live hero whose
impact transcends his overwhelming success at the polling booths,"
said one young supporter, commenting on Reagan's success in the
1984 election (Urbanska, 136). Garry Wills, one of Reagan's most perceptive biographers, believes that a key to Reagan's success is that he
entered into a mute conspiracy with his public to ignore those aspects
of reality that are unpleasant or disturbing. People, said Wills, cannot
live with the real past and its implications. So Reagan invented for
them a "true to life" past based on film and fantasy.

As the grand old man who represented an earlier, simpler, stronger
America, Reagan convinced Americans that they could have in the
1980s the world they believed existed in the 1940s, by sheer will.
"Reagan is such a great leader," said John Carlson, another young
Reaganite. "He projects optimism about the future, says nothing about

limits to growth, gives off unbridled optimism about the future" (Urbanska, 136–37). The problem is that this is not the 1940s. We didn't know then what unlimited growth does to the environment. We do now, and ignoring the knowledge can only hurt us. The problems of the late 1980s were in part the result of indulging in make-believe when reality demanded attention.

The situation of the belly gunner on a B-17 Flying Fortress provides a small but illuminating example of how the mythmaking process has damaged our ability to seriously comprehend the WWII experience. To protect the vulnerable underside of the aircraft against attack by enemy fighter planes, a gunner was stationed in a bubblelike plexiglass revolving ball turret protruding from the bottom of the ship. He was literally suspended in space, along with his machine guns, sealed off from the rest of the crew.

In his cramped turret, the gunner could not even wear his parachute. Worse still, should the electrical system of the plane malfunction or be shot out by enemy fire, he would not be able to open the turret doors. If, at the same time, the hydraulic system failed and the landing wheels could not be lowered or were shot away, the ship would have to make a belly flop or pancake landing, coming down on the turret and smashing the gunner to pulp. He would know exactly what was going to happen to him until the moment of impact, one of the most grotesque deaths one can imagine. The nature of these terrible deaths was kept from the home front audience of the war, which was most likely to see the belly gunner in an ad for Talon slide fasteners, useful to both the housewife and the flyer. Here, he was depicted as a hell-bent-for-leather hero, raining lead from his machine guns. This commercial was captioned, "Giving 'Em Hell from a 'Goldfish Bowl,'" as though fighting your war from a fish tank was a magnificent experience.

In 1945, veteran and poet Randall Jarrell tried to tell America what it was like to hang suspended six miles above the earth with only the protection of a plexiglass bubble. In his poem "The Death of the Ball Turret Gunner," the gunner is hit by flak, flying shrapnel from an anti-aircraft shell burst. The impact turns his body into mush: "they washed me out of the turret with a hose." One of my undergraduate students, imbued with the myth that every WWII soldier got a flag, a parade, and if necessary, a decent burial, wrote an essay on this poem in 1990. He wrote, "This man's death was not overlooked. I feel this man probably was praised on his burial for his services." The student transformed the awful, lonely, anonymous fate of the gunner into a

Fig. 1. Reprinted with permission from Talon American, Division of Coats & Clark

hero's death, even though there wasn't a body for the honorable burial the student envisioned.

Steven Spielberg provided the final touch in one of his *Amazing Stories*, "The Mission," aired on television in the 1985–86 season. In harshly realistic detail, Spielberg recreated the nightmare scenario: the turret jammed and the landing gear shot away. The gunner will die, and we grieve with him on the flight home. But wait. One crewman is a doodler; on a sketchpad he draws the Fortress, then crayons in new wheels with candy-striped legs. Miraculously, these wheels appear on the plane, and it lands safely. Surely, this was the best war ever.

In the chapters that follow, we shall try to look at the war as the nuanced and complex event it was—an event that left no simple lesson or moral.

two

No Easy Answers

THE FOLKLORE VERSION of World War II suggests that the war came for reasons that were straightforward and clearly evident at the time. Between the wars, so we are told, a group of dictators were in close league to destroy democracy and capitalism. These tyrants were Benito Mussolini in Italy, Francisco Franco in Spain, Adolf Hitler in Germany, and Emperor Hirohito in Japan. They committed numerous aggressions in the 1930s, which gave ample evidence of their plans for continuing conquest: Japan invaded Manchuria (1931, 1937), Italy crushed Abyssinia, or Ethiopia (1934), Franco suppressed republican freedom in Spain during the civil war there (1936–39), and Hitler absorbed Austria and Czechoslovakia (1938–39).

This simple version of history suggest that the sooner these bullies were stood up to, the easier it would be to defeat them. Conquest made them more confident and stronger, as they drew resources for war-making, such as oil and steel, from the territories they overran. But the major democracies tried to tolerate what they were doing, hoping they would be appeased by moderate expansion. The appeasers were led by Britain and France, the strongest free nations of Europe. Their "spineless" approach was particularly reprehensible because they were partially responsible for the situation through the Treaty of Versailles (1919). There they had placed all the blame for World War I on Germany and inflicted harsh penalties on it, allowing Hitler to feed off the hatred that this engendered in Germany. Only in 1939, when the dictators had maximized their strength, did Britain and France finally recognize the need to fight.

As with all myth, there is some truth here. But it is not the whole truth, and it distorts through simplification. The right course of action was usually not as clear as it may seem now. The precise time to stand up to authoritarianism was not obvious. Nor were the dictator nations a monolith with a united front that called for a uniform response. For instance, until the mid-1930s, Italy sometimes sided with Britain and France against Germany. It can be argued that the democracies gained strength by waiting to fight until 1939, instead of the earlier thirties. For example, Italy, the first state to embrace dictatorship and rearmament, hit its military peak sometime in the early thirties. By 1939 much of its equipment (such as tanks and aircraft) was obsolete, whereas Britain's war machine, designed at a later date, was closer to the state of the art.

The idea that Hitler could somehow have been contained and made to behave by fighting him earlier is a fuzzy one, and we are rarely told exactly how this would have worked. Moreover, "appeasement" is blamed for causing World War II, but such a policy was tried only in Europe. In the Pacific, where U.S. thinking dominated policy, the Allies followed a campaign of "deterrence." It also failed, as the Japanese attacks of December 1941 on Pearl Harbor and elsewhere attest. There were no easy answers, no certain solutions.

The historical roots of World War II go back well before the 1919 Treaty of Versailles, certainly to the late eighteenth century, when opposing theories about the nature of the state and of citizenship came into conflict. One view supposed that people were basically rational and capable of self-government. This position stressed individual liberties and pointed toward liberal democracy. The counterargument held that self-government produced indecision and chaos: nations needed strong leaders, leaders with vision, to dictate policy. These contesting philosophies can be seen in the French Revolution of 1789, which began in liberalism and ended in the virtual dictatorship of Napoleon Bonaparte. For many nations, the choice between structures was still open in the twentieth century; they tended to vote democracy in good times and turn to strongmen in bad.

Also coming out of the eighteenth-century age of revolutions, both French and American, was a crucial connection between citizenship and soldiering. The rights to vote and to bear arms came to be aligned as mutual privileges of adult male membership in the body politic. The positive side of this connection meant that the citizen soldier could be called upon to defend the freedom of the state. The sinister side of the association between manhood and war fed the aggressive nationalism of the nineteenth century, pitting the armies of the major nations against one another.

This leads us to notice a paradox. The nineteenth century was a period of increasing material well-being, as industrial and agricultural innovations improved the standard of living. Yet, even as human comfort increased, an influential philosophy known as social Darwinism (after the natural scientist Charles Darwin) held that in human affairs, as in nature, there is constant struggle and only the fittest survive. A nation must conquer or die. Ironically, then, the more a nation prospered, the more people worried they would become soft and a prey to their tougher, leaner neighbors. The answer lay in periodic wars to trim down the fat and keep the nation alert.

In this perceived struggle, national expansion was seen as key to survival. Western nations competed in subduing militarily weaker native peoples and turning their lands into colonies that provided the raw materials for Western industry, the markets for their finished goods, and occasional skirmishes to keep their young men on their mettle. This imperialism led to Western domination of much of the world. In Asia, only Japan stayed free of colonialism. This was important because, when in the twentieth century Japan was snubbed by the Western powers, it would take as its mission expelling the West from Asia. At the same time, the United States, pursuing its avenues of aggressive expansion, had by 1900 subdued its native population and was enlarging its dominance to include the Philippines plus other areas in the Pacific. This made it an inevitable rival to Japan for hegemony in that region, and the power struggle led directly to the Pacific war of 1941–45.

A Europe that increasingly defined the individual masculine identity and the collective national identity through combat reached its fulfillment in the World War of 1914–18. Among the results of that mighty upheaval was the destruction of four imperial dynasties. Their demise created an unstable world situation: with the smashing of established institutions and the concomitant loss of a sense of structure and safety in people's lives, insecurity became a major political factor. Further destabilization favored the rise of strongmen, who would offer release from the fear of anarchy in return for the surrender of individual freedom and international understanding. Between 1917 and 1936, eleven European states chose dictatorship.

In the east, the Ottoman empire, which had sided with the unsuccessful Central Powers in World War I, fell apart. From its corpse, independent countries emerged, some of which, like Iraq, are still struggling to shape their identity. The Western powers, partly to protect their interests in the region, acted as the midwives in the birth of these new nations. Britain, in particular, was involved, adding oversight of a large region, including a new Jewish homeland in Palestine, to its list of imperial obligations. British preoccupation with overseas problems would help to distract attention from the growing menace of Hitler.

In 1917, the retrogressive and inefficient czarist regime in Russia fell

to a series of increasingly radical revolutions, culminating in the Bolshevik state. The Bolsheviks antagonized the Western Allies by withdrawing Russia from World War I and by their militant advocacy of
world revolution, which drove them into isolation. Russia was initially denied membership in the postwar League of Nations. Fear of Communist revolution would help to foster right-wing movements in Germany, Italy, and Spain. And distrust of Josef Stalin's increasingly
ruthless, authoritarian state would further alienate statesmen in the
democracies, preventing a common front against Hitler and encouraging appeasement.

The Austro-Hungarian empire collapsed in 1918, leading to the creation of a potpourri of states in central and southern Europe. Some of
these had a weak national identity and a questionable economic or
military ability to sustain themselves. Among these was Czechoslovakia, a nation divided by ethnicity. Europe emerged from the war with
twenty-seven separate currencies and 12,500 miles of new frontier.
This was a patchwork situation, fluid and uncertain, which guaranteed
that statesmen in the interwar years would not find easy answers.

Finally, the German empire ended with the abdication of Kaiser Wilhelm II. Yet, not all the factors in Germany's situation were negative.
Renouncing the militarism of the imperial government, Germany
moved to the liberal democracy of the Weimar Republic. At the peace
treaty, France, whose northern territories had been the battleground
for the western front, wanted large German concessions, including
substantial territory, as compensation. And it wanted Germany's industrial base dismantled so it could not rebuild a war machine to again
invade France as it had in 1914 and 1870. Both the United States and
Britain opposed these extreme demands. Germany's armed forces were
limited in size, and the Rhineland was demilitarized to provide a
buffer zone against further aggression—but at the same time Germany's industrial resources in the Ruhr were reserved to it. In fact,
both in population and industrial power, loser Germany remained po-
tentially stronger than victor France.

Right-wing German nationalists later claimed that the Versailles
Treaty put all guilt for the war on the Reich. But this was not true.
Reparations were asked for to compensate the victors for their losses,
but these were more moderate than Germany intended to extract if it
had won. And such reparations were traditionally paid by the loser;
they implied nothing more than that Germany had been beaten.
Britain and France in fact had little choice: they had borrowed heavily
from America to fight the war, and America, acting on the traditional
economic principle that foreign debts must be honored, demanded re-

payment. Britain and France had to go to Germany for the money. In 1924 the reparations were put on a seemingly stable footing through the Dawes Plan, the work of an international committee headed by American Charles G. Dawes. It made German installments to the Allies feasible through American loans. The plan had merit, but it relied on American willingness to supply loans and German ability to afford them through international trade, particularly with America. Should this cycle of prosperity falter, there were disgruntled men waiting in the wings to topple the Weimar government in Germany.

Who were they? First, Germany had made the mistake of leaving largely intact the imperial military and administrative elite, many of whom despised democracy. This elite was loosely associated with other right-wing groups, including the militant Freikorps, literally free corps, or free-lance troops of veterans who were self-appointed violent defenders of German honor. The extremists had two major objectives. First, they were determined to fight and destroy the Communists, who would align Germany with Bolshevik Russia. Second, they sought to overturn the Versailles Treaty, because they rejected the idea that Germany had been defeated in World War I and that it should pay for the war. Because Allied forces had not marched deep into Germany when the war ended, they maintained that the army had not been broken but had been "stabbed in the back" by liberal German politicians, who had panicked and surrendered. Germany had been sold out, said the reactionaries.

Freikorpsmen joined other nationalists in abhorring the postwar scattering of Germans. Though Germany remained largely intact, provinces taken from France and other neighbors in the nineteenth century were given back. The port of Danzig and a strip of territory connecting it to the new state of Poland were ceded, cutting East Prussia off from the rest of Germany. Also divorced from the fatherland were the Germans living in Austria and in the Sudeten region of Czechoslovakia.

The determination to repudiate Germany's defeat, to destroy communism, and to bring all German-speaking people into one national fold provided the basis for the right-wing opposition to Weimar. The Freikorpsmen along with many other veterans refused to accept the end of the war and new world it brought. Coming to maturity in the trenches, they saw life as war and peace as preparation for war. Said one Freikorps veteran: "People told us that the War was over. That made us laugh. We ourselves are the War. Its flame burns strongly in us. It envelops our whole being and fascinates us with the enticing urge to destroy" (Theweleit, 16).

The Weimar government was able to defend itself against these right-wing authoritarians only so long as it could deliver on the promise of prosperity. But in 1922–23, the government devalued its currency to make reparation payments easier, and the consequent inflation affected ordinary people, who found their savings almost worthless. Eventually, it took thousands of marks to buy a loaf of bread. Though the Dawes Plan ameliorated this situation, the confidence of ordinary Germans in capitalist democracy had been undermined. When in 1929–30 a further economic catastrophe occurred, they turned readily to a charismatic leader who promised an end to the capitalist cycle of boom and bust. This man was Adolf Hitler. He shared the right-wing program of the Freikorps; and many of the Freikorps would serve in his National Socialist street-fighting units, called the SA or storm troopers. Like them, Hitler was obsessed by Versailles, but his regime was made possible partly by the Great Crash of 1929.

Ironically, perhaps some victor nations came out of World War I less satisfactorily than Germany. Although Britain and France had successfully defended their democratic way of life, it was at enormous cost in blood and treasure. Both were in debt. France faced a still-strong Germany on its borders and had lost a key ally, Russia, which had retreated to hostile isolation. Britain's economic power was undermined, yet its imperial obligations had increased. Throughout the interwar period, its politicians would struggle with the conundrum of how to manage on resources inadequate to its role as a great power.

British politicians believed that their situation was made more complex by fluctuations in American policy. Without the sure backing of the United States, Britain was reluctant to take a firm leadership role in Europe. At the end of World War I, President Woodrow Wilson was a key exponent of international cooperation and the League of Nations, but the U.S. Senate voted against League membership in 1920, hurting the credibility of the League.

Despite rejection of the League, America took steps to help the peace in the 1920s, sponsoring a number of conferences on arms limitation. But the public feared any binding treaty commitments that might threaten American autonomy and perhaps trap the United States in a further foreign war. We must remember that many Americans had a legitimate distrust of European political stability. Many had recently left Europe to find a new life in America, and they didn't want entanglements with the Old World. As late as 1940, 11.5 million white Americans were first-generation immigrants, and a further 23 million were second-generation, out of a rough total of 118 million whites.

They tended to favor letting Europe work out its own problems, and they put America first in a policy called isolationism.

Then, too, many American soldiers who went to France in 1917 and 1918 had been disillusioned by their reception. Expecting to be hailed as saviors, they were often treated as loud, vulgar intruders. They in turn found Europeans, with the exception of the Germans, dirty, backward, and unjustifiably arrogant. Like many returning American veterans before and after them, they brought back the word that everything was much better at home. So Americans were soured somewhat on the idealism of the international crusade and turned to the pleasures of business as usual.

The result was that American foreign policy tended to lack authority and, at times, consistency. Americans were willing to give the world an example of peaceful cooperation in an international capitalist system, but they stopped short of a commitment to make sure such a system was not undermined. The confusion in Europe was made worse by its failure to understand the American political system. For example, in Britain the head of the legislative branch (Parliament) is also the chief executive (prime minister), and so the two branches of government speak with one voice. In America the distribution of powers means that the legislative branch (Congress) and the executive branch (president) may well disagree, as they did over League membership and later support for Britain and France.

In the United States, domestic concerns and foreign policy did not always fit. America insisted that the Europeans pay back their war debts, but in 1922 they passed a restrictive tariff on imported goods making it hard for these nations to earn the dollars to pay back their loans. Similarly, loans from America were pivotal to Germany's ability to make reparations payments. Yet the federal government put no guarantees behind the Dawes Plan, so that when, in 1927 and 1928, the stock market offered more lucrative opportunities for investors, the flow of crucial dollars to Germany decreased.

As speculation on Wall Street became wilder, stock prices doubled in two years, a growth not based on a solid foundation. But the federal government took little action to help curb this speculative fever. The economy was in recession, and the inevitable loss of consumer confidence resulted in the stock market crash of 1929. As we shall see, dependence on American dollars meant that the crash impacted all major nations and led some to determine that their economic safety lay in international conquest, not cooperation. In short, Americans had genuinely hoped for an era of peace and prosperity, but the unregulated free-market system and their reluctance to be obligated abroad meant that they couldn't guide events in the direction they wanted.

Finally, the United States, along with the other democracies, did not pursue a consistent policy toward aggressor nations. In Europe, it continued to trade with dictators—even though it asked them to behave. In the Pacific, on the other hand, America felt threatened by the expansion of Japan, and succeeding administrations therefore cold-shouldered the Japanese and urged the British to do likewise. As Japan went from being a friend to being an enemy, Britain felt compelled to seek some accommodation with Italy and Germany.

The two victor nations most uncomfortable in the postwar world were Italy and Japan. Italy had had 600,000 killed and experienced only indifferent success in the fighting. In 1917 its army had been badly beaten by mediocre Austrian forces in the debacle of Caporetto, a disaster vividly described for us by Ernest Hemingway in *A Farewell to Arms* (1929). In return for such suffering and humiliation, Italy expected rich rewards at Versailles in the form of strategic territories from the defeated powers, but the major Allies rejected much of its request and gave it what Benito Mussolini called, "only the crumbs of the rich colonial booty" (Gervasi, 57). In 1922, when the powers set treaty limits to naval strength, Italy was restricted to the same sized fleet as Britain in the Mediterranean, a sea that Italy could justifiably see as its own. Though this arrangement was to protect British oil supplies, Italian nationalists perceived it as a further humiliation.

To make matters worse, the country entered peace with a depressed economy and high unemployment, particularly among returning veterans, whose dissatisfaction was a hotbed for revolution. Bloody industrial strikes convinced conservatives that Communists could seize Italy. Fearful, shocked, they were ready for a strong leader who could offer renewed national pride and economic and social stability in return for the surrender of their democratic freedoms. This was not hard for many people, who held the liberal politicians responsible for Italy's situation.

The strongman was Mussolini, who took authority in 1922 as Il Duce, the Chief. To the slow and complicated operations of democracy, Mussolini opposed the decisiveness of the man of will and force. "Mussolini is always right," said an Italian poster. Il Duce undercut communism by promising an end to labor-management disputes: workers would be guaranteed employment and fringe benefits, such as paid vacations, in return for passivity. How would resources-short Italy pay for prosperity? It would take the lands and raw materials denied it at Versailles. Mussolini, the charismatic military chief, would recreate the Mediterranean Empire of Rome (hence *fascism*, from the fasces, or bundles of sticks carried in Roman processions).

Fascism fostered the cult of personality, the image of the great man in whose hands you could safely leave your burdens. This was attractive to many veterans and others bewildered by postwar instability. In an insecure and often hostile world, the flag-waving and chest-beating of fascism gave a comforting if often false sense of collective strength and direction. Mussolini made the trains run on time, was the popular boast.

In fact, Mussolini did not exert the total power attributed to him; both the king, Victor Emmanuel III, and the pope, Pius XI, remained as competing authority figures. And fascism never achieved the efficient regulation of society claimed for it; labor unrest continued, and behind the facade of the new society, many Italians slipped into poverty. Their plight was unknown because Fascist control of the media put only the regime's successes before the public. And those who might challenge the official line were either liquidated or intimidated into silence. Newsreels showcased Italy's crack fighting units and concealed the fact that some of the army was poorly equipped and low in morale. Fascism had a flashy surface, which impressed other Europeans and led Hitler to copy its techniques in Germany.

Japan began its rise to world power status toward the end of the nineteenth century, when it emerged as the one independent Asian nation with a recognizably modern business-industrial base. Like Italy, Japan was short of resources and sought to offset this deficit by expanding at the expense of its neighbors, especially China. This country, in the second half of the nineteenth century, was a weak nation exploited for profit by the imperial states. These demanded special trading rights and "concessions," or reserved territories where they had privileged access to markets and raw materials. For Japan, a share of the Chinese pie seemed requisite for economic power. The United States, favoring equal marketing opportunities for all countries and an end to the imperial system through its Open Door policy, strongly opposed concessions and would eventually come into conflict with Japan in its attempt to make China into an economically dependent province.

Japan startled the world by easily defeating imperial Russia in the war of 1904–05. This gave it a good foothold in Manchuria, China's northern province, which had been under Russian influence. In World War I, Japan, on the winning side and closely allied to Britain, expected, like Italy, to do well in the division of spoils. But it too was disappointed. During the war, it had captured the German concession in China's northern Shantung provinces, along with other territory along the Pacific coast. It felt entitled to be recognized as the major power in the western Pacific and the premier influence in China. But it was snubbed at Versailles, where Japan's request for a statement supporting the racial equality of all nations was rejected. Japan was not seen as a full partner of the Western nations. Also, the United States championed the future national autonomy of China and put pressure on Japan to yield up its conquests there.

To the prideful Japanese, the Washington naval treaty of 1921–22, which cut their fleet to three-fifths the size of the American and British navies, was also offensive. The treaty, however, was not unreasonable, as it made Japan paramount in the Pacific; unlike the other powers, it did not also have to keep a naval presence in other oceans. But the Japanese felt the ratio implied inferior status. At the same time, in 1922, the U.S. Supreme Court, in the first of several racial decisions, declared Japanese ineligible for American citizenship. This was followed in 1923 by a ruling upholding California and Washington state laws denying Japanese the right to own property. In 1924 the barriers were completed with the Exclusion Act, which virtually banned all Asian immigration.

Though these measures boded ill for the future, Japan and America did try to work together, particularly through trade. Japan tried appeasement by withdrawing substantial forces from China and cutting its military budget. It officially acquiesced in the territorial integrity of China. But this cooperation was based on the premise that Japan could relinquish expansion and still prosper by increasing trade with America. During most of the twenties, this was true. Japan's industrial production doubled, and exports boomed—40 percent going to the United States. Yet, there were ominous signs. Japanese liberal politicians and businessmen, forces for moderation, were opposed by extreme elements in the officer corps. Arrogant and feudal in their outlook, these elements played a major role in Japanese politics, and they aspired to conquest. China, struggling to throw off colonial status, took back many of its concessions and moved to enforce uniform administration of the provinces. Some Japanese statesmen and soldiers feared that an independent China under American influence might deny them raw materials and markets.

In 1929, Wall Street crashed. During the next two years, world trade declined by one-third, and Japanese exports fell by the same amount. The price of raw silk, a staple commodity, plummeted 65 percent in one year. Workers' standard of living was cut by 33 percent. The sufferings of small farmers and businessmen infuriated many in the army, which drew upon this class for personnel. In 1930 America tried to help its depressed industries through the Smoot-Hawley tariff, which raised barriers on imported goods by 50 percent. The United States, with abundant natural resources and domestic markets, could perhaps afford to close its doors to the outside world and weather the Depression alone. But the Japanese could not.

The experience convinced some Japanese leaders that they must seek self-sufficiency through military conquest. Their first target was China. In 1931, the army in Manchuria, using as a pretext alleged Chinese attacks on Japanese property, attacked. The home government acquiesced, and by 1932 they had sufficient control to rename the region as the new satellite state of Manchukuo, under a puppet ruler. The Japanese charged Chinese provocation, but they were condemned as the aggressor by the League of Nations. Japan left the League and ultimately came into alliance with other nations—Italy and Germany—that defined themselves as the have-nots and as needing to get what they required by conquest. Japanese leaders who saw the fatal error in this policy would either be assassinated by army militants or intimidated into silence.

The financial crash and resulting Great Depression undercut the democracies' ability to show that capitalism could bring prosperity and security to all nations through the mutual benefits of trade. As the breadlines grew, so did the fear that the despairing would turn to communism or foment anarchy. Faced with that possibility, more than one country embraced strongmen, who promised a restoration of stability. The most important of these was Der Fuehrer (the Leader), Hitler.

The financial crash and global Depression hit Germany particularly hard, as it was dependent on American loans, which dried up during America's monetary crisis. Also, Germany lacked thirty-three of thirty-five raw materials needed in industrial production. Its goods had to be sold abroad to earn the money to buy these foreign commodities, but as country after country protected their home markets to help their internal industrial recovery, Germany found its export trade collapsing. With the additional stagnation caused by an agricultural glut, German's prosperity crumbled, and by 1932 six million were unemployed.

The Nazi movement, cashing in on the misery, did well in the 1930 elections, becoming the second largest political party. As succeeding chancellors (prime ministers) proved incapable of ending the Depression, Hitler inevitably became the "available man," and was made chancellor in January 1933. Having gained power by democratic means, the Nazis now moved to end genuine representative government. A fire in the Reichstag, or parliament building, possibly set by a crank, was used by Hitler as a pretext to claim that Germany faced a vast international Jewish-Communist conspiracy, virtually amounting to a state of war. In the crisis, Hitler demanded emergency dictatorial powers, which were then used to end political opposition. Germany became a one-party state. The Third Reich, which Hitler boasted would last a thousand years, had begun.

It would be easy to say that at this point Germany had opted simply to put its future in the hands of a madman. But how could this be? We would have to argue that a majority of Germans had become insane. When we think about it, such an idea is not helpful in understanding what happened, so we must seek a better diagnosis. Hitler was not mad, at least in the conventional sense. Rather, he grasped the nature of the forces at work in his time and moved to control them for his own violent vision of a greater, purified Germany.

Hitler was first and foremost a nationalist who shared the belief of many Germans that their country was destined to be a major world power. In this context, Versailles was an outrageous hamstringing of German potential and was to be repudiated. Germans living in Austria or Czechoslovakia were to be repatriated to the Reich. This assertive nationalism was not unique to Germany. Pride in country and competition between countries have marked the modern period, replacing earlier loyalties to broader definitions of human allegiance, such as the medieval concept of a united Christendom. In moving to repudiate Versailles, end reparations, and rearm Germany, Hitler was intelligible to his countrymen and to politicians of the Western world who would claim the same rehabilitation for their nations fifteen years after the war ended.

In imposing his will on German society, Hitler showed outstanding ability in two areas: first, as a dedicated soldier and, second, as a master politician who understood completely the importance of image in winning the modern audience. These twin foundations of success were noted by one of Hitler's generals, Field Marshal von Brauchitsch, who said in 1938 that Der Fuehrer "combines in his person the true soldier and National Socialist," the fighter and consumer manipulator (Keegan, 271).

Hitler had a mediocre career as a commercial artist in Vienna before finding his identity in the trenches of World War I. He wrote in his book, *Mein Kampf*, "Compared to the events of this gigantic struggle, everything past receded to shallow nothingness" (163–64). He won two

Iron Crosses for valor and decided that life is war, a struggle to see who among the species are fitter to survive. Hitler became a social Darwinist of the simplest and most dangerous kind, dedicated to German survival through the national adoption of military values and goals. "Those who want to live, let them fight, and those who do not want to fight in this world of eternal struggle do not deserve to live" (289).

Deeply impressed after the war by Italian fascism, he grafted its leading qualities onto nazism. He inculcated obedience to a leader in his disciplined followers, whose muscle was used to terrorize or liquidate opponents. These included Communists and trades union leaders, whose organizations were suppressed once Hitler had power. In return for an end to organized labor, business leaders pledged allegiance to the new order and became its tool in rearmament. Terror became an everyday aspect of government. Erich Maria Remarque, an author whose antiwar works were banned by the Nazis, wrote that "distrust was the commonest quality in the Third Reich. One wasn't really safe anywhere. And when you aren't safe you'd better keep your mouth shut" (Remarque, *Time*, 22). Even the private Nazi army, the SA brownshirts, or storm troopers, were kept in line by terror. When it looked like their head, Ernst Roehm, might try to replace Hitler, the Fuehrer's bodyguard, the SS blackshirts, killed the SA leaders in the "night of the long knives," June 30, 1934. This pleased the regular army, which had seen the SA as a threat to its position, and it now threw its power to Hitler.

Brownshirts, blackshirts, jackboots, flags, parades: in creating the outer images of nazism, Hitler was a showman who tapped into people's craving for spectacle. He understood that a job and a few creature comforts fulfill only part of human longings; people also need a cause, excitement, something bigger and more colorful than their daily work to give drama and purpose to living. Due to standardization of products and people, the conformity of behavior and appearance demanded by the big organizations that most of us work for, life is increasingly tense yet increasingly monotonous, filled with worry about mortgages and cancer. Nazism brought pageantry to daily life, the allure of military display on a national scale. Hitler was very impressed by American marching bands and copied their style. The Harvard chant, "Fight, Fight, Fight," was adapted to "Sieg Heil, Sieg Heil" (Toland, *Hitler*, 142).

In one sense, nazism was mighty good entertainment. American journalist William L. Shirer wrote that Hitler "is restoring pageantry and color and mysticism to the drab lives of twentieth-century Germans" (*Diary*, 18). A German woman recalled years later, "I loved the constant marching and singing, with flags and bunting everywhere. I wanted to join the League of German girls" (Engelmann, 27). Nazism particularly appealed to adolescents, with their chronic need to fit in and be affirmed by the group while feeling special at the same time. Nazi youth organizations gave teenagers a prestige rare in our culture; some even got to beat up unpopular teachers.

Many people find the world too complex and want leaders who will simplify it for them. Hitler understood this. The masses, he said, are weak; they want to be led. He admired American and British advertising campaigns that reduced thoughts to sound bites. So Joseph Goebbels, the Nazi propaganda minister, sold the party the way Madison Avenue sold soap powder. This was understandable to foreign politicians. But shouldn't the Nazis' treatment of Jews, Gypsies, Communists, intellectuals, liberals, homosexuals, and other "undesirables" have signaled the sickness of the movement and warned the West of its madness? Not necessarily. Prejudice is deep in most societies. Nationalism itself can be a put-down of outsiders. Antisemitism was widespread in Western culture. And the British Empire was based on the assumption of white superiority over non-Aryan peoples.

But isn't there a matter of degree here, a line beyond which persecution is intolerable? Perhaps. But where is that line? It was not until 1941 that the Nazis undertook the "final solution": large-scale extermination. Throughout the 1930s, Hitler tried to get rid of German Jews by deportation. Most Western nations would accept only a few, including the United States which would not expand its immigration quotas. The Jews were trapped in Germany. The outside world assumed that they were going to concentration camps merely to undergo a reeducation program. After the embarrassment of Allied propaganda in World War I which had falsely portrayed Germans as baby killers, outsiders were reluctant to believe stories of Nazi atrocities. Also, it was, and remains, an accepted principle of international law that a nation may imprison or otherwise discipline its own problem elements and that the international community should not encroach on this aspect of sovereignty.

The concentration camps, which by 1942 became slaughterhouses for millions, were originally detention centers—political prisons—based on foreign models. Britain, during the Boer War (1899–1902), had used such camps to restrain hostile elements of the South African population. So did Spain and America in the Philippines. The ultimate mass murder in the camps correctly shocks us. And we conclude that Hitler was mad. But it was a special madness, born of the twentieth-century experience. Hitler lived through World War I, in which thirteen million soldiers were killed and in which death was organized and carried out on a scale hitherto unheard of. In the mind of Hitler, if fine young men could be slaughtered by their nations in this way, so could criminal elements. For a man who had endured the trenches, organized mass death was a normal part of life.

Some English-speaking politicians were not unsympathetic to Hitler's racial theories, with their emphasis on the superiority of northern European or Germanic stock. They found his bullying methods uncouth but hoped that he could be worked with and that his methods would moderate as the regime matured. In particular, they responded sympathetically to his attacks on communism, which he detested as a raising of the stupid many at the expense of the gifted few. He drew support from conservatives like Geoffrey Dawson, editor of the influential London *Times*, and American newspaper baron William Randolph Hearst. A major factor in the democracies' attempt to accommodate Hitler was that they saw Germany as a bulwark against Soviet expansion. Some hoped Hitler would attack Russia and that the two systems might exhaust each other. This fear of Soviet ambitions fed appeasement. Hitler said in 1937, "The English will get under the same eiderdown with me; in their politics they follow the same guidelines as I do, namely, the overriding necessity to annihilate Bolshevism" (Toland, 448).

Then, too, at a time when many countries were mired in economic stagnation, nazism seemed to have put Germany on the road to recovery. By 1935 the country appeared prosperous, with money for public works like the new autobahns (superhighways). Hitler raised the quality of workers' lives with paid holidays, health care benefits, public parks and other free recreational facilities, and the development of a modestly priced automobile, the Volkswagen, or people's car. Such success was hard to gainsay and made the rumors of excessive Nazi brutality hard to believe.

In fact, much of the prosperity was illusory, and nazism was far less efficient than its public image. Progress was based upon using stockpiled natural resources and pouring public money into the arms industry. But the resources had to be replaced for the prosperity to grow. They could be either paid for through exports or taken by force. As Hitler had no faith in international markets after the 1929 crash, it made total sense to him to use the new armaments to take what he needed by force. These resources could then be used to produce more guns for more conquest. By 1936 Germany was on the path to war. Hitler demanded lebensraum, living space, for Germany's surplus population to expand into, to prevent future unemployment and provide resources for its factories. He would get this space from the east, from Russia. But first, he would unite the German-speaking peoples of western Europe.

We have looked at how three key states—Italy, Japan, and Germany—came to define themselves as have-not nations, lacking the natural resources and trading power of such "haves" as the United States and the British Empire. We must now examine the developments that ended in war, asking why hostilities came in 1939 rather than earlier.

To begin with, the 1931 Japanese invasion of Manchuria did not go unnoticed. The British held extensive interests in Asia. Since World War I, the annual defense budget had been planned on the assumption that there would not be a major war for ten years. In 1931 this idea was scrapped. But ironically, attention to Asia led Britain to be cautious in Europe, for it no longer had the military power to fight a three-ocean war: in the Pacific against Japan, in the Mediterranean against Italy, and in the Atlantic against Germany. The British overseas dominions looked powerful on paper but were in fact dubious assets. Australia had supported Britain's wars but could not defend itself alone against Japan. India was in turmoil over home rule. Neither Canada, nor South Africa, nor Ulster wanted to fight anywhere. In short, Britain's loss of Japan's friendship created significant problems. The United States had less respect for Japan, but it too became preoccupied with the Pacific after 1931. Neither power, however, could conceive of going to war over Manchuria, and indeed, America continued to sell war materials to the belligerents.

In 1934 Mussolini embarked on his African empire by attacking Abyssinia. Was this the time to fight? A war might have stopped Mussolini, but it would have left Hitler untouched. Italy had attacked a "native" or colored people. Though some Western states were moving away from naked colonialism, both the French and British still had substantial interests in Africa, and it would have appeared hypocritical for them to fight Italy. For France, the problem was compounded by fear of a revived Germany. France and Italy shared a border. Should they cease to be friends, Italy could stab her neighbor across that border while France was fighting Germany. This in fact happened in 1940, when Italy joined in Germany's war and hastened France's collapse. Britain didn't want a war in the Mediterranean, and anyway, many leading citizens (including for a while, Winston Churchill) respected Mussolini's energy and opposition to communism.

Nevertheless, to their credit, the democracies did not aid the invasion but led the League of Nations in passing economic sanctions against Italy. Unfortunately, this had the unforeseen side effect of driving Italy closer to Germany. Hitler, who had taken Germany out of the League, continued to supply resources-short Italy with war materials. Mussolini had doubts about nazism, particularly its anti-Semitism, which had no place in fascism. But he now felt obliged to cultivate Germany. America also weakened the embargo by continuing to trade with Italy; its oil exports fueled the Fascist war machine. President Franklin D. Roosevelt declared his moral disapproval of Italy, but he needed the Italian-American vote and, with an election coming up, could go no further. As late as 1940, 80 percent of the Italian-language newspapers in the United States were pro-Mussolini, believing that he had elevated Italy's power and prosperity. In short, the attack on Abyssinia alienated Italy from the democracies without a compensating gain. But what else might have happened? Was there an easy answer for any politician?

Perhaps a better place to stand against authoritarianism was in Spain during the civil war of 1936–39, when right-wing forces under Franco overthrew the republic with the help of German and Italian troops. Martha Gellhorn, an American war correspondent who covered Spain, believed that the democracies became morally bankrupt when they left the republic to its fate. The Republican cause made war respectable again among liberals alienated by the seemingly pointless butchery of World War I. Ernest Hemingway, who had condemned that war in *A Farewell to Arms* (1929), now saluted the Republican army in *For Whom the Bell Tolls* (1940). Yet, the situation was complicated: this was not simply a struggle between good and evil.

Many on the left were antidemocratic, crudely anti-Catholic, backward looking, and as brutal as their enemies. After Russia sent troops to Spain, the Republican cause came under Soviet domination, and many of the more moderate democratic leaders were liquidated. Conversely, not all right-wingers were Fascists; some were only conservative nationalists. Business interests in the United States and Britain feared that the Republicans would nationalize their Spanish assets and that the Soviets would dominate Spain if the Republicans won. Franco seemed a safer bet. The Firestone Corporation in fact celebrated his victories with ads saying that the general and their tires were both winners. Further, American Catholics resented Republican persecution of the Church. In short, the democracies were too internally divided to fight. And anyway, the problem ultimately was Hitler, not Franco.

In 1936 German forces remilitarized the Rhineland, the buffer zone with France. French politicians thought about fighting, but neither

French nor British generals felt they could win an offensive war. France's economy had slipped badly during the Depression, and there was no money to replace its obsolete industrial plant. Consequently, the army lacked the modern tanks and the air force bombers for an attack on Germany. Between 1933 and 1937, for example, France produced only one-tenth as many military aircraft as Germany. World War I was still unpopular in France, so that, while there was peacetime conscription, draftees could not be kept long enough to train them for an offensive war. They were trained only to garrison prepared defensive positions, like the concrete and steel Maginot Line across northern France. Britain had the Royal Navy, but it could send only two army divisions to France, fewer than it sent in 1914, and the Royal Air Force also was only just starting to receive modern planes.

It can be argued that all the democracies needed to do was exhibit a show of force, because Hitler would have backed down in the face of a resolute policy. This is doubtful. Hitler cast himself as the man of iron will, and his operational orders make it clear that German forces would have withdrawn only to defensive positions on the Rhine before turning to fight. From the democracies' perspective, the longer they had to rearm the better. Anyway, there was some sympathy for the Germans: wasn't the Rhineland German after all? At this point, there was still a hope that the international order could be stabilized by accepting a moderate revision of the map drawn at Versailles.

From 1934 on, Hitler carried out a campaign of intimidation and propaganda to undermine the government of neighboring Austria, and in March 1938, his troops occupied that country. The rest of Europe became distinctly uneasy; with the population and resources of Austria, Germany had significantly increased its offensive potential (Hitler had netted five army divisions, iron ore and oil, and $200 million in gold and other reserves). Many people now understood for the first time the real threat to European peace posed by the Nazis. Yet, Austrians were predominantly of German stock, and many of them welcomed Der Fuehrer, who was a native of that country. After all, couldn't Germans unite with Germans?

This was also Hitler's pretext for demanding the Sudetenland province of Czechoslovakia, which had a German population of three and a quarter million. Hitler claimed, with some justification, that the Germans had been discriminated against by the Czechoslovakian state, denied equal access to education, jobs, and public funding. This situation led to the Munich conference of September 1938. Here, without properly consulting Czechoslovakia, Britain and France gave in to Hitler's demands.

How could this have happened? Britain and France still felt unprepared for offensive war, and they feared attack by Germany. To comprehend this, we must understand the claims made by the air forces of the Western nations between the wars. Out of sincere belief, and to gain funding for their services, they had asserted that air power alone would win the next war. Rather than the stalemate and butchery in the bloody muck of trenches, bombers would fly deep into enemy territory and bomb its cities into submission. One such proponent of air power was Billy Mitchell in the United States. He used filmed sequences of bomber attacks on such targets as old battleships to convince the public that control of the skies was crucial to national security.

The Germans and Italians also used film to give an inflated image of the power of their air forces. They were aided unintentionally by the celebrated American flyer Charles A. Lindbergh, who was touring Europe at this time and who was deliberately courted by Luftwaffe (German air force) public relations personnel. In much publicized public statements, he pronounced the Luftwaffe the most powerful in Europe, followed by Italy's air fleet. The unreadiness of France appalled him. Shortly after Munich, he announced that, had war come, the French could not have stopped the bombing of Paris. "There was not, and is not, in France one fighting plane as fast as the latest German bombers! The French air fleet is almost nonexistent from the standpoint of a modern war" (Lindbergh, *Journals*, 85–86). He thought the British were somewhat better off but also unready for combat. Lindbergh's views were respected by the British government, and fear of the Luftwaffe was a major factor at Munich. As Prime Minister Neville Chamberlain flew home from the conference, he passed over thousands of British homes, which he believed could not be protected from air raids. Britain needed more time.

Also on Chamberlain's mind was the attitude of the United States, still struggling out of the Depression and disillusioned about the failure of the last war to bring a lasting European peace. In 1934 a congressional committee headed by Senator Gerald P. Nye had concluded that arms manufacturers had worked to get America into World War I. Understandably, a majority of Americans opposed committing troops to Europe. Moreover, Europe was remote, and many Americans didn't understand the political issues involved between the contending forces; for many, Joe Louis's fight to regain the world heavy weight boxing title was more interesting than Hitler. Nevertheless, Franklin Roosevelt did send a telegram urging Hitler to settle the Sudeten question amicably.

Britain and France had one other possible ally, the Soviet Union, which was willing to guarantee Czechoslovakia's borders, a barrier against German expansion eastward. But Western statesmen did not trust Stalin's territorial ambitions. And Poland, which lay between Russia and Czechoslovakia, refused to let Soviet troops cross its territory for fear they would stay. Poland had grievances against Czechoslovakia for the poor treatment of its ethnics in that country and, in October, attacked its neighbor. This illustrates the dilemma facing Britain and France. Was Czechoslovakia a model democracy, as had often been claimed? Or was it an artificial fabrication, patched together from pieces of the Austro-Hungarian Empire, a collection of warring ethnic groups, not worth a world war?

Whatever the answer, giving in to Hitler at Munich was undoubtedly appeasement. Czechoslovakia was forced to relinquish its fortified mountain frontier and substantial territory, which the Nazis would have paid heavily to obtain by military action. But this was not appeasement without a bottom line. Britain and France would go no further. In March 1939, Chamberlain warned Hitler that he could make no greater mistake than to suppose that he could try to dominate Europe by force without Britain resisting to the end of its power. Germany swallowed what remained of Czechoslovakia, and in April, Britain introduced peacetime conscription for the first time in its history. Hitler now demanded the end of the Polish corridor and the reunification of East Prussia with Germany. Britain and France guaranteed Poland's borders. When on September 1, 1939, Germany attacked Poland, the two democracies honored their pledges and fought.

In retrospect, it is puzzling that so much is made of Munich, since Britain and France made clear their intention to give in no further to Hitler. Had they fought in 1938, there was some chance that Czechoslovakia might have survived. But by waiting a year, Britain had the air power to defend itself in the Battle of Britain, British aircraft production having overtaken Germany's in autumn 1939. And crucially, the new air raid early warning system, radar, was near to operational, which meant that RAF Fighter Command could be there to meet the attackers and that Nazi bombers wouldn't always get through.

Of course, the West's flirtation with Hitler was unconscionable in many ways, especially its cynicism about the treatment of Jews and other Nazi victims. Also questionable was the toleration of Hitler's aggressiveness by some in the West who hoped that Germany could be a gun turned against Russia. Realizing belatedly that appeasement had failed, Britain and France made an eleventh-hour attempt to ally with Russia, but they could not accept Stalin's demand for expansion into

Finland and the Baltic republics. Any hope of alliance collapsed when Stalin and Hitler, putting aside their vast ideological differences, signed the Nazi-Soviet Nonaggression Pact in August 1939, which stated that either power would remain neutral in the event that the other went to war with a third party (i.e., they would not attack each other). This left Hitler free to invade Poland, as he would now face a war only in the west. A secret protocol of the pact agreed to divide Poland between the two countries, thus sealing that country's fate. Stalin mistakenly believed that this would cushion Russia against German aggression; Hitler's invasion of Russia in 1941 forced the Soviets to see their mistake and work with the Allies.

Developments in Europe helped to shape Japanese policy. Into the 1930s there were still significant business and political elements in Japan who wanted to get along with the Western powers and to grow through commerce. But the success of Italy and Germany in taking what they needed by force played into the hands of Japan's war party. In the summer of 1937, the army launched a full-scale attack on China. This particularly upset the United States, which had a genuine interest in Chinese independence as well as strategic interests in Asia that were threatened. The extreme brutality of the Japanese military increased public outrage. A 1938 opinion poll showed that a majority of Americans favored military aid to China though not to Britain and France. The Chinese leader, Chiang Kai-shek, and his wife were skilled diplomats, who made much of the so-called Tanaka memorandum. Supposedly written in 1927 by a Japanese minister, the memorandum was a blueprint for world conquest. It was used to stir up American feeling against Japan by playing on an old fear that Asian hordes, the "yellow peril," would swamp America by an invasion across the Pacific. The document was later shown to be a forgery, but the threat to the stability of the region was real enough.

In attacking China, Japan sought self-sufficiency through conquest. The war party believed that the alternative was to remain a minor power, living on a resources-short and overpopulated land space. The attack represented the final defeat of the liberal political and business forces, which believed (probably correctly, given Japan's trade record since the war) that the nation could achieve prominence through peaceful economic competition. The liberals believed that expansion would antagonize the United States and other Western powers upon whom Japan was dependent for vital raw materials: in 1936 Japan bought one-third of its imports from America, including 66 percent of its oil; rubber and more oil came from British colonies; another 25 percent of its oil supply came from the Dutch East Indies. With China, these states made up the so-called ABCD powers. They would inevitably bring economic pressure on Japan, and then Japan would either have to back down or expand the war to get the resources that were being denied to it.

In the spring of 1940, the United States sent the bulk of its Pacific fleet from the West Coast to Hawaii in the hope of warning Japan off. In late July 1940, economic sanctions were imposed, cutting off key war materials: aviation gasoline, lubricating oil, and military-grade scrap iron. And in August, America made a defense agreement by which the British got fifty destroyers to fight Hitler in return for Caribbean bases that the U.S. Navy could use against Japan.

Should Japan back down? In Europe, Germany and Italy were doing well: the French and Dutch were defeated. Britain had its back to the wall, and America had to put some resources into helping that nation survive. With so many of its potential opponents in difficulty, Japan gambled on a war for hegemony in the western Pacific. The region would be liberated from Western imperialists, and Japan would assume a leading role as "the first among equals" in an Asian coprosperity sphere. In September, the Tri-Partite Pact, a defensive alliance with Germany and Italy, was signed, and Japanese forces began the southward conquest with an attack on northern French Indochina. France, in Hitler's pocket, could do little to resist. The United States responded with a total embargo on scrap iron. In November the Chinese nationalists were given a $100 million loan to buy arms.

Events quickly came to a head. In July 1941, Japan swallowed southern Indochina. America froze all Japan's assets and imposed a total fuel oil embargo, as did Britain and Holland. U.S. B-17 bombers were shipped to Pacific bases; American officials warned Japan that the bombers could destroy the vulnerable wood and paper houses of Japanese cities, a threat intended to dissuade the Japanese from further aggression. But the Japanese military, convinced that America was preparing for an offensive war on the home islands, called for a preemptive strike that would seize the resources Japan needed and perhaps force the United States to make an arrangement for dividing power in the Pacific. In this respect, Pearl Harbor may be viewed as the last act in the degeneration of U.S.-Japanese relations.

The point to note here is that at no time was there an attempt to appease Japan. Western politicians always assumed that an Asian nation could be made to back down. British foreign secretary Anthony Eden, echoing FDR's views, said that "a display of firmness is more likely to deter Japan from war than to provoke her to it" (Iriye, *Origins*, ix). In fact, the policy had the opposite effect. If appeasement failed in Europe, deterrence failed in Asia. It seems there were no easy answers.

Looking back, we might say that the history of the period does not reflect particularly well on any of the major players. Yet their actions are at least intelligible in context. Who is to say that, if the world as we know it collapsed, as it did for millions after World War I and again in the Great Depression, we should act more wisely or be any better at finding lasting solutions? Our collective inability during 1992 to prevent the brutal civil wars raging in Yugoslavia, where "ethnic cleansing" again took place, and in Somalia suggests that we had not yet found international solutions to all the problems generated by the human urge to collective violence.

three

The Patterns of War, 1939–1945

WORLD WAR II began when Germany invaded Poland on September 1, 1939. Few experts gave the obsolete Polish forces much chance to win, but the speed and completeness of Germany's victory were startling. By September 14, German forces were in the rear of Poland's capital, Warsaw, and had completed a giant encircling movement, trapping the major Polish armies in a net to the north. By September 27 significant resistance had ended. Polish defeat was due not only to inferior equipment, as the Germans, too, had their share of cavalry and horse-drawn transport. Hitler's forces introduced a new method of waging war, the blitzkrieg, or lightning attack.

The Polish undertook a conventional deployment that looked back to the patterns of World War I. Major armies were spread out in largely immobile defensive positions to protect as much as possible of the northern provinces bordering Germany. Tanks were divided piecemeal as supports to the infantry. Communication with reserves to the rear was largely by rail. Poland expected a slugging match on this broad front, but Germany changed the nature of the battlefield and obviated the necessity of meeting the bulk of Polish forces head on.

The Luftwaffe quickly took out the opposing air defenses and then roamed at will between the Polish armies and their supports, severing communications and numbing their ability to react. Tanks, instead of being squandered in small numbers, were concentrated in powerful panzer (armored) units, which brought overwhelming superiority to bear on weak spots in the enemy disposition and then punched through these into the rear. Conventional wisdom would have had them then stop and battle the enemy. But the panzers kept going, striking deep into the enemy heartland, sowing terror and defeatism, while the infantry behind them exploited the breakthrough to encircle and contain the enemy. The Germans used technology and innovative planning to avoid the mass slaughter of World War I. Blocked from retreat and cut off from support, the emasculated Polish forces necessarily capitulated.

This innovative battle practice has framed our image of World War II, which is seen popularly as a mobile war dominated by fast-moving machines delivering surgical strikes in the air and on land, much like a high-tech video game. It is clean and swift. This concept was encouraged by the Germans, whose newsreel film showcased the panzer attacks and downplayed glitches in execution. On our side, the popular heroes from the war tended to be hard-driving tank generals like George Patton, who we believed exploited our superior technological know-how to outfight the Germans at their own game of mechanical warfare.

There is some truth in the image. But this kind of mobile warfare, in which relatively small forces captured huge territories quickly, primarily characterized the opening phases of the war up through 1941. In this period, German and Japanese forces defeated opponents whose equipment was often obsolete and whose generals were wedded to past ideas. The Axis needed to fight a war of breadth, of swift victories, because their armies and economies could not withstand a war of attrition. After successfully launching bold campaigns, they hoped for a negotiated peace on the basis of their gains.

When peace did not come and the pendulum swung against them as the Allies took back occupied territory, the pattern of conflict shifted considerably from a mobile one to a punishing grind-it-out war of attrition, which the Axis could only lose. Against dug-in, competent, and often fanatical Axis troops, the Allies had to apply massive firepower to winkle out resistance in ground combat, reminiscent of World War I. There were periods of fluid warfare, as in the African desert, or in France, Belgium, and Luxembourg after the Allies broke out from the Normandy beachheads. But in Russia, Italy, Normandy, and the Pacific, the fight was largely ditch to ditch, in a blasted landscape where misery for the individual soldier was maximized. Illustrating the ease with which we can exaggerate the role of armor, only 16 of 59 American divisions in Europe were armored. Of 520 German divisions in the war overall, a mere 40 were panzers.

With Poland eliminated and Germany reunited in the east, Hitler gathered strength to deal with the democracies in the west. Meanwhile, Russia moved to cushion its borders against Hitler: on September 17, 1939, the Soviets invaded and subsequently occupied about half of Poland. In the following months they forced Finland to relinquish some disputed territory and annexed the Baltic states of Latvia, Estonia, and Lithuania.

The United States had early declared its neutrality. But FDR persuaded Congress to alter the neutrality acts, which prohibited sales of war materials to belligerents, so that France and Britain could buy arms on a cash-and-carry basis. This was a crucial step in aiding these democracies. And as Britannia still ruled the Atlantic waves, guns could get through. Hitler attempted to cut this lifeline by using submarine warfare, and the battle of the Atlantic thus began to assume a pivotal role in the European war. America, though not in the war, was moving under FDR's leadership to solidarity with the free nations of Europe.

In April 1940, Hitler, concerned with guaranteeing the flow of vital raw materials such as iron ore from the north, struck Denmark, whose fifteen-thousand-man army quickly surrendered, and Norway, which put up a stiffer fight. British and French military support failed to save the situation, and the outclassed Norwegians had to capitulate.

In May, the major blow fell in the west—but not where it was expected. The French and British, preferring the defensive, awaited a German attack. But where? On their right flank, across northern France, were strong concrete bastions forming the imposing Maginot Line. The center was lightly held because it fronted the Ardennes forest, considered impassable to armor. The blow would probably fall then on the left flank, against the weak armies of neutral Holland and Belgium. Expecting this, the French and British planned to move their main forces to support the left when Hitler attacked.

But while moving northeast into Belgium, the French and British would enter a relatively narrow landspace, where they might be trapped between the attacking Germans and the coast. The Germans understood this. They attacked this left flank with their infantry, enticing the British and French to move forward into the box. Then panzers swept through the Ardennes behind them, cutting them off from the body of France. It was as though the Allies had entered a narrow room and the door had slammed behind them.

Holland surrendered quickly, and as Belgian defenses crumbled, the British and French were forced back against the Belgian coast. At this point, the Germans let slip a golden opportunity to bag the beleaguered Allied forces. While the panzers paused to regroup, the Allied navies, between May 26 and June 4, rescued 224,000 British and 114,000 French troops from the port of Dunkirk and took them to Britain. Bereft of allies, the remaining French armies fought on until June 16, when they surrendered.

Hitler expected peace with Britain. But Dunkirk had changed the British mind-set. Distrustful of France and reluctant to fight a continental war, they had shown limited enthusiasm before Dunkirk. But now, their backs to the wall, they warmed to the fight. Hitler would have to invade Britain. To do this, he would need the Luftwaffe to keep the Royal Navy from interfering with his invasion fleet in the English Channel. This meant air control, and this in turn necessitated destroying the Royal Air Force. In the ensuing Battle of Britain, fought in the summer and autumn of 1940, the Luftwaffe failed to do this.

The British fighter planes were at first outnumbered, and this led to the legend of the "few" who supposedly saved Britain against enormous odds. But the disparity was never that great, and British fighter plane production surpassed Germany's by the fall of the year. Also, the British had a radar early warning system. And with the help of Polish cryptologists, their Ultra intelligence unit had deciphered the German Enigma coding system that transmitted operational orders, so that the RAF often knew the enemy's intentions. The Germans had a further disadvantage. Many of their planes were designed for close ground support and had neither the range nor the performance for the kind of strategic air offense they were undertaking. Their fighter bombers proved particularly vulnerable to the Hurricanes and Spitfires of RAF Fighter Command. Failing to destroy the RAF, the Germans turned to blitzing British cities in the hope of breaking civilian morale, as prewar theorists said they could. But German bombers had a low payload and no chance of success. In six months they dropped only thirty thousand tons on Britain. By comparison, in a similar period during 1944, the Allies dumped twenty times as much on Germany. British morale went up under the attack, and RAF Bomber Command was to take an enormous revenge on German cities as the war increased in intensity.

The survival of Britain was a major factor in Germany's defeat, for Hitler now had an implacable enemy on his western flank, an enemy that had increasing material assistance from the great manufacturing nation across the Atlantic. The United States, said FDR, could not be a spectator in a world dominated by force. In September 1940 America introduced a military draft, and in late autumn lend-lease was announced. Britain was running out of money, and so America would "lend" it tools of war, even though the loan could not be repaid, except in favorable trade relations after the war and other concessions. America, said Roosevelt, must become "the great arsenal of democracy." The United States also extended naval protection to British-bound convoys and steadily widened the zone of American oversight to the mid-Atlantic. American and German warships were exchanging fire by the fall of 1941, as America extended a lifeline to the struggling British.

If Hitler's failure to crush Britain was crucial to the course of the war, so was his invasion of Russia. Keeping his promise to destroy bolshevism and gain Germany living space to the east, Der Fuehrer launched Operation Barbarossa on June 22, 1941. Three million Germans and their allies—Italian, Finnish, Hungarian, and Romanian soldiers—attacked in three army groups aimed at the major productive regions centered on Leningrad, Moscow, and Stalingrad. Gains in territory and captured forces were huge, but the massive distances frustrated even the German war machine. By the onset of winter, none of the major cities had fallen. And the Russians, whose men and equipment were better prepared for the bitter weather, counterattacked in December. The Axis took the offensive again in spring 1942 but failed to strike lethal blows. By fall they were stopped and would spend the rest of the war in a massively costly attempt to hold their ground.

Russia was the graveyard of the Wehrmacht (German army), which bled to death on the eastern front. By February 1942, it had lost 1,164,000 men. The Russians paid an even higher price, and without their sacrifice the Allies could never have retaken occupied Europe. As late as D-Day, in June 1944, 70 percent of Germany's manpower was in Russia, leaving Germany's western flank vulnerable to invasion. It is now clear that Barbarossa was a huge mistake, but this was not clear at the time. The American military at first estimated that Russia would collapse in four to six weeks. Before the war, Stalin had weakened his officer corps by liquidating senior men whose loyalty he suspected, and the Red Army had not performed well in Finland, due to poor leadership and obsolete equipment. But everyone in the West underestimated the resilience of the Soviet regime, the patriotism of the Russian people, and the productive capacity of their industry. The Soviets turned our armor and planes superior in quality and quantity to the Axis arsenal, and they were aided after 1941 by American lend-lease. At one point, the Russians may have had perhaps ten thousand tanks to oppose Germany's twenty-five hundred.

The swing year in the fortunes of the contending nations was 1942. It opened with renewed Axis offensives in Russia and spectacular Japanese conquests in the Far East. But it ended with the Allied nations taking the initiative back. Most crucially, on December 7, 1941, the Japanese attacked the American Pacific fleet at Pearl Harbor. The United States was now officially in the war—the third factor, along with the Battle of Britain and the invasion of Russia, that explains the Axis defeat. The relative fighting efficiency of Germany and Japan peaked and declined during this year. Both had made serious errors, underestimating the willpower of their opponents to fight a war to the finish despite crushing defeats. This was particularly true of their opinion of the United States, which they stereotyped as too materialistic and pleasure-loving to endure long the sacrifices of war.

Both Axis powers were made complacent by their early successes, cutting back, for example, on aircraft production just when the Allies were increasing theirs. The Axis countries had acquired a mistaken reputation for internal totalitarian efficiency, but the Nazi state, for example, was corrupt and inefficient. It crippled its own creative capacities by liquidating talented "undesirables." Though cooperation among the Allies was faulty, it was worse between Axis nations. By May 1942 the Nazis knew that the Allies had cracked Japanese codes, but they didn't warn Japan. Hitler expected significant military help from his puppet state, Vichy France, and from Franco's Spain, but he didn't get it. Italy was a military liability, requiring constant German bolstering. There was no way that in a war of attrition the Axis could match the Allies in numbers of men and materials of war, particularly given American productive capacity.

This did not make the task of defeating the Axis easy or the path to victory obvious. The decisions facing the democracies were particularly difficult. In December 1941, at the Arcadia Conference, America and Britain established a combined military command and confronted the tough question of which enemy should have top priority, Germany or Japan. In the month of Pearl Harbor, with Japan still making enormous gains, American public opinion favored putting the Pacific first. But American leaders agreed with the British that Hitler represented the greatest threat and could be unbeatable if he knocked Russia out of the war. The major effort must be in Europe. The Americans pressed for an invasion of France and Germany, the heart of Hitler's Fortress Europe, in 1942 or 1943 at the latest. They felt this was necessary to help the beleaguered Russians. The British thought this timetable too optimistic.

A cross-Channel invasion would require a huge American buildup in Britain, and this in turn meant winning the battle of the Atlantic, a victory by no means guaranteed. American shipping losses were heavy, partly because of inexperience with convoying techniques, partly because the lights were not immediately turned off on the East Coast and the silhouetted merchantmen made good targets for lurking U-boats. The Atlantic war would not be won until mid-1943, a victory due partly to growing American experience with convoying, and partly to Allied warships being equipped with sophisticated submarine tracking devices, such as sonar. And, at the end of 1942, Ultra broke the U-boat code, so the Allies could eavesdrop on the undersea raiders. Of 1,175 U-boats, 785 were sunk (191 by Americans). Germany sank 23.3 million tons of Allied shipping, but the democracies built 42.5 million replacement tons.

Until the Atlantic battle could be won, the British proposed the alternative of an air offensive against Germany and a land attack in the Mediterranean to weaken the Axis preliminary to an invasion of France. Why here? In pursuit of his Mediterranean empire, Mussolini had attacked Greece in October 1940. Failing badly, he pulled in the Germans, who in April–May 1941 took Greece and Crete at significant cost to their elite airborne forces. These Mediterranean air bases threatened British ships bringing oil from the Middle East. Increasing the threat, Axis forces under General Erwin Rommel on the southern Mediterranean coast of north Africa had by late 1942 driven through Libya to threaten Egypt and the Suez Canal. The British Eight Army faced Rommel at El Alamein. Should British forces be defeated, the Middle East and its crucial oil fields would be lost. The British proposed landings in the German rear at Casablanca, Oran, and Algiers, on the Vichy French African coast. The Americans agreed, though reluctantly, believing they were being used to salvage British imperial possessions. This became Operation Torch.

In October 1942 the British Eighth Army attacked, and in November British-American forces under Dwight D. Eisenhower's overall command landed on the Vichy coast behind Rommel. This successful amphibious landing against a relatively weak opponent gave the Allies experience that was later invaluable in the D-Day landings. There were difficulties. Allied intelligence failed to properly utilize sympathetic French officers who were prepared to cooperate instead of fight. Some Allied equipment proved inadequate: the Grant tank, whose cannon could traverse only 180 degrees—only half the battlefield— proved a liability in combat. GIs wearing sunglasses were killed by snipers, who caught the sun's glint on the lenses. Some British armor was lost in costly piecemeal frontal attacks reminiscent of nineteenth-century cavalry charges. Nevertheless, the outnumbered Axis forces, bereft of air cover and taken in front and rear, were driven into a dwindling pocket on the Tunisian coast and forced to surrender on May 10, 1943.

Having saved Africa and the Middle East, the next logical move was to Sicily immediately to the north—which would give the Allies a foothold in the northern Mediterranean. The Americans preferred to invade France but acquiesced in deference to British experience. The

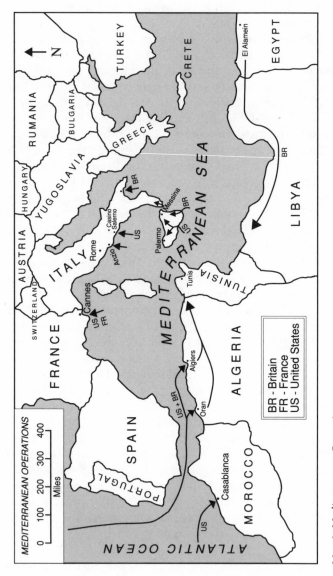

Map 1. Mediterranean Operations

British Eighth Army would drive up Sicily's eastern coast, while Patton's American Seventh Army would run block on their left flank. The target was Messina, a port on the northern coast, which if taken would stop the Axis garrison from evacuating to the Italian mainland. The aim was to cork the bottle at Messina.

The landings took place successfully on July 10, 1943. Although Allied naval gunners shot down some of their own airborne troops and other troops landed in the sea, the operation soon improved. While the British advanced cautiously against stiffening German resistance, Patton struck through weak Italian forces to take Palermo, on the west coast of the island, before turning east toward Messina. But he too now faced tough German rearguard action. Also, British and American commanders failed to properly coordinate their movements, allowing forty thousand Axis soldiers to evacuate the island before Messina fell to Allied troops on August 17. Their escape helped make the Italian campaign a tough one.

The debate over strategic aims now recurred. Winston Churchill strenuously championed an invasion of Italy, which would probably knock Italy out of the war, and force Germany to move some of its divisions from France to this front. This might make the cross-Channel invasion easier. Also, with Italian bases, Allied bombers could reach industrial targets in Germany and the Balkans. On the other hand, the plan had the disadvantage of taking troops away from the buildup for the invasion of France, which the Americans wanted without further diversions, believing that the Italian invasion would prove indecisive. Churchill and FDR reached a compromise by which there would be an attack on Italy but the resources allotted to that front would be small enough not to jeopardize the second front in France. This solution made diplomatic sense, but the two-front war probably meant that the generals in the Italian theater never had the tools to do the job properly, and the fighting bogged down into a bloody stalemate.

British-American forces landed in Italy on September 8 and 9, 1943, leading to the expected Italian surrender. But the Germans rushed troops into Italy. Taking advantage of the rugged terrain, which neutralized the Allied advantage in armor and provided strong natural defensive positions, the Wehrmacht fought a stubborn holding action, contesting every foot of ground and making the advance physically and mentally grueling for the troops. An attempt to outflank the Germans by landing in their rear at Anzio, on January 22, 1944, was contained by panzers, and though Rome fell on June 4, 1944, it was not until May 2, 1945, that German troops in Italy finally surrendered.

The strength of German defensive positions necessitated a massive

Fig. 2. The Abbey of Monte Cassino (Painting by Tom Craig, reproduced courtesy of the U.S. Army Center of Military History)

pounding of the enemy, producing enormous destruction to Italy's infrastructure. With agriculture and industry disrupted, a large percentage of the population was thrown into starvation, beggary, and prostitution. In a tragic incident, the ancient monastery of Monte Cassino, with a priceless medieval library, was ruined by Allied bombers, even though Allied ground troops suspected—correctly—that no enemy had been in the buildings. (They did then make a defensive position of the ruins.) Thus, terrain and a resourceful enemy brought about a brute force pattern of fighting that modified the surgical thrust image of combat in the war.

While the Mediterranean campaigns were progressing, the American and British air forces attacked targets in occupied Europe and Germany. Their aims were threefold: to diminish industrial production, particularly of oil and machine parts, to soften Hitler's defenses for the cross-Channel invasion, and to convince the Russians that the democracies were pulling their weight. In August 1942, the American Eighth Air Force began flying bombing missions from British bases, and in late 1943, the American Twelfth Air Force attacked targets in Germany and the Balkans from Italian fields. Yet the buildup took time. In autumn 1943 U.S. bomb tonnage represented only 15 percent of the theater total, and it did not reach parity with the RAF until February 1944.

In mid-1941 the British abandoned the illusion that they could hit military-industrial targets with surgical strikes. RAF bombsights were so inaccurate that only one of four bombs fell within five miles of the objective (Schaffer, 36). Precision bombing could be done only in daylight, which meant huge losses of bombers to air defenses, so the RAF went to nighttime "area bombing" of industrial areas in hopes of creating broad damage and demoralization.

Americans, disturbed by the collateral damage done to civilian districts by the night raids, stuck to daylight bombing. It was hoped that the B-17 Flying Fortress and the B-24 Liberator had the firepower and speed to defend themselves in daylight while delivering bomb loads onto targets with pinpoint accuracy, thanks to the Norden bombsights. In practice, American daylight raids were very costly for some time. In July 1943, 100 planes and 1,000 crewmen were lost. A further 75 airmen had mental breakdowns (Schaffer, 64). The October 14 raid on the Schweinfurt ball bearing factories cost 60 of the 291 Fortresses committed (Ellis, 197). Conditions improved with the introduction, in December 1943, of the P-51 Mustang, a long-range fighter capable of providing to-the-target protection. But losses remained high. In the

February 20–26, 1944, raids on aircraft factories, the American Air Force lost 226 bombers, 28 fighters, and 2,600 men (Weigley, *American Way*, 339–40).

The daylight sacrifices did not pay off in bombing accuracy. Under perfect conditions only 50 percent of American bombs fell within a quarter of a mile of the target. Fighter attack, flak, smoke, and cloud cover lowered efficiency. American flyers estimated that as many as 90 percent of bombs could miss their targets (Perrett, 405; Eckert, 260). Along with British area bombings, this caused huge "collateral damage" (to civilians), not only in Germany but in France and other occupied countries, creating resentment of the Allies. For example, attacks on the submarine pens at Saint-Nazaire and Lorient destroyed the surrounding French towns but left the pens undamaged. "No dog or cat is left in these towns," wrote German Admiral Karl Dönitz. "Nothing but the submarine shelters remain" (Franklin, 105).

How do we judge the strategic air offensive against Fortress Europe? There isn't a simple answer. On the one hand, hopes that air power would provide a cost-effective, clinical, and humane method of destroying the enemy's power base proved illusory. Neither Axis nor Allied air attacks slowed overall production or destroyed civilian morale: both went up under duress. The official U.S. *Strategic Bombing Survey* (1946) estimated that it cost a million dollars in planes, bases, crews, and bombs to do a million dollars in damage (Perrett, 437). Since the Allies could afford the cost more than the Axis, the Allies won.

Air attacks extended the cruelty of war. At least 635,000 German civilian men, women, and children died, along with thousands in the occupied countries (Irving, 41). Even if the Norden bombsight had proved reliable, the distinction between military and civilian targets was largely lost in total war. When bombers attacked a factory, a railroad marshalling yard, a dock, an oil refinery, or an electrical power system, they hit civilian workers and their families in the surrounding working-class housing. The longer a war continues, the greater the desensitization to enemy suffering, and the less concern about "collateral damage." By June 1944 the Luftwaffe was defeated, and Allied planes roamed at will, seeking "targets of opportunity," which inevitably included many nonmilitary structures.

This pattern reached its extreme with the destruction of Dresden, an undefended city that had neither industrial nor military significance. On February 13 and 14, 1945, the city was bombed three times by the RAF and U.S. Eighth Air Force, creating a fire storm that killed up to 135,000 people and destroyed irreplaceable examples of medieval architecture. Military historian James M. Morris concluded that, by the time Germany surrendered, virtually nothing of any significance was left to bomb.

On the other hand, the air offensive did make significant contributions to the Allied victory in western Europe. Although German industrial production climbed, the rate would have been higher without the bombings. By using their bombers as decoys in daylight raids and accepting a high cost in crews, Americans drew the Luftwaffe into a battle of attrition that virtually destroyed it by D-Day, vastly helping the success of the invasion and saving the lives of Allied ground forces. From March to September 1944 the transportation network in the invasion area was targeted; this campaign proved highly effective in stopping the Germans from getting their armored reserves into battle. Finally, as distinguished American military historian Russell F. Weigley argued in *The American Way of War*, attacks on Axis fuel production, begun in March 1944, were spectacularly effective and left both tanks and planes immobilized through lack of gas.

By 1944, the Axis was fatally weakened. Italy had surrendered and, in the west, the Soviets made huge advances. By October, Finland, Romania, Bulgaria, and Hungary were out of the war. Yet the conflict could not be ended without a frontal attack on the western face of Hitler's Fortress Europe: France. The D-Day invasion, beginning June 6, 1944, was completely successful: it was the biggest cooperative amphibious operation in history, involving troops from America, Britain and its Commonwealth countries, the Free French, and other European exiles. On day one, after a massive air and naval bombardment, Allied paratroops attacked key coastal locations, followed by waves of 176,000 men in four thousand landing craft. It was a remarkable feat of planning and coordination. Success was aided by Allied intelligence, which tricked Hitler into believing that the major landing would come further north, at Calais. Awaiting this, he held back crucial armored reserves, which were destroyed behind the front by Allied aircraft. By the end of June, a million Allied troops were ashore, along with 177,000 vehicles and 586,000 tons of supplies. With the fall of Cherbourg, a deep-water port that replaced the temporary artificial harbors, the ability to sustain the beachhead was assured.

The Germans were stubborn opponents. At Omaha Beach, veteran panzers nearly succeeded in denying Americans the beachhead. The landing was also handicapped by the American failure to realize the need for specialized equipment to sweep the shore of obstacles like underwater mines. The Wehrmacht, though bereft of air cover and armor, made excellent defensive positions out of the thick Normandy

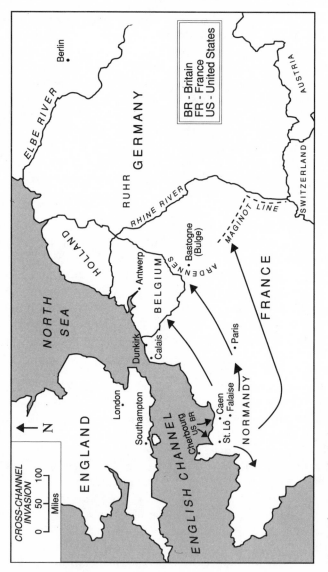

CROSS-CHANNEL
INVASION

Miles
0   50   100

N

ENGLAND

London

Southampton

ENGLISH CHANNEL

Cherbourg
US BR
Caen
St. Lô Falaise

NORMANDY

NORTH
SEA

Dunkirk
Calais

Paris

BELGIUM

Antwerp

HOLLAND

Bastogne
(Bulge)

ARDENNES

FRANCE

MAGINOT LINE

RHINE RIVER

RUHR GERMANY

ELBE RIVER

Berlin

SWITZERLAND

AUSTRIA

BR - Britain
FR - France
US - United States

Map 2. The Cross-Channel Invasion

hedgerows (made of earth, stone, and trees), which had to be cut through by bulldozers fitted with plough blades.

Allied tanks did not have the firepower needed to spearhead a break-through without massive artillery or air support fire. The infantry, too, called for a deluge of shells or bombs to clear the path ahead and save GI lives. "We let the artillery fight the war as much as possible," said one U.S. infantry officer (Ellis, 384). The result was massive destruction on a wide front. The devastation hindered Allied progress. Cherbourg was so battered it took three weeks to clear it for traffic. Caen, the first major British objective, was pounded into rubble, which blocked the roads the armored vehicles needed.

Finally, on July 25, the American First Army, under Omar Bradley, broke out of the pocket at Saint-Lô and reintroduced mobility to the battlefront. Part of Patton's Third Army, exploiting the gap, swung west to try to free the ports of Brittany, while the rest wheeled east to drive across France. The pace was so fast that a large part of the German Seventh Army was in danger of being outflanked and trapped between the Americans and the British and Canadians, who were now advancing in the north. The Germans were able to hold open an escape route at Falaise long enough for thirty-five thousand men to escape entrapment. They were helped by clumsy British-American coordination. But ten thousand Germans were killed, and thirty thousand surrendered. Meanwhile, a further U.S.-French landing in southern France strongly reinforced the Allies and led to the fall of Marseilles, a port whose facilities greatly aided Allied supply. Paris was liberated on August 25, and the swift American advance continued into northern France. By mid-September, the Germans were largely out of France and Belgium.

Meanwhile, the British advanced on the left toward Holland, with Antwerp as the target. Further ports were needed to keep the armies supplied with fuel, and shortages began to seriously slow progress. Antwerp was a logical choice. British Field Marshal Montgomery took the city in early September, but he failed to dislodge the Germans along the banks of the estuary from the sea to the city, so that shipping access was hindered until November 29. Montgomery's attention was distracted from Antwerp: for some time, he had been urging Eisenhower to give him the bulk of the remaining fuel for a drive that might collapse German resistance before the end of the year. He proposed a daring thrust through the Netherlands that would flank Germany's West Wall defenses and plunge into the northern regions of the Reich. The plan was imaginative but too ambitious: it relied on taking and holding four rivers and three canals to open a path for Allied armor. The high command ignored Ultra's warning that panzer strength in the area was greater than expected. The upshot was that Operation Market Garden failed, and as winter approached, the Allied offensives ground to a halt opposite Germany's Siegfried line of defenses.

Hitler now launched his last major offensive in the west. He hoped to repeat the success of 1940 by again attacking in the Ardennes and driving through weak American forces in what was designated—in an incredible intelligence failure, given the experience of 1940—a quiet sector. German armor would then drive to the coast at Antwerp, dividing the Allied armies and defeating them piecemeal. On December 16, 1944, twenty-five German divisions, taking advantage of bad weather that kept Allied planes grounded, attacked. In hard fighting, they dented the American line but could not pierce it, creating only a "bulge." Although the Germans achieved complete tactical surprise, they did not have the strength for a breakthrough. This was not 1940, and the Germans were not facing a weak, inexperienced opponent. When the weather cleared, Allied air power blunted the German advance. American ground forces struck back, including elements of Patton's Third Army, which in a remarkable feat wheeled out of line and drove hard from the east to help beat the Germans back in the Bastogne area. The Battle of the Bulge spent the Wehrmacht's last strength, and Germany lay open to assault. The western Allies crossed the Rhine on March 1, 1945, and met the Russians at the Elbe on April 25, as they poured in from the east. Hitler committed suicide on April 30, and German nazism collapsed with him.

Germany, along with much of continental Europe, lay in ruins; this was the havoc that Hitler had wrought. Believing that in World War I Germany had surrendered while there was still a chance of victory, he preferred total destruction to the repetition of this failure. Thus, a war of brute force destruction was made inevitable, in which Germany's resistance went beyond any logical defense of state interests and provoked national destruction.

In the Wehrmacht, the Allies faced an opponent too skilled to be beaten with the same ease displayed by the panzers in 1939 and 1940. In both east and west, the armies had to be hammered into destruction. A conflict fought to unconditional surrender had brought about such destruction that a disturbing ferocity was provoked on both sides. In the ruins of European cities, we learned of our ability as a species to wreak havoc on each other and on our environment in proportions hitherto unimagined.

In the Pacific, the pattern of war was marked in its early stages by lightning offensives. Japan's conquests were a remarkable feat of plan-

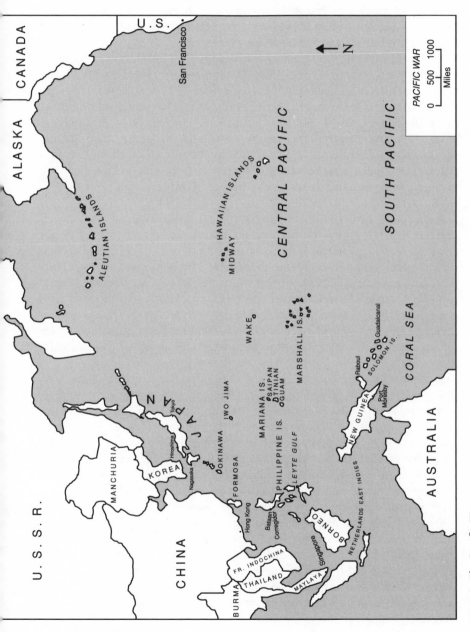

Map 3. The Pacific War

ning and execution. In three months, imperial forces overran territory half the size of the United States. On December 7, 1941, Japanese carrier-based planes attacked the American Pacific fleet at Pearl Harbor, sinking 4 battleships and 3 destroyers and severely damaging numerous other vessels. They also destroyed 160 aircraft and disabled 128 others, for a loss of only 29 Japanese planes.

At the same time, the Japanese struck at the Philippines, Thailand, Malaya, Wake Island, Guam, and Hong Kong. In February 1942 the British bastion of Singapore fell easily, followed by the Netherlands Indies in March and Burma in April. The Japanese also took strong positions in New Guinea and the Solomons. Only in the Philippines, where U.S. and Filipino troops clung to the Bataan peninsula and Corregidor, was the conquest held up. But by May 6, 1942, these had also fallen. The Japanese were on the doorstep of Australia and needed only to take the Hawaiian islands to exclude the United States from the Pacific.

A number of factors aided Japan's lightning war, including Western arrogance. Used to easily quelling poorly equipped and trained Asian armies, the West did not believe until too late what their intelligence reports told them about Japanese strength. The command at Pearl Harbor became complacent about the warnings. Even after the war began, General Douglas MacArthur in the Philippines failed to properly disperse his aircraft. Over half the modern bombers and fighters in the theater were still parked in neat rows, a regular shooting gallery, when the Japanese hit Clark Field. MacArthur had not accepted this possibility.

Much to the West's surprise, they were outclassed technologically in the opening rounds. The Japanese Zero fighter plane outfought any Allied plane, and in 1941 Japanese pilots may have been the best trained anywhere. American submarines were handicapped by inferior torpedoes, and the B-17 bomber proved ineffective against naval targets, two weapons crucial to stopping Japanese invasion of the Philippines. Japanese armies also surprised their opponents by their logistical skill: they moved faster and further than Occidentals believed possible, negotiating terrain Westerners deemed impassable.

Western armies, highly bureaucratized and heavily dependent on lines of communication for their many material needs, required anywhere from eight to twenty-eight service personnel to keep one man on the firing line. In the Japanese army, each man subsisted lightly, and the ratio was more like one to one. Put crudely, their military animal dragged a lot less tail, so they took ground quickly. The Japanese were also helped initially by an ironic flip-flop in Western attitudes.

Never characterized as simply human by their enemy, the Japanese went from being seen as subhuman before December 1941 to being seen as superhuman immediately after. In 1942, American and British Commonwealth troops collapsed before relatively small Japanese forces, which had acquired an almost supernatural status.

Why, then, did Japan's war effort fail? To begin with, the Japanese, unlike the United States and its allies, never saw the war as one for total conquest and domination of its major opponents. Contrary to belief at the time, no Japanese leader seriously considered invading the United States. Japan fought for a place in the sun, alongside Westerners. The best Japanese military minds, such as Admiral Isoroku Yamamoto, knew that in a war of attrition Japan must lose. Their hope was to initially take such a vast area of the Pacific that the price of taking it back would be too daunting and Westerners would acknowledge Japan's right to a sphere of influence in the region. (At their furthest extent, Japanese conquests ran from the Aleutians and the tip of Alaska in the north to New Guinea at Australia's border in the south.) Japan's aim was the sharing of power.

Racially stereotyping their opponents as coarse barbarians not imbued with the finer military spirit, the Japanese underrated their enemies' staying power—especially that of Americans, whom they saw as corrupted by their high standard of living. They failed to grasp the absolute resentment their actions, particularly the surprise attack on Pearl Harbor, had generated in their enemies: unconditional surrender—the eradication of Japanese militarism—would dominate Allied thinking up through the dropping of the atomic bombs.

If the war continued, Japan had some hope of holding out by drawing upon the resources of the regions conquered to refurbish its war machine. But the Allies rebounded too quickly, taking back territory and choking off Japan's maritime trade routes, for this possibility to be made good. Also, through arrogance and brutality the Japanese military alienated other Asian peoples who might have worked with them. Japan was forced to fight a war to the death on chronically inadequate, dwindling resources. Japan in the east, like Germany in the west, at first won a war of width, of breathtaking seizure of territory, that temporarily obscured its inability to win a war of depth. Japan's economy, like Germany's, could not compete in attrition with the combined power of its enemies, particularly the United States.

As the tide changed, the weaknesses in Japanese military thinking and technological applications also became apparent. Often forgotten, but central, is the fact that Japan in the 1930s had tied itself to the albatross of the endless China war. A disproportionate percentage of the

Imperial Army was tied down in China. Allied assistance to Generalissimo Chiang Kai-shek, together with the opening of subsidiary mainland fronts in Burma and on the borders of India, helped to sap Japan's land-based fighting strength.

Japan's naval technology and fighting methods, innovative in the beginning stages of the war, quickly lagged behind the Allies. Japan lost naval air battles because its ships and planes did not have radar, a basic tool for locating the enemy. Despite embarking on maritime conquest, the navy neglected vital elements of domination in modern sea warfare. Some senior officers continued to see the battleship as the heart of the fleet, even after their own bombers had shown the vulnerability of ships to air attack. For example, aircraft carriers were seen primarily as floating platforms from which to attack land targets, not as vital weapons in the high-seas fleet, a belief based on the Japanese experience of flying ground support missions off the China coast. The result was fatal errors, such as at Midway, where Japanese carrier planes attacked the island defenses of Midway first, instead of seeking out the enemy's fleet. Consequently, American naval flyers caught the Japanese refueling on deck and smashed their carrier force.

Similarly, Japan did not build sufficient submarines to interdict the Allied invasion fleets that took back Japan's conquests. And, acting on a tragically antique sense of honor, the high command for much of the war would not allow submarines to sink merchant vessels; only warships were seen as fair game. Hence, Japan failed to cut the life-giving supply lines that fed and armed the forces closing in on their home islands. Submarines were also frittered away in futile attempts to supply Japanese garrisons on beleaguered Pacific islands. The boats carried too little cargo capacity to be effective in this role.

Their use here followed from another error. Japan's survival depended on merchantmen taking supplies to its troops on the Pacific perimeter and bringing back raw materials to turn into weapons of war. Its merchant marine was the third largest in the world in 1941, but it was decimated by Allied air and underwater attacks. Adequate convoying techniques were not developed, and the Japanese were blind to the crucial role of radio technology in antisubmarine warfare. Most Japanese vessels had no listening devices to locate boats underwater. Partly, the problem came from lack of resources and tools to build new machinery, but partly, too, it reflected a continuing struggle between conservatives and innovators in the Japanese navy. Officers of the old school, steeped in traditions modeled on the British Royal Navy of World War I, were often resistant to change.

From mid-1942 onward, the conclusion of the Pacific war was not in fact in doubt. Even the apparent Japanese coup at Pearl Harbor contained an omen of disaster, for the crucial weapons of a Pacific naval war, the three carriers, were away from Pearl. The Japanese, concentrating on the battleships and land-based aircraft, got none of them. The United States retained sufficient naval power to end Japan's seaborne invasions in two pivotal battles. The Allies were also helped by Magic, the deciphering of Japan's diplomatic codes, which gave precious advance intelligence regarding enemy intentions. On May 7 and 8, in the battle of the Coral Sea, Allied naval and land forces turned back a Japanese amphibious group bound for Port Moresby in southern New Guinea, opposite the Australian coast. Japan's southward thrust was stopped. A month later, during June 3 to 6, Japanese forces steaming toward Hawaii were precisely identified by Allied intelligence and "ambushed" in a crushing defeat at Midway, ending their expansion in the central Pacific. A diversionary attack on the Aleutians to the north failed to draw off the American fleet. And the small Japanese invasion force was isolated and eventually defeated by American and Canadian forces operating from Alaska.

With Japan's Pacific initiatives ended, the Allies began to strike back. The first targets were Japanese troops in New Guinea and the Solomon islands to the east, who were establishing positions from which their aircraft could interrupt Allied communications with Australia. In the summer of 1942, American and British Commonwealth forces drove back the Japanese in New Guinea. In August, American forces assaulted three of the Solomon islands: Gavutu, Tulagi, and Guadalcanal. Savage fighting on the latter did not end until February 1943, but the Japanese army had suffered its first major defeat of modern times. Combined with the Coral Sea and Midway, these actions turned the war around.

Some who fought in the Pacific, including General MacArthur, believed that this theater was neglected because of FDR's promise to Churchill to put Europe first. In fact, the administration devoted serious attention to the Pacific, which it saw as a special American sphere of interest—so that there was in fact a huge buildup of American strength in the Pacific. In December 1943 there were more troops and equipment in the Pacific than in Europe. By 1944 the U.S. Navy had three times Japan's 1941 strength. In the fight for Okinawa, typical of late-war battles, (fought April to June 1945), a starving Japanese garrison of 120,000 faced 250,000 Americans with enormous firepower.

The plethora of American resources allowed for a two-pronged strategy in the Pacific. From Australia in the south, MacArthur, army commander in the theater, pushed northwest, severing Japan's transportation network with the resource-rich Netherlands Indies. He then retook the Philippines, restoring America's bruised martial pride and providing bases for a bomber offensive against Japan. Meanwhile, a navy and marine offensive, under Admiral Chester Nimitz, used Hawaii as a staging post to push westward across the central Pacific. Nimitz had two major objectives: the Marianas, linchpin of Japan's supply system in the central Pacific, and the Formosa-China coast, from which bombers could also be launched against the Japanese home islands.

This two-offensive strategy has been criticized as a needless duplication of effort that cost lives and resources best used in other ways: the failure to choose between the two invasion routes reflected a political desire to avoid interservice rivalry between the army and the navy rather than any legitimate military purpose. On the one hand, it can be argued that the central Pacific route was the more direct and that MacArthur's thrust against the well-defended Philippines should have been avoided. On the other hand, it can be said that for Filipino and American morale, the return of MacArthur was indispensable and that the navy would have been better employed in total effort against Japanese commerce rather than in island taking. In the end, both arguments may be colored by hindsight. At the time, the Japanese Empire seemed so strong and its military so effective that assaults from two directions to pin down their resources seemed sensible. And, the strategy worked.

Savage early fighting suggested the felicitous policy of "island hopping." The Japanese expected that they could wear down the Allied will to fight and forge a compromise peace by exacting a huge toll for each island retaken. For example, they thought that Raboul, a bastion of 100,000 Japanese on the northern tip of New Britain Island, stood in the way of MacArthur's advance. The retaking of Raboul would be enormously costly to the Allies. But the Joint Chiefs of Staff realized that, given that Japan had lost command of both sea and air, Raboul could simply be bypassed, leaving the garrison to sit out the war, isolated and starving.

They were right, and this set a pattern for the remainder of the war in the Pacific. By October 1944 MacArthur had leapfrogged his way north into the Philippines. Here he fought the decisive battles of Leyte Gulf, which smashed Japanese resistance in his area. At this point, MacArthur can be legitimately criticized because he became almost obsessed with mopping up Japanese resistance in the Philippines, taking out isolated pockets that unnecessarily cost lives and damaged the environment. In mid-June 1944, Nimitz's forces struck the Marianas, capturing Tinian, Guam, and Saipan, 1,350 miles from Japan's capital. The ring was closing. By February 1945, the marines were fighting for Iwo Jima, only 750 miles from Tokyo.

However, the Japanese fought with desperate bravery and, after Saipan, with increasing effectiveness. At Saipan and earlier, the Imperial Army tried to contest the initial landings, only to be devastated by enormous American firepower falling on the open beach areas. After Saipan, the Japanese waited inland in carefully prepared defensive positions that were difficult to locate and eradicate. And they fought with desperate courage, often attacking in mass suicide assaults rather than surrendering. The result can be seen at Iwo Jima: although only eight square miles of land, it cost the marines 27,000 casualties to take. On Okinawa, attacked April 1, nearly all the 120,000-man Japanese garrison perished after inflicting 48,000 U.S. casualties.

At the same time, kamikaze attacks were being launched against Allied warships supporting the landings. These were suicide assaults flown by young and barely trained pilots whose crude planes had only enough fuel for a one-way trip. Due to the successful Allied attacks on Japan's industries and shipping lanes, competitive fighter aircraft could no longer be produced. Nor was there enough fuel to fully train pilots. Therefore, adolescents tried to ram crude machines, equipped with no navigational aids but crammed with explosives, into enemy ships. This was a desperation strategy and was not approved by the growing peace party in Japan.

Most kamikazes had no chance of getting through the fighter and flak screen. Nevertheless, these attacks were terrifying to the men who faced them and suggested to the Allied high command a fanaticism that was utterly irrational. In a further instance, the battleship *Yamato*, without air cover and running on soybean oil, was sent out in April 1945 to attack the American fleet. It had no chance and was sunk with huge loss of life. These kamikaze attacks, along with the bitter Japanese island defenses, colored Allied thinking about what would be needed to force Japan to surrender.

Like Germany, Japan was subjected to intense bomber attacks. Starting in June 1944, new B-29 Superfortresses, with the highest bomb load of any Allied plane, began to hit Japanese industrial targets. Then, in early 1945, General Curtis Le May, heading the Twenty-first Bomber Command, initiated the incendiary bombing of cities, whose residential districts of wood and paper houses were especially vulnerable to fire. On March 9, three hundred B-29s hit Tokyo with napalm, creating an inferno of 1,800° Fahrenheit. Sixteen square miles of the city and 85,000 people were destroyed. Fire raids followed on Nagoya, Osaka, Kobe, Yokohama, and other cities, with similarly devastating results. In all, sixty-one cities were bombed, destroying 40 percent of their surface area and causing 672,000 casualties.

Given the stupendous Japanese losses, we may ask why the government did not surrender. For one thing, some leaders, particularly in the military, still felt that the home islands could be defended. And the Code of Bushido dictated a sacrifice that went beyond the rational interest of the state or the people. Also, the peace party lacked effective leadership, especially as the emperor, though increasingly convinced of the need for peace, took a passive role. The peace cause was not helped by the Allied call for unconditional surrender, first promulgated at the 1943 Casablanca Conference. Japanese leaders feared this would mean the removal of the emperor, who played a quasi-religious role in Japanese culture, symbolizing the soul of the nation. His survival was seen as key to retaining political and psychological stability in the stricken nation. The government did put out tentative peace feelers through a third party, the Soviet Union, which was not yet in the Pacific war. The Western Allies knew about this through Magic intelligence intercepts, but they doubted the seriousness of Japanese intentions and feared to make a direct response in case this should be interpreted as indecisiveness, encouraging the fanatics in Japan.

In this atmosphere of stalemate and mounting destruction, the decision was taken by President Harry Truman (FDR had died on April 12) to use the two atomic bombs in existence on Japanese cities. The first was used on Hiroshima on August 6, and the second on Nagasaki on August 9, killing roughly 135,000 people and forcing the surrender of Japan. At first, most Americans approved of the bombs being dropped, particularly as the problem of radiation was then not widely understood. But in the next five years, a further 130,000 people died of the bombs' effects. And in 1946, a major American journalist, John Hersey, graphically described in his book *Hiroshima* the suffering caused by the bombs. With humanity now living under the shadow of nuclear war, a debate was sparked, which has not ended, over whether the bombs were necessary.

The arguments surrounding the use of the bomb are too complicated to be summarized here, but pivotal is the question whether Japan would have surrendered without either the use of the bombs or an invasion of the home islands, scheduled to begin in November. Should invasion have been necessary, Japanese defensive skills and determination might have cost a million American casualties and enormous devastation to Japan. Some military men believed that Japan would collapse without an invasion, because attacks on shipping and industry had devastated the country's defensive capacity. Others disagreed. But even if an invasion were avoided, more Allied lives would be lost in the weeks of bombing and sea warfare that still remained. In the climate of 1945, an environment of destruction and escalating hatred, it is simply impossible to expect that Allied leaders would have considered sacrificing Allied servicemen to save Japanese civilians. Moreover, as not using atomic bombs would have meant continued incendiary attacks, concern over Japanese civilians seemed moot.

Could the bomb have been demonstrated without destroying a city? Some of the scientists who worked on the weapons wanted this. The risk here was that, if the test bomb failed to work properly, which was possible, its impact would be squandered. Then, as the Allies had only two, the second would have to be dropped on a city and, if it failed to provoke surrender, there was no follow-up possible. So a demonstration was ruled out. This is understandable.

What is more questionable is that only three days were allowed to elapse between the two atomic attacks. Two days after Hiroshima, Russia declared war on Japan, sealing its fate. The peace party was gaining ground, particularly as most senior army officers now accepted the inevitability of defeat. Nothing would have been lost to the Allies by waiting a further few days and perhaps guaranteeing the position of the emperor. Ironically, the latter was done—after Nagasaki and the Japanese surrender. The truth is, concern over civilian deaths and the initiation of the nuclear age have been more apparent since the war than they were at the time. Humanity had been forced to witness enormous destruction all through World War II. By 1945 the killing had reached such enormous proportions that the bombing of one more city did not have the aspect of moral horror that it might have now. In such a time of death, the unimaginable had become the acceptable.

In the Pacific, Japan's grim defense of the islands necessitated the same brute force that Hitler's refusal to yield ground produced in Europe. The Japanese were skilled defensive fighters, making careful use of the terrain to create positions that were expensive to take and difficult to destroy. Inevitably, the Americans responded with firepower: there was plenty of ammunition, and it saved lives. As in Europe, every foot of ground in the path of advancing forces was pulverized. It is estimated that 1,589 artillery rounds were fired to kill each Japanese soldier. In the final fight with the battleship *Yamato*, planes from one American carrier alone fired 1.5 million rounds of small-caliber ammunition from their machine guns.

Japanese suicidal fanaticism produced a corresponding insensitivity to killing on the part of Allied soldiers, who butchered their opponents in staggering quantities—over 100,000 on Okinawa, alone. The ecology of some islands was so badly damaged that it had not recovered twenty years later.

It was necessary for world peace and the future of democracy that the Axis be overcome. This should not, however, lead us to glamorize modern technological warfare, which has an almost unlimited capacity for human and environmental destruction, because of the sheer number and effectiveness of the weapons we have created. For the men who fought in the Pacific or in Italy, for the civilians who suffered in the blitzing by one side or the other, World War II was a brutalizing experience. Anonymous mass destruction was the dominant characteristic. As David Divine, a historian of the air war, commented: "To accept that this was a war of sophisticated weaponry has become a convention in the West, but it was in reality a war of desperate attrition, and victory in the end hinged upon human death" (Divine, 263).

four

The American War Machine

AMERICANS were justifiably proud of their contribution to the Allied victory in World War II. In the 1930s, isolationism and the America First campaign had convinced the Axis that Yankees had been too softened by their consumer culture to wage effective war. Herman Göring, head of the Luftwaffe, boasted that Americans could produce razor blades but not artillery; they were an unwarlike people. Some Americans feared he might be right.

Yet, following Pearl Harbor, the nation came alive, like a giant awaking from sleep, it was said. American industry provided the needs of its own military and contributed substantially to arming its allies. America was the only Allied nation able to field and fully equip major armies in both western Europe and Asia.

However, there is a tendency in popular thought to magnify America's contributions. The American war machine is sometimes seen as not one factor but the only factor in the Axis defeat. Lieutenant-Colonel Oliver L. North in his book *Under Fire: An American Story* (coauthored with William Novak, 1991) wrote that this was "the war that America won for the world" (64). Americans outproduced and outfought everyone else. American industry saved the world. Americans were good with machines. And all American machines were good. American soldiers were the best on the planet; highly committed, superbly led, and superior in morale and morals. The draft was fair, and the military functioned like a well-knit, integrated family.

So did the nation. The cause was not marred by racial tensions. There was harmony. Men went to war, and women took over the production line. Everyone put a hand to the wheel, and Rosie the Riveter became the symbol of a can-do country. It was a splendid community effort in the best war ever.

This legend was born during the war. In comic books, a primary molder of public opinion, America had no allies; the enemy was a pushover because of American guts and technology. General Brehon B. Somervell, reflecting popular sentiment in 1942, said that "when Hitler put his war on wheels he ran it straight down our alley. When he hitched his chariot to an internal combustion engine, he opened up a new battlefront—a front that we know well. It's called Detroit" (Keegan, *Soldiers*, 236).

The real picture is complex. Although industry had a powerful role in winning the war, it also had difficulties. Not all GIs were well adjusted or keen to play their role. The draft and the military structure worked well, but they also produced ethnic and gender tensions. And it is not true that all the men fought and all the women worked. Of sixteen million military personnel, 25 percent never left the United States, and less than 50 percent of those overseas were ever in a battle zone. Only 8 percent of wives had husbands in the military; a majority of married men were civilians working at home. Most women were housewives: of thirty-three million women at home in December, 1941, seven out of eight were still there in 1944, at the peak of wartime employment. Nine out of ten young mothers didn't work (Anderson, 78; Campbell, 77, 82; Hartmann, 34, 226).

Of women who did work, only 16 percent were in war industries (Gluck, 10), partly because men didn't want their wives in the grimy, often dangerous war plants, where they were also open to sexual advances, particularly on the night shift. A 1943 Gallup poll showed that 70 percent of married men opposed war work for their wives and that 75 percent of female homemakers agreed (Gluck, 12; Hartmann, *Home*, 82). GI surveys showed that the soldiers' dream was not Rosie the Riveter but Mrs. Miniver, Hollywood's idealized middle-class housewife (played by Greer Garson), who kept familiar family behavior alive during anxious times. Many middle-class women would have felt degraded by sweaty, blue-collar factory work. And wives worried, too, that if they became self-supporting their husbands were more likely to be drafted.

To get a realistic picture of the war machine, let us begin with its industrial arm. The tendency to overstate the significance of American production is understandable, because the achievement was remarkable. For most of the 1930s, congressional military appropriations were minimal, averaging $180 million annually, of which the navy got the lion's share. Though there was a jump in 1938 with a billion-dollar appropriation, the Senate cut expenditures in the following year. On September 1, 1939, when Hitler invaded Poland, the army could fully equip only 75,000 of its 227,000 personnel.

Even when government became alert to the danger, some businesses dragged their heels. It was difficult, for example, to get automakers to turn from consumer to military production. Still affected by the Depression, they feared neglecting the domestic market. Though tanks and trucks were needed, Detroit turned out a million more cars in 1941 than in 1939. Even after Pearl Harbor, Standard Oil insisted on honoring its chemical contracts with I. G. Farben, a synthetic rubber manufacturer for Hitler's military; for nine months of the war, the Axis thus received American aid. U.S. production of synthetic rubber lagged when the supply of natural rubber from Southeast Asia was cut off by Japanese conquests.

Despite such problems, the sum of American wartime production was massive. In round numbers, America produced 300 thousand planes, 77 thousand ships, 372 thousand big guns, 20 million small arms, 6 million tons of bombs, 102 thousand armored vehicles, and 2.5 million trucks. Such output aided Britain, Russia, and China through lend-lease. Yet lend-lease was not a one-sided arrangement. Giving British soldiers guns saved American lives and stopped the bombs from falling in American streets. Europe to the east and China to the west were America's first lines of defense. In return for equipment, America got important trade concessions and strategic British bases, which helped to establish America's postwar superpower presence around the world. Moreover, through reverse lend-lease, Britain provided the United States with services and goods, including access to military inventions.

Lend-lease was more important to Britain than to the Soviets. America contributed 25 percent of British equipment but only 4 percent of Russia's total output (Calvocoressi, Wint, and Pritchard, 445, 476). Russian home production was in fact great, despite the fact that many plants were captured or destroyed by the Germans. At its peak, Soviet industry turned out 40 thousand planes and 30 thousand armored vehicles a year, plus 150 thousand big guns and 500 thousand machine guns. Further, when we add that one in ten Russians died to destroy Hitler, it is clear that the contribution of the Soviet war machine was considerable (193, 480).

Although many Soviet units had to fight with obsolete equipment, the increasing quality of Russian armaments surprised their opponents. For example, the T-34 and heavier KV-85 tanks were at least a match for the German Tigers and Panthers. America also produced much first-rate war material, such as the M-1 rifle, one of the best shoulder arms of the era. The proximity fuse, developed in 1943, used a tiny radio to detonate shells close to the target. It was so effective that for months the Allies did not use it on land for fear the Axis would capture one and copy it.

However, other equipment was less impressive. The bazooka anti-tank weapon was inferior to the German panzerfaust, taking two men to operate and leaving painful powder burns on the holder's face. American WWI-style automatic rifles were slower and clumsier than German light machine guns. Some anti-tank mines became unstable in subfreezing weather, and truck loads blew up in the severe winter of 1944–45. Submarine and torpedo design at times lagged behind the Axis: for example, German boats were faster and featured a snorkel device that obviated the need to surface at night to recharge batteries.

American and British tanks were largely weaker than German in throw power (the weight of shell that could be fired) and armor thickness. The Grant was mechanically unsound, and the thin eleven-inch tracks of the Stuart sank in soft ground. The Sherman, standard equipment for American and many British tank crews late in the war, had design deficiencies. Models with a gasoline instead of a diesel engine burned easily when hit: crewmen called them "the Ronson," after the famous cigarette lighter. The armor was too thin and the 75-mm gun was outclassed by the German 88. Conventional wisdom said it took five Shermans to kill a Panther (Keegan, *Second War*, 399–401).

This was only partly the fault of the engineers. Russell Weigley pointed out that military planners were also culpable. Their formative professional memory was of the mobile frontier forces that battled the Plains Indians—the cavalry—so they tended to stress speed at the expense of firepower and armor, instead of finding the optimum balance. The result was that American tanks were vulnerable and needed intensive air or artillery support to pound all before them. This helps explain the brute force nature of Allied operations in western Europe, particularly in 1944. Without a tank powerful enough to make rapier-like thrusts through enemy lines into their rear, Allied attacks sometimes had the quality of blunt hammer blows, relying on mass destruction to offset the weakness of the spearhead weapon (Weigley, 257–67).

By an irony, the very plethora of American production sometimes encouraged a reliance on blanket firepower instead of finesse. Americans had plenty of ammunition, and this led to the philosophy that it was best to saturate everything ahead to save friendly lives. After 240-mm howitzers pounded the French town of Maizieres-les-Metz to get rid of German snipers, an American infantry surgeon "saw that it was in complete ruins, from one end to the other" (Colby, 269). *Time* magazine, taking the approach to an extreme, urged the systematic total destruction of thirty-one strategic German cities to ease the job of the ground troops (Hopkins, 462).

The manufacturing of unprecedented quantities of deadly instruments was accompanied by a naive attitude on the part of some production personnel, which has affected Americans' relations with the rest of humanity. Only the United States was not both a destroyer and a victim of destruction in the war. Unlike other belligerents, U.S. civilians didn't experience firsthand the awful effects of modern weapons. A nurse on a plastic surgery ward might tend men with no eyes, noses, or mouths, and those who worked in war plants could suffer ill health from the poor conditions, such as lung problems from fumes and cancer from chemicals that colored their skin orange—but they were neither bombed nor burned. And some failed to imagine what this might be like. There were parties in Washington when the atomic bombs were dropped and 23 percent of Americans were disappointed that America didn't have more to drop (Gervasi, 619; Dower, 54). Sensitive soldiers who saw war's carnage were shocked to get letters from relatives asking how many enemy they had killed and urging them to get one more for the home folk. Some who confessed horror at the war's reality were called cowards (Gray, 135).

Living apart from the rest of suffering humanity, Americans were vouchsafed an ignorance of war's reality that allowed them to cherish an innocent belief in the clean and bracing atmosphere of battle. A cheerful, naive pride in America's war production, unsullied by disturbing insights into what the products did to people, was encouraged by the advertising industry. The government enlisted the advertising sector to help sell the war. This made sense, in that no country had so effective a ready-made mechanism for the swaying of public opinion. And by letting business handle propaganda, the government saved money. Because America was not a battleground, it was easy for people to become complacent about the war effort. Madison Avenue reminded them daily of why the United States was fighting.

Advertising had inherent problems as an educational tool. It is by nature emotional, rather than intellectual; it sells feelings rather than ideas. And those feelings have to be positive and cheerful, so that we will feel good about the product. As cultural historian John Costello commented, "If you want to sell a housewife Jell-O you don't tell her: 'Madam, it is highly probable that your son is coming home a basket case, or at least totally blind, but cheer up, tonight choose one of the six delicious flavors and be happy with America's finest dessert'"

(121). In short, ads had to be upbeat and sell happy endings; they showed gung ho troops cheerfully using new products to kill the enemy or relaxing with a Coke after the adventure of a bombing run.

The commercials encouraged warm feelings, even affection, for terrible weapons, associating them with other, popular consumer items from the same companies. Weapons were not so much tools for maiming as a simple tribute to American know-how, no more threatening than a new rat trap or toilet bowl cleaner. Take the flamethrower, which shot from a hose a jet of napalm or oil burning at 2,000°. To the men who used it and suffered from it, this was a horrifying if necessary weapon for winkling out stiff resistance in caves, tunnels, and buildings. "Hellfire," one veteran called it (Sledge, 36). Men hit by the flame would flare up like Roman candles. The smell of roasted flesh was sickening. So hated were the weapons that their operators were rarely given quarter by any army but were killed on the spot. Ads deceived civilians as to this reality. One in the New York *Times* during February 1945 showed a flamethrower killing Japanese under the heading "Clearing Out a Rats' Nest" (Dower, 91–92). Another said the flamethrower was "convincing the world of America's right to live the American way" (Fox, 69). The same message might have sold a Chevrolet.

Many GIs resented such glorification of fighting, but in a media-dominated age their view got buried. Advertising convinced civilians that they knew as much about fighting, and were as central a part of the war machine, as the men in combat. "You are a *Production Soldier*: America's first line of defense," boomed one poster. "Give 'Em Both Barrels," charged another, that showed a rivet gunner and a machine gunner battling the enemy together. Ads implied that if you bought a war bond your sacrifice was on a par with that of the men in the front lines. Even the little boy who collected scrap iron was described as a hero in one commercial. The upshot was that, as Eric Sevareid put it, Americans came to believe wars are won by buying and selling, not by killing and dying (215).

This attitude left a legacy. Wars are sometimes unavoidable; World War II certainly is a case in point. But they should be undertaken soberly and in the clear knowledge of the terrible and lasting suffering they cause. Then only the most grave and necessary reasons will provoke conflict. Americans are sometimes guilty of waging war by inadvertence: of condoning military intervention without taking responsibility for knowing what their military machine will do to its targets. For example, some feminist historians talk about the wartime expansion of the arms industries only in terms of the greater employment opportunities this created for minorities. Relatively few seem to think this placed a related responsibility on these employees to educate themselves about the actual consequences of the work they were doing. They could remain in a state of innocence about war. Indeed, some feminists both claim that women are more peace abiding than men, absolving them of responsibility for war, *and* boost the image of Rosie the Riveter, who was part of the war machine.

In World War II it became difficult to question the defense spending and the defense industry. During and after World War I there were those who warned against the growing role of the arms industry in national life, but, as America became the "arsenal of democracy," defense contracts were no longer controversial. The corporation, once seen as an enemy of individualism, emerged as a vital symbol of Americanism. The role was hammered home by advertising, which made a vital connection between brand name manufacturing, American values, and world peace.

Americans now bemoan big government and federal intervention in all aspects of life, often without realizing that this phenomenon was vastly increased by World War II. Government agencies such as the War Production Board and the Office of Price Administration regulated economic and social life in the interests of the war effort. Government did a good job. But, at the same time, the central bureaucracy more than tripled. Big government worked closely with big business, which received the overwhelming majority of military contracts. These ties remained after the war ended, forming the embryo of the military-industrial complex that profoundly shaped American policy in the decades after the war. Joe Marcus, head of the Civilian Requirements Division during the war, reflected that "the single most important legacy of the war is . . . the military-industrial complex. In the past, there were business representatives in Washington, but now they *are* Washington" (Terkel, 326–27).

Along with mushrooming institutions came the concept of the organization society, in which the roles of the individual intellect and conscience were diminished and loyalty to the group, being a team player, was emphasized. It seemed disloyal to criticize the government while the country was at war, so America's intellectuals voluntarily censored their doubts about such issues as area bombing, calls for exterminating the Japanese, and belligerent flag-waving. It felt wrong to in any way obstruct a cause that was so clearly right, even if this meant stifling qualms about national policies and attitudes.

Merle Curti, a student of American thought, noted that the war saw the emergence of an aggressive nationalism that replaced the more self-critical, skeptical spirit of the thirties (158). Scientists developing weapons of mass destruction, including biological warfare and the atom bomb, to preserve military security worked behind a cloak of secrecy that precluded open and rational public debate on the wisdom of producing or using such weapons. Consequently, when President Truman thrust humanity into the nuclear age, nobody in the democracies had voted on, or really debated, the momentous issues involved.

The universities, normally sanctuaries for those whose vital role is to stand aside from the passions of the moment and who have the intellect and training to take the long view and to offer the sensible second thought, undertook research projects that aided the war effort. But freedom of conscience was curtailed and scholars became civilian soldiers in the military machine. Thus Harvard was midwife to the birth of napalm. University professors still accept grants to work on germ warfare and other doomsday projects under the doubtful rationale that it is not their job to debate the purposes to which the research will be put. Their surrender of individual moral responsibility in favor of national defense needs takes its precedent from the war period.

In no area was the power of organized society to impinge upon the freedom of thought and action of the individual more manifest than in the selective service. The draft was highly effective for the purpose of winning the war. In 1939 the U.S. Army ranked forty-fifth in size in the world. But by 1945 sixteen million Americans had worn the uniform, of whom ten million, or just under two-thirds, had been drafted. It is popularly believed that the WWII draft was more fair than the Vietnam era draft and caused much less resentment. This is largely true. The 1940s draft drew more widely and resulted in a better balanced and possibly more mature fighting force than that of Vietnam. The first draftees were nonfathers aged twenty-one to thirty-five years. After July 1, 1943, eighteen-year-olds and some fathers were drafted. As a result, the average age was twenty-seven, versus nineteen for Vietnam.

It has been argued that the WWII inductee was better adjusted because he saw that the attack on Pearl Harbor violated American sovereignty. Vietnamese communism never clearly threatened America. Also, the 1940s draftee had less to lose, coming out of the Depression and a poor economic situation. The upwardly mobile young man of the 1960s was giving up a significantly better domestic situation and therefore felt more deprived by military service.

This may well be so, but it is best not to overstate the comparative ideological commitment of the 1940s soldier. When the peacetime draft was introduced in 1940, calling for the induction of eighty thousand men aged twenty-one to thirty-five, it was deeply resented and branded as militarism. When, the following year, Congress extended the term of these men, the House approved the measure by only one vote, and many servicemen vowed to go "over the hill" in protest (Burk, 434–35).

Pearl Harbor turned this attitude around, and most drafted men accepted their lot. But the rush to volunteer soon ebbed and was followed by an increase in marriages and births aimed at avoiding service—the start of the baby boom. One official estimated early in the war that "about half the increase in marriages must be traced to barefaced draft evasion" (Costello, 193). George Patton observed that many draftees had little of the enthusiasm of 1917, when America entered the last war. They stumbled into draft boards drunk or with farewell hangovers (Farago, 78). From there they marched glumly to the trains that took them to boot camp.

In his novel of wartime life, *The Fall of Valor*, Charles Jackson described a party of New York inductees going to Grand Central Station to embark for a southern camp. They were sheepish, shuffling, silent. "They straggled along hangdog and silly; they stared at the sidewalk in a ludicrous grin, or straight ahead, unseeingly" (20–21). Small boys jeered at them. An army wife, seeing on a train close-cropped recruits in their ill-fitting uniforms, felt like crying: they were "like freshly sheared sheep being led to a sheep dip" (Klaw, 14–15).

Draft evasion, standing at 5 percent, was lower than the 12 percent of World War I. But college deferments, more than double those of 1917–18, helped to defuse white middle-class resentment. This in turn led some to accuse draft boards of class bias. One Bronx, New York, taxi driver, whose adolescent son had been taken, called his board "a bunch of crooks" who "don't touch those rich college kids" (Gervasi, 435). By 1944 there was considerable hostility to the draft among the underprivileged, particularly as the deaths and mutilations of friends and family members mounted. On VJ night, when Japan surrendered, some draft board offices were defaced and vandalized.

Black Americans were the victims of draft discrimination. Tennessee, for example, refused to put blacks on the boards. Blacks had a lower deferment rate than whites only partly because they rarely could afford to finish high school or go on to college (Stouffer, 1:494): their needs for deferment were not seen sympathetically. Blacks were often denied conscientious objector status; the Black Muslim faith, for example, was not categorized as a legitimate religion (Foner, 146).

Conscientious objectors of all races fortunate enough to have their appeals accepted found that there was no segregation in prison. But they were treated as felons, rejected by the community, and sometimes beaten up and harassed by guards. There were about eighteen thousand conscientious objectors, a third of whom served prison terms; the others did civilian public service (Nelson, 167–68). It took a postwar Supreme Court decision for all conscientious objectors to get their civil rights back and expunge the felon label.

Some of the procedures used by selective service officers to rate draftees may be questioned. Regarding the physical and mental condition of recruits, the statistics say that, of eighteen million men examined between 1940 and 1945, 29.1 percent were rejected. In the first year, 1940–41, a whopping 50 percent failed to pass. Of these, 10 percent failed through illiteracy, the rest from psychological or physical defects such as bad teeth, poor eyesight, or venereal disease. As the need for men grew, the standards had to be dropped, and by 1943 many previously rejected men were being inducted. Some induction officers felt that America was scraping the bottom of the barrel.

Perhaps so, but there is reason to suspect that some methods of selection and their underlying assumptions were faulty. For instance, among the eighteen-to-twenty-one-year age group, a leading problem was flabbiness. Boys out of condition could not do ten squats; many had to be helped up after five. Softness was blamed on "momism," and some male psychologists asserted there was a national crisis of masculinity brought on by women pampering their boys. In fact, most of these young men needed only regular physical exercise and did not have to be rejected.

Thirty-two percent of the rejections were made for psychological reasons, but these were based on as few as four standard questions, such as, "How do you feel? Do you like the army? And worst of all, Do you like girls? The boy who replied that the opposite sex frightened him could be rejected as latently homosexual. America alone of all the belligerent nations rejected men not for the overt commission of a homosexual act but for an alleged leaning in that direction. If a stripped recruit seemed uncomfortable with his nakedness, if he was a hairdresser or had effeminate gestures, he usually failed (Bérubé, 16, 20–21; Ellis, 10–11). A common joke was that if you didn't want to be drafted, the easiest way out was to shave your armpits, wear perfume, and affect a mincing step during your physical (Gorer, 96).

The root problem here lay in a reliance on behavioral science techniques that were pioneered in America but that were at a relatively early and crude stage of development. Behavioral scientists suggested that you could quickly and easily deal with large masses of humanity through the application of standardized test questions. Because these were arrived at through rigorous scientific research, they would take the subjectivity and guesswork out of decisionmaking. You could, it was thought, tell if a recruit was latently homosexual by asking a correctly devised short question. The fact is that too much faith was placed in standardized performance evaluation methods: humanity is more complex than they suggested. Social scientists tried to apply industrial, production line, quality control techniques to people, but people cannot be graded like cans of peas. This was one of the worst aspects of the growth of the organization society, with its insistence on machinelike regularity. And it hurt the performance of the army in the field.

We commonly think of the WWII army as a rough-and-ready, can-do organization that won the war partly because it was more flexible and more innovative than its opponents, particularly the Germans, whom the Allies stereotyped as hidebound Prussians fighting according to rigid, heel-clicking dogmas. The reality was more complex. U.S. Army Colonel Trevor N. Dupuy studied Allied versus German performance in the 1944 Normandy campaign. Despite complete Allied air superiority and massive numerical advantages on the ground, the Wehrmacht outfought its opponents, inflicting a 50 percent higher casualty rate than it sustained (234–35).

This led the distinguished Israeli military historian Martin Van Creveld to compare German and American military structures to understand the apparent disparity in fighting efficiency. The result was *Fighting Power*, upon which much of the following discussion is based. Van Creveld maintained that Americans employed too much top-down management, meddled in issues best left to subordinates, and demanded obedience to orthodox rules and doctrine that robbed the frontline soldier of initiative (32–33). Too often he had to ask permission to call in fire or to exploit a situation in his immediate sector. In the navy, submarine commanders had to file a contact report and get permission to fire before engaging a surface vessel. This often meant the prey escaped.

Some Americans observed that discipline was poor among American prisoners of war compared to British or German. They dealt badly with such matters as fair distribution of food rations, which often degenerated into fistfights. They did not keep themselves clean and committed suicide at an abnormally high rate. This was because junior officers were allowed little freedom of action and were not used to taking command. Thus they could not exercise effective leadership requiring initiative, especially in circumstances where there were no rules or directives from above to rely on and where the organizational structure was missing (Kaplan, 175; Wright, 7, 141, 151; Cubbins, 152).

The Wehrmacht encouraged more initiative at the lowest levels, even on the part of the private soldier, and it was expected that those on the ground would use their intelligence to exploit the immediate situation without waiting for directives from above (Van Creveld, 32–33). The American army, emphasizing behavioral management, was hierarchical, with rigid caste walls separating the ranks. The Germans, on the other hand, were more democratic. They encouraged camaraderie between officers and men, building a team spirit in which even the private soldier felt he was an important element of an elite group (38, 129–131).

Because there was less centralized management, there was less paperwork going up and down the chain of command. For example, in the American army, every officer each month had to fill out a standardized, quantifiable report sheet on his subordinate officers, plus a fuller twice-yearly performance evaluation. This was required even in combat. Once, an infantry office sheltering in a shattered pillbox on the Siegfried line in February 1945 had settled down to sleep when "about midnight, a runner came up with a bunch of papers. I got under a blanket with a flashlight and found I was supposed to fill out an efficiency report on each officer who had been in the company during the past six months. I could not believe it" (Colby, 411).

The Germans asked only for an informal rating every two years, though a superior could remove a man in the field if, in his subjective judgment, the situation demanded it. Men on the spot were expected to make sound professional decisions based on common sense (Van Creveld, *Fighting Power*, 63–69). The result was that the American army developed a huge clerical staff to handle the enormous bureaucratic flow; by 1944, 35 percent of personnel were in clerical posts. The Wehrmacht had a much better teeth-to-tail ratio: in 1944, 54.35 percent of overall strength was in combat troops, versus 40.6 percent in the U.S. Army; 70 percent of German officers were in fighting units, whereas only 36 percent of American officers were; many more Americans were staff officers, dealing with reports (58–60; Campbell, 19).

American practice, said Van Creveld, erred when it emphasized bureaucratic neatness and regularity over immediate need and practical application. For example, soldiers were normally assigned to a classification within two days, often on the basis of standardized aptitude tests, which assigned them to clerical, technical, infantry, or other status (also see Stouffer, 1:293–94). Because the system functioned for the convenience of the managers rather than the men at the front, classifications were hard to change, even in an emergency. A field commander might have too few infantry, while there was a surplus of depot troops in the theater. His frontline units, through combat and exposure, might be in worse shape than his rear echelon people, but it was often difficult at the ground level to shuffle their roles (Marshall, 15–17). German field commanders utilized men as they saw fit, and classifications operated more as intelligent guidelines than rigid categories.

In short, overmanagement and concern with procedure frustrated sharp responses to problems. Most telling, the constant form filling produced a tick-the-box-and-pass-it-on mentality. Confronted with the patent impossibility of trying to scientifically quantify the performance of their subordinates each month, supervisors treated the forms as a farce and ranked all officers in the top 25 percent of ratings. This meant that real problems with incompetent or exhausted officers didn't always get dealt with (Van Creveld, *Fighting Power*, 146).

In an army drawn from the democratic society with arguably the most personal freedoms on earth, overmanagement could cause great friction. All military systems must restrain individual freedom in the interests of the group, which must act together to be effective. But soldiers often perceived regulations as going beyond what was necessary and becoming petty tyranny, known to GIs as *chickenshit*. Chickenshit could be refusing a soldier a pass to visit his newborn child and its mother in the local hospital (Klaw, 83–84) or harassing a combat soldier on R and R (rest and recreation) in a rear area for having dirt spots on his uniform or not saluting smartly enough (Fussell, *Wartime*, 80ff). George Patton was notorious for chickenshit: he would berate men in a combat zone for not wearing a tie or for having their trousers outside their leggings; he would creep through latrines to catch and punish soldiers defecating without their helmets on.

Contrary to Hollywood films, the army was not a big happy family of mutually respectful ethnic and class groups headed by beloved, fatherly officers. Intellectuals, for example, who in films came to see army life as a wonderful antidote to their effete bookworming and wimpy social criticism, were in reality often wretched and appalled by their introduction to military practice (Stouffer, 1:55–59, 65–66; 2:82–83). Along with Jews, they were frequently the bait of training sergeants, who saw them as the privileged snobs of society. Basic training, aimed at demolishing the recruit's civilian personality and rebuilding him to the military's design, was hard on many but was particularly rough on the educated. Herded together, stripped of the vital space crucial to privacy, the men felt like animals who had to do everything from eating (like pigs at a trough, said one) to urinating in public (Jones, *WWII*, 31).

Very typically, during the early stages of the war, regular noncommissioned officers were less educated than the recruits under them, which led to mutual antagonism and often humiliation for the privates. Marine recruits were forced to march around the barracks with their gun in one hand and their penis in the other—or were made to recite the correct way to kill a "Jap" by "a shot in the balls" (Sledge, 10, 18). The military machine strove to mold men into sameness. John Steinbeck, watching soldiers file aboard a troopship in their round, potlike overseas helmets, thought they looked like so many mushrooms, vegetables bereft of individual identity. The soldiers themselves had learned that they as individuals didn't count: America would survive, but many of the cogs in the war machine would not (Steinbeck, 15, 19; Jones, *Red Line*, 230).

For the better educated, conditions often improved after basic training, with the chance for officer candidate school or assignment to a relatively safe, clean job in a technical or clerical division. For others, the tension and misery might continue, sometimes as a result of ethnic, gender, or class discrimination. All ethnic minorities were represented in the armed forces. Mexican-Americans volunteered in numbers far higher than their proportion of the population: 350,000 of a total 1.4 million did duty and won seventeen Congressional Medals of Honor. Thirty thousand Japanese Americans served, even though many of their parents were denied American citizenship and their families were in detention centers at the time they were drafted. A Japanese-American unit in Europe was America's most decorated outfit. Out of a potential pool of 334,000 American Indians, 29,000 served.

All of these minority groups faced some prejudice from the white majority, but at least many served in integrated regiments or divisions. This was good for their morale in most cases, though some native Americans came home with a confused identity, feeling neither mainstream American nor simply Indian, and had to wrestle with this dilemma after the war.

The greatest prejudice was faced by black Americans. The buildup of the defense industries and the expansion of the armed forces on the eve of war were welcomed by African-Americans, who had endured a disproportionately high unemployment rate in the Depression. But they were discriminated against throughout the war machine. The U.S. Employment Service for some time allowed employers to demand photographs from applicants to screen out persons of color. Those fortunate enough to get jobs in war industries usually found themselves in the lowest paid, most menial positions. Few achieved skilled or supervisory status. Conditions in the job market improved somewhat after a threatened protest march on Washington in 1941. But widespread discrimination continued, largely because the federal government would not enforce fair practices.

Discrimination in the military hurt blacks more than discrimination in the industrial sector. Since the American and French revolutions, bearing arms had been associated with the right to claim full citizenship privileges. Both races knew this, and it had much to do with African-Americans being denied combat status, so that they could not demand civil rights after the war (Stouffer, 1:493–94, 511, 519, 568–69). More than a million blacks, or 8 percent of the total military, served. But 78 percent were in service branches, compared to 40 percent for whites (Foner, 134ff). For most of the war, the navy would let blacks go to sea only as mess boys (waiters), and they were almost totally excluded from the air force. One black veteran—who served in the quartermaster corps, shifting supplies—recalled, "We were really stevedores. Many of those young blacks wanted to be in combat units" (Terkel, *Good War*, 275). Even the celebrated Ninth and Tenth Cavalry, black units whose fighting record went back to the San Juan Hill in Cuba and the Indian wars, were dismounted from their tanks and put to work "unloading ships, repairing roads, and driving trucks" in North Africa. To allay public outcry, the men were forbidden to discuss the situation with anyone (Foner, 158).

The work of the black soldiers was often dirty and dangerous: supply carriers went ashore right behind the first assault waves; road builders were exposed to artillery and sniper fire. But these jobs were neither glamorous nor noticed by the public. Late in the war, when the shortage of combat troops forced the administration to put black troops on the front lines, they performed as well as white troops. African-Americans received more than twelve thousand decorations and citations.

Most American units, like British colonial forces, were segregated throughout the war. Black officers could not command white men. Black men and officers could not dine with whites, frequent the same clubs, or use the PX (post exchange store). Several black soldiers were killed and others wounded for trying to integrate army facilities (Terkel, 150). Others received dishonorable discharges for resisting discrimination. White MPs beat up black soldiers and white girls caught together. Even blacks' blood plasma was refused on the totally unscientific basis that it would "mongrelize" the white race.

High-ranking officials, such as Army Chief of Staff General George C. Marshall, were blunt about believing in innate white racial superiority. Secretary of War Henry L. Stimson justified not appointing black officers on the grounds that "leadership is not embedded in the negro race." He also doubted that they had the brains to pilot planes, even though the few black air combat units did well; for example, the all-black 332d Fighter Group received a Presidential Unit Citation in March 1945 (Blum, 11, 184; Winkler, *Home Front*, 59; Terkel, 341).

The services also encouraged sexual and gender discrimination. Male homosexuals who survived induction were the target of continuing persecution. Lesbians were less threatening, as there were fewer women in the forces, physical intimacy among females (such as kissing and touching) was more accepted in the culture, and lesbians were stereotyped as "butches" with masculine traits that were considered an asset in the military. The military showed a preoccupation with rooting out homosexuality that mirrored the concern with heterosexual cleanliness and innocence within the larger society. Periodic witch hunts disrupted the normal functioning of units and created widespread unease among the men, numbers of whom committed deprivation homosexuality. That is, secluded from women over long periods, lonely, and facing death, normally heterosexual men sought consolation and affirmation of life by coupling with other men—on troop trains, ships, and in foxholes.

Men found guilty of occasional offenses were given a dishonorable discharge, seasoned habitués got heavy prison sentences, often running over a decade. The treatment of the accused was traumatizing: suspected men were chained, put in stockades where they wore special labels, and sometimes mentally and physically abused by MPs. They were then tried before boards, where they had no legal counsel. By war's end, about ten thousand men had been condemned in this way. They were stripped of medals and honors and disgraced in their home communities, for their draft boards were informed of their crime. Inevitably, the information was passed along to potential employers.

The pursuit of homosexuality wasted time and resources. There is no proven correlation between sexual preference and military performance. In fact, the military has repeatedly acknowledged the efficiency of homosexual personnel. On one American warship, the best torpedo officer was "a notorious Queen" who wore a hair net and bathrobe (Bérubé, 184). Given that 10 percent of any nation's males are usually homosexual, the services reduced their potential manpower pool. Moreover, many homosexuals had a higher than normal ideological commitment to the war, since the Nazis had targeted homosexuals for liquidation. Rejection of American homosexuals negated their patriotism and idealism.

Women also desired military service, and they too sometimes faced negative public attitudes. Despite the image of the Nazis as ruthlessly regimenting society, Germany was less successful than America in getting women to leave the home and take nontraditional employment for the duration. The number of working women in the United States increased by 60 percent, to a total of 16 million. And 350 thousand women served in the forces: 150 thousand in the army, 100 thousand in the navy, 22 thousand in the marines, and thousands more in the Coast Guard and the reserves (Segal, 116–18).

The male establishment, civil and military, at first resented the female presence as implying that men alone could not protect America. One congressman fumed, "Think of the humiliation! What has become of the manhood of America?" (Costello, 41). Yet it soon became clear that, with the high rejection rate of male inductees, America needed women in uniform. In 1943 the army undertook a massive recruiting campaign to enlist half a million women. As an incentive, for the first time in army history, women would receive full pay and benefits as soldiers, including veteran's entitlements. The WACs (Women's Army Corps) did as well as men in the areas allotted to it. Eisenhower relied heavily on WACs as staff personnel in planning and communications. There were eight thousand WACs on the European mainland when Germany surrendered. In the Pacific, MacArthur praised them as "my best soldiers" for their hard work and good discipline (49, 51). Yet women at no time represented more than 2 percent of the military machine, and service for females failed to be popular.

Why? To begin with, the military retained traditional views of gender. America alone refused to place women in battle zones; most were restricted to typically low-level "woman's work," such as typing or, for black women, mopping floors and emptying waste baskets. The percentage of women who filled clerical posts in the military was greater than in civil life. Female officers could not issue orders to male personnel. Married women were not welcome, and their families were denied dependency allowance. Pregnant soldiers were discharged. So were menopausal personnel, because male officers thought that this natural life change permanently incapacitated women. Females faced promotion ceilings and other bars to professional advancement. Black women were kept out of the defense industry, and when they complained they were referred to situations as domestic servants. Most nursing schools refused admission to black women, and the army would let them tend only black soldiers. The navy begrudgingly accepted four black nurses.

The media patronized professional women. Press reports consistently dubbed WACs the Petticoat Army and their barracks Fort Lipstick. Even good war reporters like Ernie Pyle condescended to them, calling them "gals," and any story on women in the field included a reference to their giggly ways and their "frilly panties" hanging on a washing line by their tents (*Your War*, 78). The condescension to women was pervasive enough that the official War Department *Guide to Great Britain* (1942), issued to GIs bound for the United Kingdom, warned them not to take their attitude overseas. Britain was the first nation to conscript women, starting in 1942. Women helped defend Britain against the Luftwaffe, and their campaign ribbons were earned. Female officers commanded men. The *Guide* told American troops that treating these personnel with disrespect would earn the enmity of the British.

Some Americans could not imagine women making a military contribution beyond giving sexual favors to male personnel: there were pervasive rumors stateside of immorality among service women, and it was even said they staffed brothels for officers. Surveys showed that 90 percent of GIs bought into these rumors. Such crude hostility hurt recruiting, as women shied away from being dubbed whores (Costello, 61). GI animosity was increased by the army caste system. For example, female medical personnel served in all theaters, and the bulk were commissioned officers. By army law, only officers and not other ranks could date them. In the sex-starved atmosphere, this created resentment and resulted in some rape cases.

Most crucial to the low recruitment of female personnel, however, was the fact that when women enlisted they took rear-echelon slots that would otherwise have been available to save men from frontline service. Women were reluctant to join up when doing so might send a man to die. Evelyn Fraser, a WAC, recalled: "When we came along, the men in clerical jobs were none too happy. We replaced them for combat overseas." The feeling against women serving was not helped by the WAC recruiting slogan, "Release a man for combat" (Terkel, 123).

Many GIs, understandably, did not want combat posting (Stouffer, 1:173). And there was resentment among some infantry about the disproportionate share of sacrifice they bore. Because most black males and all women were barred from combat, and because better educated white males got technical or desk jobs, a disproportionate share of the fighting and dying fell to underprivileged and unskilled white males.

The infantry had the lowest prestige of any service; it got maximum risk with minimum compensation. The air force, marines, and paratroops offered danger but glamour, and the technical branches were comparatively safe and offered professional training. White men whose scores were in the bottom half of the Army General Classification Test were assigned to the "foot sloggers." This does not mean that American infantry were not of a high overall caliber, or that there was not pride in being a fighting man, but a degree of demoralization and surliness was inevitable. A study by the army showed that not all combat troops were the happy-go-lucky boyish warriors pictured by the media (Stouffer, 1:161–62, 287, 296–98, 309, 312, 329–31).

This seminal study was carried out by the Information and Education Division of the army, under the leadership of Samuel A. Stouffer. His team found that the infantry had the lowest morale and that some combat veterans felt they had a rotten deal. Seventy-five percent of men who had been in combat believed they should be sent home and others sent to take their places. Most confessed they would get out of combat if they could, and a safe (nonmutilating) wound was seen as a ticket to freedom. The study concluded, with notable candor, that two factors held men in the lines: they didn't want to let their buddies down and they didn't want their families to lose their pay and benefits if they were court-martialed for refusing to fight. Coercion was critical (Stouffer, 1:186–88, 192–94; 2:312).

Men in the infantry were hostile to rear-echelon troops, whom they saw, often irrationally but understandably, as shirkers and sharpsters who stole supplies intended for combat troops and got fat on the black market (Mauldin, 135; Terkel, 56–57). Battle veterans felt slighted because base clerks got the same campaign ribbons they did (Litoff, 253). Joe Hanley, an infantry veteran, recalled the sense he had that he was cannon fodder, willingly sacrificed by a society glad to get him out of the labor pool: "Nobody really cared about you whatsoever. It was a big surprise to everybody when you came home. What are you doing here?" they asked (Terkel, 273).

The infantryman's particular sense of alienation was simply part of all servicemen's more general sense of distance from civilians. The military made far less money than the people at home, and they commented bitterly on civilians who, while living well, complained about poor coffee and the gas shortage. Labor strikes generated GI anger, as did business greed. Manufacturers who risked the soldiers' safety by cheating on armor thickness or quality of weapons' parts were particularly loathed (Mailer, 743; Mauldin, 128; Murphy, 145). Men overseas were made uneasy by reports of sliding moral standards on the home front. One soldier returning from leave told his buddies: "Everything's in a mess. Busiest people after this shindig will be the divorce lawyers" (Murphy, 235). An officer wrote home, "Everyday or so a soldier comes in and tries to find out how he can stop his allotment to his wife or get a divorce. So many of the wives are doing their husbands wrong" (Litoff, 209).

Many Americans believed that the WWII military was America's most ideologically committed fighting force. Hollywood boosted this image by having a leading character in each war movie deliver a speech to his appreciative buddies on the need to be out there fighting for freedom. Richard Leacock, who fought in Burma, said of these pictures: "I remember those Hollywood films where people sat in their trenches and had ideological discussions about the beauties of democracy at home. Oh bullshit!" (Terkel, 376).

This may have been one of the least ideologically motivated military machines in American history. A survey of enlisted men found that only 5 percent fought for idealistic reasons, such as a clear understanding of the threat to democracy posed by fascism. A Vietnam-era poll, by comparison, showed an ideological commitment against communism closer to 14.5 percent (Van Creveld, *Fighting Power*, 82). According to Stouffer's team, only 13 percent of GIs could name three of the four freedoms America was fighting for; 33 percent knew none of them. (Announced by FDR in August 1941, they were freedom of speech and of religion, freedom from want and fear.) Ernie Pyle observed no reaction among GIs to the news that the Senate had ratified the establishment of the United Nations. They didn't see it as their business (Stouffer, 1:433; Pyle, *Your War*, 299–300). Educational critics took this ideological disinterest as evidence of failure in the educational system (Wylie, 86–87).

The army tried to compensate with a troop orientation program, including the *Why We Fight* film series. But according to David L. Cohn, who monitored the program, too much material was at an elementary school level. For example, one booklet tried to explain the threat of nazism by comparing Hitler to a small-town major who told you how to raise your kids and where to work. Both instructors (usually reluctant junior officers) and audience were often bewildered by the program materials (Cohn, 7, 33).

British and French troops were determined to effect major postwar social reform in return for their sufferings, particularly as a disproportionate share of bombs had fallen on working-class districts where the underprivileged lived. They talked of redistributing wealth, of health and welfare benefits, of the end of class privilege. American troops, when asked what they wanted, cited no social changes: they craved a piece of the action going on at home: prosperity, defined as a new car, a good job, a piece of pie, and a baseball game. The songs the troops liked, such as "Don't Sit under the Apple Tree" and "White Christmas," reflected their lack of idealism and their longing for American life (Steinbeck, 23, 25; Gervasi, 513, 548; Pyle, *Your War*, 15; Hersey, 73–74).

This is not to say that the bulk of troops were cynical about the need to prosecute the war. After Pearl Harbor, it seemed clear that America had to join the Allies. There was a pragmatic sense that here was a job to be done and that the only way through was to get on with it. And they were probably right in being somewhat skeptical about the ultimate meaning of the four freedoms for the larger postwar world (Stouffer, 1:431). Then, too, as William Manchester, a marine who fought in the Pacific, said, this was not a rebellious generation. There wasn't a counterculture, and people conformed more readily; they feared social division (246–47). Nevertheless, the soldiers had a limited commitment. They only wanted to do their bit, and then they thought others should take over. Very few felt they should serve until the war was won. Civilians were most likely to see service as a war-long obligation, combat veterans the least likely (Stouffer, 1:451).

Felt obligation dropped sharply among men in battle zones as the war's end neared. Men overseas also tended to be more critical than the rear-echelon troops of the army, its leadership, and their own situation. They particularly resented officers' privileges, such as better leave packages and liquor allowances (Stouffer, 1:155–56, 168, 364, 370–71, 401). Some thought their officers lacked leadership and fighting ability, and hated them more than the enemy. This was partly because most junior officers came of out training schools rather than from promotions in the field and, therefore, had less combat experience than their men; their mistakes cost lives (Gorer, 26).

As victory neared in 1944–45, many soldiers' enthusiasm for the war effort dropped, especially those in Europe as Germany crumbled. The sense was, hey, most people now, especially back home, are going to make it through this war and live happily ever after. Why should I get shot at this stage in the game? Many men went AWOL (absent without official leave); Paris was full of them. Forty thousand soldiers deserted during the war; 2,854 were court-martialed, and at least one was shot. When we look at combat in the next chapter, we shall see why men might decide they could no longer serve Uncle Sam (Ellis, *Sharp End*, 243, 269; Fussell, *Wartime*, 151; Stouffer, 1:195; Terkel, 389).

In summary, the achievement of the American war machine was remarkable. It is doubtful that the Allies could have won without American participation. With America in the war, it is equally doubtful that they could have lost. American troops fought well, under good leadership, and with plenty of the tools of war. But American performance was not the only factor in Allied victory. Nor was the American war effort free from error, strife, or injustice. When we create a myth about the past, such as the belief in the perfect American WWII war machine, we create morale problems for ourselves in the present. We sell short our own effort. Although we try hard, our efforts don't always work; we have ethnic and gender tensions, social divisions. If everything worked so well back then, it follows that later generations must be inferior.

Moreover, when nostalgia drives us to depict a war as a golden age in our cultural development, a time of cheerful production, team spirit, prosperity, and patriotism, we trivialize the event by slighting the real suffering that took place; we make it into a carnival. And we lose sight of the fact that war is inherently destructive—wasteful of human and natural resources, disruptive of normal social development. We risk initiating human catastrophes in the questionable belief that history shows that wars will cure our social problems and make us feel strong again.

five

Overseas

AMERICA was not a battle zone in World War II, and most Americans never had to confront the devastation of war firsthand. What was happening overseas was censored by the government and media, so that civilians had only a limited exposure to reality. The full truth, it was thought, would not be good for morale and the war effort. Ads showed the troops as happy warriors, boyish and eager to be at the front, like a scout troop at camp. GIs gave candy bars to enemy kids, did not shoot prisoners, and tried not to harm civilians. The military was portrayed as a surrogate father, taking care of the boys' morals. The *U.S. Infantry Journal* officially condemned the use of profanity by the troops, and the gritty truths of military life were screened from the public. The GI phrase to describe the chaos of war, *situation normal all fucked up* (snafu), was translated as *fouled up* for the stateside audience.

Journalists resorted to frequent euphemisms. When Ernie Pyle reported that the soldiers wanted to "make love to" Olga, a woman who broadcast anti-Allied propaganda from Berlin, he meant they hoped to rape her, but he couldn't say it outright (*Brave Men*, 42). American mothers, delicately ignoring the killing work their sons were being sent overseas to do, formed organizations to worry the army about the men's morals in such areas as sex, drinking, and gambling. The army dutifully responded to public demand by denying alcohol to the ranks and shrouded much of what happened overseas.

Many GIs who had not been in combat looked and acted very young. Europeans noted that some GIs behaved "as if they were children," chewing gum, playing ball in the street, drinking Coke, and reading comic books (Shukert, 128). They seemed immature because they had not grown up amid war and because their parents had worked to prolong in them the sheltered innocence that Americans feel is a part of their national dream. Away from home and normal restraints, they often acted with an unconcern that was both refreshing and frightening.

War is, by definition, destruction. It can have a sinister charm. Constructing a building is creative, but it takes time, special ability, and training. Crushing a building can also be creative, in a secondhand way, but it can be done quickly by someone with little talent. This is why children smash toys they otherwise cannot handle: they try to perform through crushing. "The way I messed up that house was beautiful," says a machine gunner in Harry Brown's *A Walk in the Sun*. "I could do that fifty times a day" (166). An infantry lieutenant who got to fire a 155-mm howitzer found that its power was "thrilling," and he was "mightily impressed by the blast" that made his carbine seem like a "popgun" (Colby, 409–10).

This sense of power lent to the soldier by potent weapons was not unique to America, but the destructive urge was exacerbated in Americans by two factors. First, the American war machine was so powerful. It produced earth-moving machinery, such as bulldozers, and ear-pounding munitions in such quantities that the environment was inevitably changed profoundly by the impact. Second, Americans had less concern for the existing landscape than did other peoples, who respected the integrity of the natural features and architecture of their homelands.

Americans noted that the British, to protect their rural environment, built military facilities around landscape features: "the air base was completely mingled with farm, field and spinney," recalled an air veteran (Kaplan and Smith, 44). Americans used their powerful machinery to scrape the countryside clean and put their camps square and squat on the landscape: "ugly, barren, temporary . . . bases that had been nailed together overnight," as one soldier remembered (Baker, 269). Herman Wouk commented on the Pacific: "With the coming of the Americans, the once-tropic islands had taken on the look of vacant lots in Los Angeles" (351). Eric Sevareid worried about the potent combination of green American youth, powerful technology, and insensitivity to nature. The GIs "had the minds of simple children," he said, "but their hands were wizards' hands." Like "a blind Gulliver," they swept up fragile Lilliputian peoples and places, scooping out the earth with giant mechanical fingers (233).

Americans in Asia, like other Westerners, acted with racial arrogance. They mostly behaved better in Europe and were welcomed with gratitude by their allies, but some still exhibited aggressive ethnocentricity. Americans, said Sevareid, walked the earth as though they didn't care who owned it (230–33, 487). Most had no interest in learning from other peoples, and they lived only to get back home (Terkel,

157). Their great loathing was for Arabs, whom they met in Africa, and for Asians of the Pacific region, but they even held the British and French in contempt for their lack of consumer goods and modern gadgetry such as refrigerators (Pyle, *Brave Men*, 31; *Your War*, 27, 299; White, 21). While many were paragons of good manners, some were not, feeling that the rules of good behavior applied only at home. This minority festooned trucks with blown-up rubbers. They threw packs of condoms and candies at passing civilians (Costello, 238). They looted freely, for which they were sometimes shot or otherwise punished if it happened in friendly territory. But their misdemeanors were often overlooked in Italy, Germany, and Japan, where such robbery was termed "liberation" of enemy property. Some enthusiastically took part in the black market (Lindbergh, 947–53; Terkel, 376).

Some white GIs took their racial prejudices overseas and demanded that others conform to their views, wrecking businesses that served black troops. The British accepted black Americans simply as Allied soldiers, but the U.S. army insisted that facilities for their troops in Britain be segregated. British girls who dated black soldiers were beaten up, and several of their escorts were killed, by either white GIs or MPs (Smith, 138–51; Terkel, 369; Shukert, 13–14).

Sexual relations are a problem whenever any nation's soldiers are away from home. Americans in both world wars worked hard to keep their "boys" pure. The post office confiscated too-explicit pinups mailed to soldiers. Purity groups fought the issue of prophylactics or the organization of official brothels under proper medical supervision. USO shows were expected to keep the troops entertained and wholesomely satisfied without sex. The result was that the military had to treat their handling of sex as a covert operation. The establishment of prophylactic stations close to approved brothels in rest areas had to be kept secret. But the lack of sex education among GIs hurt military efficiency (Costello, 81, 86 132–34, 152, 222, 241).

War is inextricably bound up with death, and the proximity of death produces a need to affirm life, which inevitably centers on the procreative act. Soldiers had sex, wherever and whenever possible: 75 percent of GIs overseas, whether married or not, admitted to having intercourse. Unchanneled sexual need produced rape, occasionally even murder (Costello, 89, 97, 232–36, 261). Away from home, where nobody knew them, some GIs forced themselves on women. American soldiers treated Australian women so badly that their behavior led to two pitched battles with Aussie troops. And any woman associating with an American was automatically assumed to be a prostitute (Lindbergh, 902). GIs fathered tens of thousands of illegitimate children in

Britain. In war-torn countries, they took advantage of women's desperate need for food, cigarettes, and even clothing to trade them for sex. Respectable women had to prostitute themselves to survive in shattered Rome, Naples, Paris, and Berlin (Perrett, *Country*, 438; Gervasi, 563; Shukert, 96–99).

The venereal disease (VD) rate soared. In the northern European theater, it caused more American casualties than the German V2 rocket (Campbell, 28; Ellis, 304–6). At one point in the Italian campaign, VD cases outweighed battlefield wounds. In France, the rate went up 600 percent after the liberation of Paris. In Britain, the government and the American military finally joined in a sex education campaign that brought the contamination rate down by 66 percent (Costello, 225–26, 243, 248). But too often, Americans were handicapped by homefront pressure to preserve the illusion of innocence at the expense of pragmatic intervention.

The same was true of alcohol. It must be the ultimate act of willful naïveté to pretend that a man engaged in killing other men will be morally corrupted by a bottle of liquor. Only the American army tried to keep its ranks dry (though, because of the military caste system, the prohibition didn't apply to officers). The result was an army obsessed with obtaining booze. Whiskey became a form of currency, with a fixed value in trading for other items; a Samurai sword was worth so many bottles (Lindbergh, 906; Ellis, 289–90). Those without the wherewithal for barter distilled their own substitutes. Aqua Velva aftershave lotion from the PX and grapefruit juice made a popular mix, somewhat reminiscent of a Tom Collins (Jones, *Red Line*, 91). A five-gallon can of fruit and a handful of sugar, left in the sun to ferment, made a cloying but potent brew called "swipe" (Jones, *WWII*, 130). A similar concoction involved a coconut and raisins, notorious for vicious hangovers (Hilsman, 112, 139). The less inventive drank medical alcohol or torpedo fluid, which killed the unlucky (Garfield, 133–34).

Some troops also scrounged pep pills and got hooked on them. At least 10 percent of American troops took amphetamines at some time. Benzedrine was very popular; 25 percent of men in the stockade (field prison) were heavy users (Holmes, 246–47). Morphine, used as a pain killer, produced addiction among thousands of the wounded (Hilsman, 98–99). Deprivation tends to lead to obsession with the object of denial. Paul Fussell, a veteran of the European theater, said the infantry's canteens contained booze as often as water (*Wartime*, 101–2).

In no area have Americans retained more unreasonable ignorance than in their innocence about combat. Any combat situation will provide a certain stimulation. War gets us away from the humdrum of daily life, the monotonous routine, anxiety about mortgages or medical bills. There is an adrenaline flow rarely attained in civil life, and issues become clear-cut: live or die. Veterans speak of a team spirit and camaraderie rarely found in the competitive marketplace at home. Some people never lose their appreciation of fighting's brighter aspects. Some have it for a short while but then become traumatized or appalled by the constant exposure and only later in life come back to a positive, even romantic, view of battle.

Oddly enough, it is often the better educated soldier, who can rationalize and abstract his experience, who finds meaning in combat. But for the average man of any class or temperament, prolonged exposure to combat is highly debilitating, physically and mentally. About 25–30 percent of WWII casualties were psychological cases; under very severe conditions that number could reach as high as 70–80 percent. In Italy, mental problems accounted for 54 percent of total casualties (Keegan, 156; Holmes, 259; Ellis, 246–49). On Okinawa, where fighting conditions were peculiarly horrific, 7,613 Americans died, 31,807 sustained physical wounds, and 26,221 were mental casualties (Sledge, 311–12).

The symptoms of combat breakdown varied. A man suffering from what in World War I was called shell shock (shattered nerves from too-prolonged exposure to bombardment) might display an abnormal sensitivity to noise and sudden light (the characteristics of an exploding round) and become helpless. A psychiatric casualty in North Africa said, "I just want to be where it's quiet; I don't want to ever hear a gun again" (Wecter, 546). Some were debilitated by stomach pains and migraines (Litoff et al., 235, 255). An early warning signal was often the "thousand yard stare," a vacant expression fixed on the far horizon, usually accompanied by a total disregard for one's personal safety under fire (Pyle, *Brave Men*, 270, 451). Men often knew when they were close to or passing over the edge of normality. They hallucinated the dead coming back to life, wept unaccountably or uncontrollably, became prey to morbid fears that they would "do something terrible, like kill somebody [on his own side] or shit on the floor." This was the nightmare of a soldier in Ceylon, whose friend died in his arms and who subsequently had to be placed in convalescence (Sledge, 269; Terkel, 375).

The cruelest myth about combat stress is that cowards break down and heroes don't. In World War II, psychiatric casualties were often seen as "mommies' boys," spoiled brats without manliness (Strecker, 171, 21–23). This was the view of General Patton, who notoriously twice hit men in army hospitals suffering from stress. He held the popular but mistaken view that, while all people feel fear, cowards are those who give in to it. Heroes overcome their fear. "Americans pride themselves on being he-men and *are* he-men" (Farago, 231). Those who let down this magnificent ethic were ridiculed and punished (Patton, 340, 356, 382). The problem with this concept is shown by the fact that the second man Patton hit had fought with distinction in North Africa and Sicily, but his nerves began to give way after his wife had a baby that he feared he would not live to see. When a friend was badly wounded, his resolve caved (Farago, 183–87; Terkel, 288).

This example exposes the Hollywood myth that men who survived their first exposure to fire become battle-seasoned veterans who would be fine from then on if they were of sound character. But there was no such thing as getting used to combat, and the more you saw of it the more likely you were to break down (Marshall, 123–24). Battle-seasoned troops were also the least likely to appreciate Hollywood-style heroics, for they had the keenest awareness of how such meaningless stunts could get them killed.

The attempt to divide men into heroes and cowards avoided some major complexities: for example, a man might be steadfast on a beach but crack up in street fighting or be able to take any amount of shelling but go to pieces in a dive bomber attack. Sometimes, heroics came from exhaustion and hopelessness. It is probable that, when Audie Murphy performed the deeds of killing enemy soldiers that made him America's most decorated man, he had passed into a stage of battle fatigue where he despaired of surviving and had a reckless desire to get his death over with. Ironically, in seeking an end to his anguish, he became a hero (135, 158, 208).

The charge that men who failed in combat had grown up too much under the influence of women, tied to mom's apron strings, was examined by the Stouffer team of army researchers. They found no evidence that psychiatric casualties had more protective or possessive mothers. There were, however, other clear reasons for combat stress. First, we teach children that killing is a sin. The better this lesson is learned, the more traumatizing will be the taking of life (Stouffer 1:136 and 142). In Europe, only 25 percent of American infantry fired their weapons in battle; in the Pacific, the percentage was only a little higher. Men might stay on the firing line but not be able to kill—and these men were not cowards. The bulk of killing was done by heavy weapons platoons, artillery, and aircraft, which released missiles from afar (Marshall, 50ff).

Killing carried with it a grave psychological burden. When William Manchester killed his first Japanese, a sniper concealed in a house, he cried, threw up, and wet his pants. He begged over and over: "I'm sorry" (7). A soldier might rationalize death because the enemy was evil: "it is very wrong to kill people, but a damn Nazi is not human, he is more like a dog," wrote one officer (Litoff et al., 258). Possibly, but the problem was that the German enemy looked like, bled like, even smelled like oneself. It was somewhat easier to kill the Japanese, because they seemed very different and, unlike the Germans, were known to have committed widespread atrocities upon Americans.

At some level, the soldier was caught between competing and incompatible values: killing was both reprehensible and admirable. Similarly, he was the victim of conflicting loyalties: to be of service to his family, a man had to stay alive and provide for them; to be of use to his nation, he had to be willing to die. The tension between these incompatibles produced nervous breakdowns (Stouffer, 2:84; Marshall, 78–79).

Most important, the high breakdown rate among American troops (in the German army it averaged 2–2.7 percent) was due to the questionable policy that put the whole weight of war's horror on the small percentage of men designated irrevocably for combat. In chapter 4 we noted that American inductees quickly received a permanent classification (technical, clerical, infantry), and there was no effective limit to the term of service, so that a rifleman was likely to stay in the infantry until he was killed, badly wounded, or the war ended (Stouffer, 2:87).

The inevitable GI sense of being expendable was increased by the unfavorable teeth-to-tail ratio in the army, often as high as twenty-seven service people to one combat personnel, so that the army was perennially short of fresh combat troops. In 1943, for example, the army enlisted 2 million men, but only 365,000 were flagged for combat. Consequently, men at the front could not be given even short breaks and might be on the line constantly for weeks. Any brief rest they got could be no more than a hundred yards from the front (Ellis, 41, 296–99).

To alleviate the situation, a policy was introduced allowing theater commanders to rotate a limited number of men home each month. But combat needs meant that normally far fewer than the allotted number could be spared; the constant dashing of hope for relief added to demoralization and combat fatigue (Tregaskis, 203, 251). Said General Omar Bradley: "The rifleman trudges into battle knowing that the odds are stacked against his survival. He fights without promise of either reward or relief" (Holmes, 261). The odds Bradley was talking about were these: in three months of combat, an infantry regiment would suffer 100 percent casualties (Van Creveld, *Power*, 75). The sense of doom could lead to reckless behavior or suicidal bravado, like that of marines in New Guinea who played Russian roulette—gambling on who would be killed by the one round in a pistol chamber, revolved before each player put the gun to his head and fired. You might as well die one way as another (Lindbergh, 852). A GI with Audie Murphy in Italy said, "Home is the place where they send you when you lose an arm or a leg" (50).

Further organizational errors compounded the problem. In retrospect, it is clear that divisions should have been smaller so they could have been rotated out of the line without causing huge gaps at the front. Replacements could then have joined the divisions at rest and trained with them, becoming fully integrated members of the team when they moved into combat. Men recovered from their wounds should have been returned to their old outfits to encourage unit esprit. As it was, replacements, including recovered veterans, went into a central pool and were fed piecemeal into the line, so that group loyalty was not built up. This was bureaucratically convenient, but it meant that rookies were often thrown into combat with no chance to adjust to their situation. Some didn't even know how to handle the weapons assigned them (Marshall, 16, 42). They were often resented as outsiders by the old-timers, who gave them the most dangerous jobs to do in order to protect their buddies. The returning wounded were similarly treated. Some of the least necessary psychological casualties resulted from men being thrown into the meat grinder, friendless and without time to adjust to their units (Stouffer, 2:273, 278).

The result of keeping troops at the front too long was an inevitable drop in combat efficiency. A soldier in the line for, say, ten days would reach a maximum level of experience and competence. This would sustain through about the next twenty-five days. After that, his usefulness would decline until, after sixty days, he would be worn out, and by seventy or so he would often need hospitalization. Some of the 146th Engineers, who fought to exhaustion against the Germans in November 1944, were said to be "like a broken violin string, they had been stretched too far for too long" (Currey, 201). Thus, inexorably, the hero of ten days would become the coward of eighty days whom Patton slapped. One arrested deserter, who had fought through Africa, Sicily, Italy, and southern France, said all the men he had trained with were killed. He was promised repatriation, but his rotation never came. "I can't stand the infantry any longer. Why won't they transfer me to some other outfit?" (Gray, 17).

What was it about action that brought a man to this pass? Combat was not like the ads that made war glamorous. Nor was it like the movies,

Fig. 3. The anguish of combat (Drawing by Howard Brodie, reproduced courtesy of the U.S. Army Center of Military History)

which never showed blood. Even today's films, with their supposedly vivid special effects, fall far short of the reality. Admiral Gene LaRocque, who served from Pearl Harbor on, said: "I hated to see how they glorified war. In all those films, people get blown up with their clothes and fall gracefully to the ground. You don't see anybody being blown apart." He concluded: "You see only an antiseptic, clean, neat way to die gloriously" (Terkel, 189).

If it wasn't antiseptic, neat, and clean, what was combat? What was it that made madness the last defense against the combatants' surroundings? Let's take the fighting forces overseas. Stress began with the troopship that took men away from America, for most their first break from home. Loneliness was intense, particularly among married men, who knew they might not again see their wives and children. The sense of being a herd of animals marked for slaughter began here (Stouffer, 1:107–8).

Troopships were often modified merchantmen, their holds full of macabre scaffolding that converted cargo space into acres of bunks reaching into the upper darkness of the cavernous space. Men might have to climb ladders to reach beds twelve or more levels high. Often, the holds stank, and this, combined with the roll of the ship, made men sick. They vomited on those below. When possible, the decks were flushed with hoses, but this was difficult because, if too many men were cleared to one side of the ship to cleanse the other, the change in weight could make the boat roll over and capsize (Decker, 2). Ships at sea were rife with rumors: a U-boat wolf pack was assembling to sink the convoy, a deadly epidemic was sweeping the boat (Steinbeck, 20–21).

Sooner or later, the troopship would take the men to a hostile landing on a foreign beach. Often, belts and ties were taken from the particularly young or excitable the night before disembarkation; said one female nurse, "they were very, very young. In their fearful anticipation, they might do themselves damage" (Terkel, 286). The beaches were dreaded by foot soldiers, because they maximized the worst features of combat (Stouffer, 2:67–68). A man would climb down the ship's netting to the assault boat, often in a pitching sea, carrying 85 to 135 pounds of equipment. If he missed his footing and plummeted into the water, he would sink and drown (Manchester, 162).

The landing craft, chugging slowly toward the shore, was a sitting duck. On board, most were silent, some wept, others vomited (Ellis, 60–64). In a beach landing, the inconceivable became normal. At Kuralei, a direct shell hit flung a barge of men high in the air, and the boat came down on them. The few who survived were shot in the water by Japanese snipers (Michener, 308). Going ashore in southern France, during the landings that followed the D-Day operation, J. Glenn Gray recorded that the boat next to his was blown apart, scattering parts of men everywhere. The shock made a fellow officer lose his voice for three days (113–14). At Tarawa, a coxswain went mad from piloting his boat through body parts run after run (Fussell, *Wartime*, 273). And a wounded battalion commander who crawled onto a pile of bodies to avoid drowning in the surf was recovered the next day, insane (Manchester, 228). To make a shattered naval officer take his men within wading distance of the shore on D-Day, Elliott Johnson had to shove his pistol in the man's mouth and order his every movement (Terkel, 253).

The beach itself was a surreal hell. Ernie Pyle described the D-Day shore: for a mile out, the coast was littered with shattered boats, tanks, trucks, rations, packs, buttocks, thighs, torsos, hands, heads (*Brave Men*, 366–67; Jones, *WWII*, 118). Hostile fire swept the beach, creating more confusion and casualties among the men, who naturally went to earth in the face of such carnage. Young soldiers milled around, often crying, soiling themselves. Timuel Black, an African-American GI, recalled that on Utah Beach on D-Day there were "young men crying for their mothers, wetting and defecating themselves. Others tellin' jokes," unreasonable jocularity also being an emotional response to horror (Terkel, 276).

The men had to be forced forward, off the beaches. Conventional theory in World War II taught that fear was natural but that you must not give in to it; you must move forward. Often, this made sense: if you stayed prone, you would finally be hit (Stouffer, 2:196). But in the days and months that followed the initial landings, the troops would force themselves to get up and push forward over so many naked expanses, each time expecting death, that finally putting one foot ahead of the other became an act of heroic will. And one day, the feet would no longer respond on command.

> I must lie down at once, there is
> a hammer at my knee.
> And call it death or cowardice,
> Don't count again on me

wrote poet Louis Simpson ("Carentan O Carentan," *Dream*, 75–76).

Once the soldier moved inland, he entered an arena eerily empty of the enemy. One observer described the battlefield as small groups of men apparently out on a hike; occasionally one would gesticulate and fall

(Sevareid, 388). Contrary to film staging, where we see men point guns at and shoot individual enemies, in real modern war long-range weapons have abstracted the enemy to the far horizon: he is rarely seen; only the incoming rounds give notice of his presence. Men dying at the hands of unseen antagonists added to the terror of combat (Marshall, 44–47).

Modern war is unreasonable to the person engaged, because it denies the individual knowledge of the factors needed to provide for personal safety. In addition, the soldier's senses are assaulted by noise, chaos, and shocking images of violence (Stouffer, 2:83). Bullets would rain down from a fighter plane that came and went so fast nobody saw it (Brown, 52). Shells landed among trucks on a crowded highway, spewing flesh and twisted metal, preventing movement. The incoming rounds might arrive from the rear, called friendly fire, which falls on its own side far more often than any army is willing to admit. General Mark Clark's boat was nearly sunk by friendly fire as he went ashore at Anzio (Gervasi, 531). General Leslie McNair was killed in Normandy when Americans bombed their own lines. There were thirteen such major errors and countless minor ones from D-Day until the Ardennes. On every field, from Morocco to Peleliu to the Bulge, troops reported casualties from targeting errors made by their own side (Gellhorn, 141–42; Currey, 199; Colby, 47–49; Pyle, *Brave Men*, 436).

The soldiers rarely saw much, but the sound of both their own weapons and of the enemy's was deafening. "You don't see much. Mostly you hear it, especially in the jungles.... Oh God, your ears ring for hours after," said a veteran of the Japanese war (Terkel, 376). The men on the ground most feared projectiles that came down from above—shells, mortar rounds that descended quickly from a sheer trajectory, bombs that they had no defense against and that they could never burrow into the ground far enough to escape. A dive bomber made you feel your backbone would be laid bare by every concussion. About 85 percent of physical casualties were caused by shells, bombs, and grenades; only 10 percent or less by bullets (Stouffer, 2:234; Holmes, 210).

A platoon might be hit by incoming fire, and then the fighting suddenly would wash on to somewhere else, leaving the soldiers stunned and bewildered as to what had happened and why (Brown, 33). One man might have gone to ground—and, there, counted the buttons on his jacket; another might have ripped up the earth with his bare hands. Some men had fired their weapons, probably without a target

(Hersey, 94–95; Brown, 45, 124). Others had wept, vomited, defecated in their pants. Someone might have died in panic, like the sergeant who was blown to bits when he reached for a grenade in his pants pocket and pulled out only the ring pin, activating the weapon while it was still on his person (Jones, *WWII*, 53). Then it was over. Unlike the movies, few firefights reached an acceptable resolution: there was no climax in which a battle was won, a mission accomplished. There was a rain of blind destruction; men were hit, the landscape blasted; then nothing but the moaning. Survivors were left with a disjointed, episodic sense of what had occurred (Jones, *Red Line*, 229–30; Pyle, *Brave Men*, 452).

The mysterious, even incomprehensible, nature of the battlefield provoked intense caution among the infantry. They were reluctant to move forward until artillery and aircraft had plastered the path ahead, giving a brute force quality to the offensive. Officers and noncoms who were too eager were resented—and occasionally killed—by their men (Terkel, 41; Litoff et al., 247). Men who cracked up and became a danger to their own side in battle might be killed through necessity. A machine gunner in the Bulge who went mad and could not stop firing his weapon was shot by GIs whose only chance of survival was to surrender to the attacking Tiger tanks (Wallace and Burns, 8–9; Sledge, 101).

In civilian life we find many ways to transcend our basic animal origins. Natural functions are discreetly and hygienically handled, we smell sweet, and many of us are privileged to work with our minds, transcending the bodies that cage us. The combat soldier was forced daily to witness man as animal, scratching and gouging to live, dying, and decaying. He knew that we excrete from every pore, that we stink, and when we die our bodies become garbage. He lived with endless animal misery. He wore ill-fitting clothes and toted huge burdens. He looked like a hobo (Manchester, 256). When not under the stress of combat, he endured endless monotony and the fatigue of long marches (Mauldin, 40, 46). He was always tired. One remembered: "My eyeballs burn; my bones ache; and my muscles twitch from exhaustion. Oh, to sleep and never awaken. The war is without beginning, without end. It goes on forever" (Murphy, 46).

The foot soldier rarely got a decent meal and often in the front lines went weeks without hot food. Much of his diet was dehydrated: powdered eggs and dried vegetables. He lived endlessly on K rations: spam and dried sausage, crackers and chewing gum. Or C rations: cold stew and candy bars. He needed cigarettes for their warmth and comfort. The front lines reeked of them, along with vomit, for the food soured his stomach (Ellis, 280–85; Fussell, *Wartime*, 145; Murphy, 116). A soldier poet who served in the 101st Airborne Division wrote:

> Most clearly of that battle I remember
> The tiredness in eyes, how hands looked thin
> Around a cigarette, and the bright ember
> Would pulse with all the life there was within.
> (Simpson, "The Battle," *Poems*, 19)

Men suffered abscessed teeth, stomach ulcers, skin diseases, and other manifestations of malnutrition (Garfield, 133).

The infantryman was filthy, and many of them said that this was worse than the shelling. He had only rare opportunities to wash himself or his clothes (Tregaskis, 181; Brown, 24–25). At least 50 percent of combat soldiers soiled themselves at some time; a last order before battle was, "keep your assholes tight" (Manchester, 380). Men lived in their own filth. Tank troops often had to defecate and urinate in their vehicles (Ellis, 152). Troops in foxholes had to foul their positions or risk death by exposing themselves. They might use a ration can to scoop the waste over the top of the hole (Pyle, *Your War*, 151; Murphy, 115). One marine was constipated for months after his superior officer was shot by a Japanese sniper while squatting for a bowel movement (Manchester, 71, 257, 358; Hilsman, 94–95).

The physical environment became another enemy. In the desert, men suffered from hot winds, sand in their food, and lack of water. In Italy they struggled against freezing temperatures, torrential rains, savage rushing rivers, and carefully defended mountain passes with narrow approaches along cliff edges (Murphy, 34). Marines in the central Pacific fought on bleak, hot, cinderlike coral atolls, which shattered like shrapnel when hit by explosives. To the south, the forbidding jungle enveloped troops in its claustrophobic dark heat (Mailer, 46–47, 666). It was host to a legion of natural dangers, from snakes, insects, and land crabs to tropical diseases such as malaria, cholera, typhus, and even elephantiasis, which attacked the glands (Manchester, 95–96, 215). One soldier's testicles swelled to the size of watermelons (Hilsman, 71–73). To combat malaria, the troops were given atabrine, which had the side effects of nausea and yellow skin coloration. Many threw the medication away.

Everywhere, there was mud. In all theaters, rain turned earth to slime. Men struggled against it in foxholes, it buried them alive, and they drowned in it when shells threw mounds of it upon them (Manchester, 374). It puckered their skin and rotted their feet. As many as 70 percent of nonbattle casualties during bad weather were trench foot

(Currey, 84; Colby, 359). When Eugene B. Sledge tried to clean up from the fighting on Peleliu, the mud in his hair ripped the teeth from his comb. It had decomposed his socks into slimy webs that pulled the flesh from his feet (Sledge, 153, 260, 288). And all around were flies and maggots, for this wasteland of mud and excreta was also a charnel house wherein the dead lay rotting (Ellis, 185; Mauldin, 198–99). Decay accompanied the troops wherever the pace of battle bogged down and the bodies could not be removed (Sledge, 142–44).

On Peleliu, where the opposing lines were so close that it was too dangerous to try to reclaim the dead, bodies oozed into the pervasive slime. Land crabs fed on them, as did dogs on other fields, such as at Cassino, where they ate out the tender throats (Jones, *WWII*, 128). An officer was riveted by the body of a Louisiana boy: "The flies had arrived already and were feasting on the blood in his open mouth" (Gray, 109). The stench from the bodies, said one reporter, made your eyes run and your breathing difficult, made you vomit. "The sight of death is nothing like its smell" (Sevareid, 409). Freezing temperatures cut the smell, but then bodies were petrified in the grotesque contortions of violent death, and they turned a startling claret color (Patton, 220).

Sometimes there were too many dead for individual burials. On Okinawa, the marines were "stacked like cordwood" and then buried in communal graves, as were the Japanese (Terkel, 179; Colby, 311). Many corpses were too disintegrated to be reclaimed: vehicles squashed them into the earth (Sledge, 302); explosives blew them into bits. At one burial, the only recognizable parts were a scalp and a rib cage (Cubbins, 196–97). A GI who saw the remains of German panzers caught in Allied crossfire said, "There was nothing," just a pair of boots and "flesh hanging" in the tanks (Decker, 21). Reporter Martha Gellhorn, examining a Sherman tank that had taken a direct hit from a German 88-mm shell, saw only "plastered pieces of flesh and much blood" (128).

There were seventy-five thousand missing in action (MIAs) in World War II. Most had been blown into vapor. A WAC who assisted families coming to Europe to visit their relatives' graves said: "I don't think they know, in many cases, what remains in that grave. You'd get an arm here, a leg there" (Terkel, 125, also 286). A member of the quartermaster corps who dug the graves said he never got used to the stink. "I think maybe if every civilian in the world could smell that stink, then maybe we wouldn't have any more wars" (Eckert, 305).

Only in heroic battle art do the dead assume restful poses, regarded with reverence by their comrades. James Jones said that the living automatically resented the dead: "*Nobody* wanted the poor bastard now"

Fig. 4. A jeep squashes the torso of a dead enemy (Drawing by Howard Brodie, reproduced courtesy of the U.S. Army Center of Military History)

(*Red Line*, 159; *WWII*, 86). The reason was that violent, unexpected death was ugly, embarrassing. It reminded you that, in the scale of things, you were of infinitesimal value, a piece of matter, as bombardier Joseph Heller put it. "Set fire to him and he'll burn. Bury him and he'll rot like other kinds of garbage" (450). There was no distinction, said Norman Mailer, between a corpse and a shoulder of lamb (224).

Often there was little romance in the way combatants became casualties. William Manchester was wounded by a shell blast blowing parts of his men into his back. (46, 69–70). A tank officer found he was choking on bone fragments from his shattered left hand (Patton, 276). A GI was killed by his buddy's flying head, another by the West Point class ring on his captain's severed finger (Fussell, *Wartime*, 270). One young soldier watched in horror as a tank rolled over his legs (Colby, 75). A new phosphorus shell, developed in 1944, threw out pellets, which ignited with air to cause massive burns: one member of a forward observer team cracked up when two buddies, hit by friendly fire, flared up "like Roman Candles." "No more killing, no more killing," he sobbed (Terkel, 260). The most feared wounds were in the brain, eyes, abdomen, and genitals.

There was some comfort in the fact that medical discoveries helped the wounded to survive at a far better rate than in previous wars. Medical advances cut the immediate death rate of wounded at the front from 8 percent in World War I to 4.5 percent in World War II. Four innovations were vital. Penicillin, produced in quantity by 1943, was a crucial antibiotic; it was also pivotal in combating syphilis. Sulfa drugs gave immediate help in preventing wound infection. Shock, a prime killer in previous wars, was treated through injection of a glucose saline solution, which replaced lost blood plasma. But most important were supplies of fresh plasma, which reversed the slide into shock.

These emergency measures were administered by medical corpsmen. The wounded man was then sent to the battalion aid station, where the wound was properly dressed. If he required major treatment, he was transported to the portable hospital, where surgery was performed. This was the MASH (mobile army surgical hospital) of World War II. From here the soldier would be either sent to a rear hospital to recover and be returned to active duty or, if incapacitated, evacuated home. Thanks to such sophisticated medical techniques and organization, only one in ten field casualties died, a notable achievement. Unfortunately, some had to live with permanent disability and lasting pain. "The heroes were packaged and sent home in parts" (Simpson,

"The Heroes," *Poems*, 20). Some of the wounded were humiliated and outraged by their predicament; they were not the stereotypical happy warriors. James Jones said they viewed the world with a cold, unforgiving stare (*WWII*, 147).

Although sailors and airmen normally did not have to endure the filth and charnel house conditions that ground troops did, their experiences were also stressful. The decks of a fighting ship in action became littered with pieces of men (Fahey, 231). One sailor saw his mate blasted through a metal ladder, which cut him into symmetrical chunks (Jones, *WWII*, 25). When a ship went down, many men struggling in the water were dragged down by the undertow. Then underwater explosions blew them back to the surface, entrails curling from burst stomachs, blood pouring from noses and ears. Men on the surface were coated with oil, which attacked their eyes and lungs. They might or might not be rescued before exposure claimed their lives.

Airmen in such theaters as Britain and Italy lived comparatively well when not in the air. They had showers, hot food, and recreational facilities. Yet even in Britain, life in temporary buildings, called Nissen huts, was often primitive; crewmen huddling in damp clothing on muddy floors around smoky coal stoves, while wind whistled through cracks in the walls (Kaplan and Smith, 48, 51). In zones with intemperate climates and little developed infrastructure, such as Alaska or the central Pacific islands, life could be as stark as for the infantry.

Unlike ground troops, many airmen could hope to be rotated home after a specific number of missions, but this was not always the case. In Alaska in 1942 there was no rotation for the Eleventh Air Force, because there were no replacements. The men said you only got home in a coffin (Garfield, 125). In Europe a tour was normally twenty-five missions, but during 1943–44, when the air force was waging a war of attrition with the Luftwaffe, the average life of a crew was fifteen sorties (Kaplan and Smith, 23). Air crews, like other combat troops, cracked up (Cubbins, 68). Occasionally, a pilot went mad in the air and crashed his plane (Tapert, 66). "There's a point where you just get to be no good; you're shot to the devil—and there's nothing you can do about it," said a naval pilot in the Pacific (Tregaskis, 250). To try to help, crews in some theaters well along in their tour got a week's R and R plus a three-day pass every five missions (Kaplan and Smith, 143–45). But it hardly compensated for what the men went through. Why?

Let's take a bomber crew on a raid over Germany. A mission began with the crew's dressing. This was important. Many were superstitious: their safety depended on dressing in a certain order or carrying a lucky charm. If you got things wrong, your number came up (24). Next came the briefing and psyching yourself up for combat. Stress mounted. The bombers might wait an hour or more on the runways for the all clear that led to takeoff (97). Once airborne, the flyers were at continual risk. Where the bombers cruised, it was always winter, with temperatures 20°–50° below zero. The cold was intensified by the bomber's speed, which generated a 150-mph wind. With no insulation or heating, the crew were highly vulnerable. A gunner might lose his fingers if they froze to his weapon (7). Condensation from the oxygen masks dripped down into windpipes and could freeze there, cutting off the oxygen supply: a man could black out and die before he realized the danger. Vomiting into the mask from fear or airsickness provided similar risk. Usually it was the job of the copilot to check every ten minutes that everyone was all right (110–11). Meals for flyers had to be carefully chosen, avoiding foods that caused gas, because in the low-pressure atmosphere, pockets of gas in the digestive tract expanded, causing intense pain. Men had to defecate into their suits to relieve the agony (Hilsman, 50).

The bombers flew in a tight box formation, which allowed their machine guns to give maximum mutual protection through an envelope of overlapping fire. A bomber wing or group might throw out thirty tons of steel a minute. But the tight formations also increased the risk of crashes, particularly as vapor trails from the engines created a thick haze, through which the planes flew blind. And the trails gave away the presence of the bombers to enemy fighters which, sooner or later, would come up to fight (Kaplan and Smith, 104).

Fighting in the air, as on the ground, was characterized by noise and confusion. With no soundproofing, the racket made by ten or more machine guns clattering at once was almost unbearable. Shell cases flew everywhere (Gervasi, 462; Eckert, 264). The air became filled with debris and hurtling fighter planes, some of which were your own escort. In the mayhem, you might hit one of your own fighters: the gunners' rule was, if it points its nose at you (meaning its guns were brought to bear), you fire (Cubbins, 33).

More feared than the fighter planes was ground fire—shells that burst around you, hurling chunks of flak or shrapnel through the flimsy skin of the bombers. Once the bomber formation locked on target, the planes could not deviate from their flight path. Ground gunners knew this and put up a "box barrage," which filled a section of air with flak, through which the bombers must fly. Bert Stiles recalled a shell coming up through the belly of his ship and bursting ten feet above it. A chunk of shrapnel clipped off the pilot's kneecap (Kaplan and Smith, 136). Ira Eakin remembered a direct hit on a top gun turret: all that was left of the gunner was his upper teeth stuck in the plexiglass (128). The wounded who couldn't make it home were strapped into parachutes and shoved out, in hopes the enemy would treat them.

If your ship was crippled, you had to ease out of the formation before parachuting out or risk that you would be pulled into the propellers of the planes behind (Cubbins, 31). One pilot saw a main exit door hurtle past his cockpit, followed moments later "by a man, clasping his knees to his head, revolving like a diver in a triple somersault. I didn't see his 'chute open" (Eckert, 263). One B-17 turned slowly out of formation, its cockpit a mass of flame. The copilot tried to jump from the window and was smashed by backdraft into the tail plane (ibid.). Pilot William Snaith was lucky. When his cockpit exploded he was blown clear of the wreckage and parachuted safely to earth, albeit badly burned (Cubbins, 178).

The planes that survived the outward-bound journey still had to get home, often limping, badly damaged and with gaping holes from flak and fire, their props dead, their landing gear collapsed. If you ditched into the sea, you had a 35 percent chance of being rescued before you died from exposure (Kaplan and Smith, 10, 116). If you made it home, you had to live with what you had seen and with the guilt of knowing you were secretly glad others had got it instead of you.

Air crews knew the depths to which humanity can sink (Terkel, 198). Their ultimate burden was that they knew intimately the inhumanity of which we are capable: that man as an animal, away from social surroundings and civil discourse, can be a savage (Sledge, 156; Manchester, 382). They could be cynical about human life. Ernie Pyle worried about the outlook of young pilots who laughed about how Germans had blown out of trucks they had bombed, their bodies exploding like firecrackers (*Your War*, 107). Pilots in the Pacific freely admitted that they machine-gunned hostile flyers in parachutes; the enemy did the same to them (Lindbergh, 857). Though most airmen never had to see the carnage their bombs caused, the dreadful wounds and mutilations, they could hardly be blamed if they lacked compassion for civilians. Didn't they manufacture the flak and cannon shells that shattered their planes and bodies?

But it was the lot of the men on the ground to truly experience the full unreason of war. As children and adolescents, they had been taught not to kill, but now they were being asked to kill in defense of the national interest. Often, the etiquette of war didn't make sense: you could slice off an opponent's face with an entrenching tool but not shoot him with an exploding bullet; you might incinerate him with a flamethrower but must spare the civilians who made his weapons. To survive, you sometimes had to do grotesque things that nobody could have warned you about, like kill a man by sticking your finger in his eye socket (Sledge, 109). That some men under stress lost sight of the fine distinctions should not surprise us. What is more remarkable is that most retained their sense of humanity: as we have said, perhaps 75 percent of infantrymen in the war rarely fired their weapons (the percentage appears to have increased late in the Pacific war).

Inevitably, however, there were atrocities. For example, before the invasion of Sicily, General Patton told his men to accept no surrender from enemy soldiers who continued to fire within the highly lethal 200-yards range. At Biscari, U.S. troops killed thirty-four unarmed prisoners who had given up at the correct distance, but these GIs had seen buddies killed, and they didn't feel that a few yards made any difference (Patton, 109; Weingartner, 24–39). Intelligence officers in all armies admitted that prisoners were sometimes tortured, even killed, to extract information (Gray, 203; Terkel, 374–75; Jones, *WWII*, 225; Lindbergh, 955). This is part of the moral unreason of war. This conduct is often condemned, but the torture and killing had the same rationale as the dropping of the atom bombs, of which many Americans still approve: that is, that the action saved friendly lives. Why was torturing prisoners to obtain vital information reprehensible when dropping the atom bombs was not?

Men in all armies shot prisoners because they were too exhausted to tend to them properly. They might be termed murderers, but they were often terminally tired, desperately trying to survive. Prisoners, particularly wounded ones, added to the complexity and hence also the risk of the combat soldier's situation (Sevareid, 388–90; Manchester, 381; Terkel, 556–57). This is why Audie Murphy told new men to take no prisoners and to kill the Axis wounded (206, 249).

In Europe, the SS were particularly likely to get no mercy because of their reputation as Hitler's fanatical, cold-blooded killers. The Seventy-Eighth Artillery Battalion of the Second Armored Division called itself "Roosevelt's Butchers" and openly claimed that it shot all the SS soldiers it caught (Decker, 19). In the Pacific theater, toward the end of the fighting, Allied soldiers became hardened to slaughtering Japanese soldiers, because the enemy themselves appeared to have no respect for life. Throughout the war, the Japanese military committed atrocities on both enemy soldiers and civilians, including the notorious Bataan death march, during which American prisoners were force-marched to death. As the Allies took back territory, Japanese soldiers would often launch hopeless but terrifying suicide attacks against Allied troops rather than surrender. Their ferocity and unreasoning dedication convinced some Western soldiers that only extermination could stop their determination (Dower, 11, 47–48, 51, 78–79). Some American soldiers showed no interest in taking Japanese prisoners (Lindbergh, 853, 856). To some, the Japanese was a cunning and dangerous animal, not a full human being. In the last battles of the war, Japanese soldiers were butchered in enormous numbers. For example, on Okinawa, 7,613 Americans died, but 107,539 Japanese were killed.

The fighting in the Pacific finally developed a mutual ferocity that had its own horrific momentum. The enemy dead were mutilated by both sides. Americans boiled the flesh off Japanese heads and sent the skulls as gifts to loved ones in the States. Ears, hands, and sexual organs were dried for keepsakes (Fussell, *Bomb*, 46–48; Tregaskis, 15). Marines used their K-bar knives to gouge the gold teeth from dead and dying soldiers (Terkel, 59; Mailer, 225). Garbage was dumped on the enemy dead, and men urinated into their mouths (Lindbergh, 859, 883). Some marines were seen playing toss into the open skull of a dead Japanese, and one officer shot the heads off corpses' penises for sport (Sledge, 123, 198). Such behavior can occur when ordinary men are placed in extraordinary circumstances.

Perhaps we are now in a position to appreciate why the breakdown rate among combat troops was high. Loss of personal freedom, sexual deprivation, physical misery, chronic exhaustion, and immersion in a chamber of horrors coalesced to produce strain beyond endurance (Stouffer, 2:78–90). There was bitterness. Only 18 percent of combat veterans in the Pacific in 1943–44 said they were usually in good spirits (Stouffer, 1:162). They resented the pain. A GI whose arm was blown off in the Arno Valley in Italy cursed God and America, because he suffered "for something I never did or knew anything about" (Fussell, *Bomb*, 33). And a soldier at Anzio wrote:

> Praise be to God for this captured sod
>   that rich with blood does seep;
> With yours and mine, like butchered swine's;
>   and hell is six feet deep.
> That death awaits there's no debate;
>   no triumph will we reap.
> The crosses grow on Anzio,
>   where hell is six feet deep.
>
>   (Murphy, 125)

John J. Conroy, a Marine who was shell-shocked and full of shrapnel bits and who had seen most of his buddies killed on Guadalcanal, wrote bitterly: "the medicos here optimistically say I'll pay for it the rest of my life" (Wecter, 545-46).

The saving grace was that most of the personnel in any theater never saw combat. For those who did, the trauma eased over the years. Eddie Costello, a flyer who became a journalist, said the war was four years of nervous diarrhea and a sore anus. But later, the survivors "take what happened and enlarge it, embroider it, and come out maybe not smelling like a rose, but smelling a little better than I do" (Terkel, 205). Some rationalized the slaughter they had seen in the war's last stages on the basis that the enemy was clearly evil and therefore deserved it. "I'm more of a pacifist than I ever was," wrote Second Lieutenant Kermit Stewart, who fought in the Philippines, "but as long as there are vermin like Japs and Nazis, they have to be exterminated." (Tapert, 238). But this didn't work for everybody. Some men continued to have nightmares about the war. And we should remember that 25 percent of WWII veterans still in veterans' hospitals have psychological wounds. What they were forced to witness so appalled them that they recoiled permanently from our world. They will never return from overseas.

six

Home Front Change

THE MAJOR ROLE the U.S. armed forces played in overcoming the Axis is an important part of the pride Americans take in World War II, but it is not what ultimately makes that war the best war ever. At the center of the popular view of the war is a picture of a rich, united, and confident America. It is this vision of home front strength and prosperity that makes the era appear as a golden age.

In the Great Depression, America's mighty economic machine seemed to stumble, become impotent. Millions were unemployed and millions more lost hope of improving their lives. Confidence in capitalism was seriously eroded. Though the situation was improving by 1939, the economy was still in low gear, and government, despite all its New Deal plans and agencies, didn't appear to have the answers. Unemployment stood around 8.9 million. Then came war, normally a scourge of humanity, to increase the burden of human misery.

But here is the remarkable thing. The nation not only rallied, the war inaugurated the greatest era of prosperity in human history. The U.S. gross national product increased 60 percent during the war. And while living costs rose 30 percent, total earnings went up 50 percent (Nelson, 99). By 1945, the United States owned two-thirds of the world's gold reserves, half its shipping, and more than half its manufacturing capacity.

Over time, and as later problems have seemed harder to overcome, this economic miracle has loomed large in the nation's imagination— to a point where anyone who was alive in the 1940s is assumed to be gifted with special powers. Evan Thomas, writing in *Newsweek* (Jan. 12, 1992) urged that President Bush, in his State of the Union address, call upon his generation to once more take the lead in resolving current U.S. difficulties. Paul Taylor, of the *Washington Post*, had a month earlier wondered if America's mood of self-doubt came from fear that the passing of this can-do generation would mark the decline of the national genius. Was the American Century nearing its end? The *Cincinnati Enquirer* (Dec. 4, 1991), beneath a large picture of Bush and FDR superimposed on a background of war workers building B-17s, said that for decades America had trusted its leadership "to the generation of men who served in World War II." But this generation would soon pass, and how would America fare then for leadership?

World War II and the Depression are now nearly as far back as we can go in living memory, and so they loom large in our active folk story. And many who lived then were too young to understand it in depth; they remember only that the war was a great victory. Others have filtered their recollections over the years, forgetting the strain and pain—just as, when remembering a vacation, we forget the rainy days and bad motels. This is selective recall. In the same way, the achievements of the 1940s have, with time, become more spectacular than they really were. Not only was America prosperous, there were no ethnic or gender problems, families were happy and united, and children worked hard in school and read a great number of books. Americans knew who they were and what was right.

There is a lot of exaggeration in this; at times, faith in the can-do generation borders on ancestor worship. Thus Evan Thomas, after calling for the WWII generation to save us, admitted that about all most surviving members could do to help is use less Medicare and give back some of their social security pensions. Two major points need to be made about the home front boom of the war era. First, the economic recovery of 1940–45 came out of unique circumstances; it provides no magic formula to be applied whenever America is in trouble. Second, prosperity, important as it is to America's sense of well-being, is not a cure-all for social problems. Change, even positive change, is disruptive. America in the war was wrenched by change. And while the war brought good times for many, it put strain on the family and on ethnic, gender, and class relations. Despite the myth that all Americans were well adjusted back then, many felt great anxiety about their society and its future.

The unparalleled prosperity of the war period led to a popular belief that wars are normally good for the economy. Many people expected the Gulf War of 1991 to lift the country out of incipient depression, whereas it had the reverse effect. A comparison of the two situations suggests why. In World War II, unemployment left over from the Depression was sopped up when sixteen million potential workers were

Fig. 5. FDR, George Bush, and B-17 bombers (Drawing by George Longfellow, reproduced with permission from the *Cincinnati Enquirer* and George Longfellow)

absorbed into the military, leaving those at home to take advantage of the economic opportunities. The Gulf War, by comparison, was fought by professionals already in the forces, so that there was no absorption of the worker pool.

Perhaps 60 percent of the industrial plant that could be tooled for military production—to make tanks, planes, and so forth—lay idle in 1939. In 1991, the military used huge existing stockpiles from an arms industry that had already overproduced during the cold war, so there were no sluggish defense plants to jump start. In addition, Britain and France in 1939 had huge contracts with the United States for arms, boosting the American economy. This did not happen in 1991.

America in 1991 already had huge debts from immense deficit spending, whereas in 1940 America could afford a radically higher level of government investment to prime the economic pump, as the nation's wealth had not up to then been significantly tapped for public purposes. This ability of government to spend liberally was key. Despite the idea that the primary agency of economic recovery was private enterprise, it was in fact government spending acting upon an underutilized economy that energized the system. Private enterprise did not have the capital to bankroll a boom. Had the government spent as much during the Depression to pump the economy as it did during the war, it would have achieved the same spectacular results. In the two years 1939–41, Congress paid twice as much for defense as it had spent on the New Deal in the past eight years. Between 1940 and 1945 the government spent $323 billion, largely on the war effort. Even by Pearl Harbor, the rate of military spending was two billion dollars per month (Nelson, 142–43; Blum, 90–91).

Thus, public spending was crucial in financing recovery. But it was not without long-term costs. It is wrong to think that World War II somehow paid for itself and that wars are therefore unalloyed economic positives. The immediate cost of the war was $381 billion. Only about 44 percent of the bill was paid by direct taxation. To cover two-fifths of the remainder, the government floated bonds; it financed the rest through bank loans. The result was that the national debt more than quintupled, from $50 billion to $260 billion, and has not been under that figure since. It was not until 1970 that the original cost of the war was paid off, and America will be paying pensions and other war-related benefits well into the twenty-first century (Clayton, 661–63; Nelson, 99).

All of this could be handled in the context of 1945 America, because the country was a rich creditor nation with an unprecedented worldwide demand for its goods. More recently, as America's competitors have increased in economic efficiency and power, America's economic takings have failed to handle the deficit. Thus the tradition of deficit spending established in World War II did not set a precedent that would work for less favorable economic times.

A corollary myth is that a well-organized war effort will unite people in a common cause. As a generalization, this has value: most Americans did support the war effort. But the emergency situation also changed the American way of life. As an example, many people today work for large organizations and feel small and powerless. They dream of a time when small farms and businessmen worked for themselves, a time when, if you built a better mousetrap, the world would beat a path to your door. World War II undermined the world of the small producer in business and agriculture, completing the triumph of large corporations and inaugurating the organization society in which most of us work. In 1941, there were over two million small businesses. Many went under quickly, as products they sold went off the market due to war shortages. Independent car dealers and washing machine distributors are good examples.

In awarding production contracts, the government properly sought the most advanced technology, standardized parts, and economies of scale. This meant that orders went to the big producers, not the small craft shops. America's ten biggest corporations got 33 percent of the war contracts. The next largest forty-six companies received a further 42 percent (Nash, 135–36). Not all these giants made arms. Coca-Cola got a massive boost with a contract to supply its soft drink at a near monopoly to the forces. It controlled 95 percent of the overseas PX (post exchange) market, and the government assisted it in adding fifty-four more bottling plants to the five existing in 1940. Wrigley's got a boost when its gum was put in GI K rations. Corporate profits, after taxes, rose by 68 percent during the war (Blum, 107–8; Ellis, *Sharp End*, 288–89; Nelson, 108).

As the big got bigger, the little were squeezed out. Two months after Pearl Harbor, *Business Week* reported the loss of 200,000 small employers (Winkler, 13). The growth of big industry led to further radical change. Cities such as Knoxville, Tennessee, and Atlanta, Georgia, which were home to war industries, experienced mushrooming growth. In just two years, the Detroit area of Michigan received $11 billion in war contracts. Such cities became host to huge migrant populations. Many migrants were attracted by high factory wages, others were floating workers from collapsed small businesses and economically depressed small towns. Some were farmers displaced by army camps and training ranges and by the same move to big production that was changing industry. The new training base at Hinesville, Georgia, for example, threw fifteen thousand families off the land, while a Procter and Gamble shell-loading facility uprooted eight thousand. The number of farms in the United States declined by 17 percent (Nash, 139).

Over 15 million civilians moved during the war, and 700,000 people from rural Appalachia migrated to cities like Dayton, Muncie, and Detroit (Campbell, 219). Willow Run, site of a new Ford plant outside Detroit, grew from fifteen thousand to forty-seven thousand inhabitants almost overnight (Campbell, 170–71; Nash, 145). One resentful Willow Run native commented: "Everybody knew everybody else and all were happy and contented. Then came that bomber plant and all this influx of riff-raff, mostly southerners. You can't be sure of these people." A newcomer, equally disgruntled, said that Detroit was "a city without a heart or a soul" (Winkler, 44).

The inevitable housing shortages led to poor living conditions. By October 1942 in the country as a whole, 1.2 million families were doubled up in one-family units. Basements and garages, trailers, tents, and coal sheds were rented out as homes. Some new homes, quickly built to meet the crisis, had neither water nor sewage lines. By 1945, five million families were in substandard dwellings, like cellars and woodsheds (Hartmann, 166). Many natives of the exploding areas helped the migrant workers, offering free meals to travelers and accommodations at fair prices. Others exploited them. One Connecticut landlord boasted he could rent beds to women workers on three separate shifts, so they were occupied round-the-clock (Blum, 103).

Overcrowding was worst in the neighborhoods allotted to black workers. In San Francisco, people in the ghetto doubled, and Chicago's increased by 33 percent. The thrusting together of dissimilar ethnic and regional types generated distrust and hostility. In large areas of the country, segregation in housing, education, and recreational facilities was legal, so when emergency conditions forced working-class whites to live and work with blacks, violence often resulted. In June 1943, prolonged friction between blacks and whites living next door to each other in a predominantly Polish and Irish section of Detroit resulted in riots. It took six thousand National Guardsmen to restore order. The cost included thirty-four dead, a million lost work hours, and two million dollars in property damage. There were similar riots in New York and elsewhere (Nash, 145–52; Tyler, 101).

Many plants, such as North American Aviation, wouldn't hire persons of color. To combat this, FDR established the Fair Employment Practices Committee to investigate hiring abuses. Although it had a small staff and no power to enforce its findings, there was improvement. Where the workplace and worker facilities were integrated, there might be peaceful acceptance of change, but some employers faced white retaliation. White women at a Western Electric plant in Baltimore struck rather than share a restroom with black women. Pleas to put the war effort first didn't always work: a white man in a wildcat strike at a Packard plant said, "I'd rather see Hitler and Hirohito win the war than work beside a nigger on the assembly line." The sociologist Gunnar Myrdal found a majority of whites in the South and the West agreed (Tyler, 99).

However, Afro-Americans saw in the booming war economy and in the crusade against the Nazi superman ideology factors that could immensely improve their place in society, and they showed a growing interest in civil rights. By 1943, black workers and sympathetic white colleagues started to try to integrate restrooms and eating places, despite being served eggshells in their burgers and garbage sandwiches. These pioneers paved the way for the civil rights movement of the postwar era.

Hispanic workers also faced hostility. In addition to American-born Hispanics, large numbers of Mexican workers entered the country in response to labor shortages on the Pacific Coast and in the Southwest. White uneasiness grew when Mexican-American teenagers, like many other adolescents, began forming street gangs and challenging the traditional restraints on their behavior. Identifiable by zoot suits (long tapered jackets and baggy pants tied at the ankle, and worn with broad-brimmed hats, an outfit also worn by many young blacks), these youths antagonized white GIs who thought they were flouting the very values they were going off to fight for. (It was rumored, incorrectly, that Hispanics weren't doing their share in the military.) In June 1943 the "zoot suit" riots exploded in Los Angeles. For almost a week, off-duty white enlisted personnel roamed the streets, assaulting Hispanics. When the police intervened, they usually arrested the Hispanics, sometimes for their protection. Don McFadden, then a sixteen-year-old mechanic, saw servicemen drag a boy off a trolley and beat him senseless: "Here's a guy riding a streetcar and he gets beat up 'cause he happens to be a Mexican" (Terkel, 144–45).

Also on the West Coast, Japanese-Americans became the focus of fear and hostility after Pearl Harbor. Most of the forty-seven thousand Issei (Japanese born abroad and therefore banned from citizenship) and eighty thousand Nissei (American-born children of the Issei, who were citizens) lived in the Pacific region. They were removed to detention

Fig. 6. The police arresting Hispanics during the zoot suit riots, June 1943 (Photograph reprinted courtesy of the Library of Congress)

centers in the interior, suffering a $400 million loss in forced property sales. The Supreme Court upheld the removals in 1944. Although most inmates were released later that year, few received any compensation until the 1980s. These removals, although intended to prevent Axis subversion, actually hindered the war effort, because they demoralized a loyal segment of society and required the diversion of military resources to build and guard the camps.

Adding to the strain imposed on housing and transportation facilities by the civilian population movement, millions of service person-nel were in transit throughout the war from one military base to an-other. The camps were often bleak facilities, and bars and houses of prostitution usually sprang up around them—places soldiers could go to ease their loneliness. There were also cheap souvenir stores selling such items as silver-plated dog tags and china ornaments to send home. Many new military bases were in the South and the West, where legal segregation was standard, on and off base, and black per-sonnel suffered serious harassment. In a Kentucky railroad depot, po-lice beat up three black WACs who used a white restroom. Elsewhere in the state, three WACs were roughed up and arrested for sitting in the front of a bus (Tyler, 94; Hartmann, 40).

Northern blacks, unaccustomed to Jim Crow laws, had numerous run-ins with southern laws that consigned them to the backs of buses and theaters. Governor Eugene Talmadge of Georgia ordered bus dri-vers to carry guns and to force black GIs to comply with Jim Crow seating (Tyler, 93). Some white troops supported black soldiers, and the military at times tried to protect its personnel. But the Justice De-partment was reluctant to challenge local mores: when a black GI was killed by a bus driver in Alexandria, Louisiana, the department would not take up the case. In streetcars, restaurants, and theaters in the South, black soldiers had to sit behind German prisoners of war, who were accorded the rights of white men. Lena Horne, the famous singer, refused to perform in one USO show because German soldiers were seated in front of black GIs (Terkel, 149, 153; Hartmann, 193).

Service personnel were often followed around the country by their spouses and children. Although many townsfolk treated military de-pendents well, some cold-shouldered them, resenting the influx of an unstable population. Unused to seeing migrant females in large num-bers, some civilians saw these army wives as "loose" women who "couldn't get enough" and who should go back home (Klaw, 50, 100). Some guest house owners, fearing for their reputations, wouldn't allow GI husbands in their wives' rooms, so couples had to meet in alleys and phone booths (14–16). Housing around camps became so over-crowded that small sheds were put up, big enough only to hold one bed. In many houses, women had to wait in line to use the building's one stove and one bathroom. Women with children often couldn't get accommodation at all. Women of color had the worst time. At Camp Stewart, Georgia, wives and mothers of black soldiers had to carry army identification papers to keep the local police from arresting them as prostitutes (Tyler, 96–97). On the other hand, officers' wives were often able to get luxuries like soap and prompt dental appointments (Klaw, 20, 24; Litoff, 69, 99; Campbell, 191–98).

The movement of millions of people created a breakdown in traditional behavior patterns, which fed a growing anxiety over morality and the integrity of the family. And some people away from the watchful eye of relatives and neighbors did violate hometown mores. Homosexuals found safety and opportunity in the anonymous crowds of the big cities, using parks and youth hostels. Heterosexuals also found greater sexual freedom. A 1942 survey revealed that only 25 percent of single men and 40 percent of single women abstained sexually. Between 1939 and 1945, there was a 42 percent increase in the illegitimate birth rate, to ten per thousand newborns. With couples separated by the war, marital fidelity declined, and the divorce rate rose—from 16 percent in 1940 to 27 percent in 1944. By then, three million marriages had broken up under wartime strain (Costello, 5–7, 202–3; Winkler, 46).

Adding to the stress on traditional marriages was a government-business campaign to get married women to do paid work, reversing the conventional wisdom that said a wife should be a full-time home-maker. By 1942, the white male unemployment pool had dried up, and new worker groups were needed. Married white women were the most obvious labor source, and so propaganda badgered and enticed them into the labor market. "Mrs. Stay-at-Home" was the target of one ad saying that women were not doing their share (Gluck, 13). A 1943 editorial in the *Baltimore News Post* told unemployed wives: "Sister you'd better reform" (Anderson, 28). The War Manpower Commission asserted that "women have been allowed to fall into habits of extraordinary leisure" and were "getting by just by being 'a good wife and mother'" (Rupp, 97). Women were also told that they had over-parented their children and that "momism," the spoiling of male adolescents, was responsible for the high failure rate of army inductees to reach basic physical and mental standards of toughness (Wylie, 208; Strecker, 67).

The upshot was an influx of married women into the job market. In 1944, for the first time, married female workers outnumbered single female workers, representing 72 percent of the increase in employed women since 1940 (Gluck, 13; Winkler, 50). By then, 19 million women had paid jobs (Anderson, 4). We should not exaggerate the extent of real change that this represented: despite the Rosie the Riveter image, two-thirds of adult females were still full-time homemakers (Hartmann, 21–24). Moreover, 11.5 million of those in jobs were working in 1940 (Gluck, 7). And for only a handful of women was this their first job; most had worked before marriage. Nevertheless, the change in the lives of many families was real enough.

Not everyone supported women being war workers. Conservative journals such as *American Home* and the Catholic *Commonweal* urged women to stay home. A judge in Seattle ordered a working woman to quit when her husband threatened divorce (Anderson, 82). Many Americans thought that married female factory workers were immoral and assumed that adultery was rife on the night shift. Male workers were openly hostile to women applying for the same work they did.

Many women felt great guilt about shirking their family responsibilities and tried to do two jobs, one in and one out of the home. They got some help from day-care centers for infants, but these were often expensive and inconvenient, and they carried a stigma of parental neglect, so most women relied on family help with children and worked hard to accommodate both family and employer. One woman, who worked nights, got home at 7:30 A.M. After a short sleep, she got up to shop, clean, wash clothes, and cook for her husband and daughter (Gluck, 190). Another rose at 5:45 A.M. to cook the family breakfast before punching in at work at 7 o'clock. "Some nights," if she didn't manage to get dinner on the table by 6 o'clock, her husband "was mad" (Hartmann, 83–84). Food stores were asked to stay open one night a week to enable women workers to shop. By early 1944, the strain on working women had led to high absenteeism.

When it became clear late in 1944 that the war was being won and that women were no longer needed in the work force, the media began encouraging women to return home, partly because of a growing fear that children were being neglected. The worry was no longer about momism but about the emotional and behavior problems of unsupervised adolescents.

Both the Depression and the war appeared to lessen parental authority. In the 1930s, the father's stature had been diminished by his unemployment or reduced wages, which undercut his place as breadwinner and the voice of authority in the family: Geoffrey Gorer noted that, in a row over who should use the family car, a father usually lost to his son (chap. 3). Fathers and elder brothers were often away at war, so important role models were lost. If the mother worked too, the stage seemed set for wildness among unsupervised children. Adults worried about adolescent hostility and rebellion, which was expressed in growing numbers of street gangs. Cutting school increased; in Detroit, truancy jumped 24 percent between 1938 and 1943. More girls got pregnant. And the venereal disease rate rose: between 1941 and 1944, New

York City's VD rate among girls aged fifteen to eighteen years old increased 204 percent (Winkler, 46–47).

This delinquency was part of a larger trend: the birth of teen culture as a separate and distinct phase of the American life cycle. Other factors were at play in this development besides the weakening of family ties; many of those aspects of adolescent group behavior that concern social critics today were already becoming apparent in the youth of the war years. To begin with, there appeared to be a decline in the authority of the schools and in the intellectual quality of education. The denunciations of the teaching profession at the time make clear that upholding educational standards was difficult in wartime.

Charges that are made against education today were common by the eve of war. Standardized tests, used to cope with large class numbers, were accused of producing a drop in analytical and writing skills. The Englishman Geoffrey Gorer observed that American tests were usually checklists of unrelated facts and dates. He charged that, compared to European systems, "the standard required at any given age is low" (74). Eric Sevareid called high school the "most fruitless" period of life. "It is astonishing how little one is taught in these schools." Civics, for example, meant little more than the rote learning of the Bill of Rights (11–12).

The armed services found students were poorly prepared in math, science, and foreign languages. Mass entertainment competed with books for the attention of youth, as students devoured film, radio, and comic books. Philip Wylie, a social critic, said that youth could no longer speak or write properly (92). It was estimated that by 1941 most teens listened to two to three hours of pop music per night. Teen devotion to singers like Frank Sinatra worried adults who saw teenaged girls mob him in the streets and swoon in pseudosexual ecstasy at his concerts. One reporter said that Sinatra "generated the nearest thing to mass hysteria in the country" (Gervasi, 440). A pervasive antiintellectualism was already apparent among many students: the school heroes were the athletes, and humanities courses were seen as boring and irrelevant to "real life."

The war only exacerbated these problems. The draft caused a drop in the quality of secondary teachers, but Congress in 1943 killed a bill that would have raised teachers' pay in order to attract better people (Blum, 239). In urban areas swamped by population influxes, schools had to go on split sessions, and their facilities were run down by overuse. The draft had another direct impact on secondary and higher education: to speed boys through to induction, schools and colleges cut the requirements for graduation. And the needs of the army and navy also caused universities to offer fewer liberal arts courses and more technical and vocational subjects.

Military development projects, funded by federal grants, moved the focus from pure to applied scientific research and forged a link between university research and defense programs that continued after the war. Campuses became host to military training units. By 1942 Harvard had 4,500 troops training on its campus; the president of the University of California at Berkeley described his school as "a military tent with academic sideshows" (Hartmann, 103–4). A 1943 report by the American Association of University Professors, the watchdog society for academe, warned that the needs of the military were not only dictating curriculum but forcing the hiring of airplane mechanics and other technicians as teachers. The report also alleged that universities were using the emergency as an excuse to fire professors with unpopular views, eroding academic freedom in the name of patriotism.

Assertive patriotism also hurt the quality of debate in secondary schools. World history and current events had often been poorly covered by educators and the press before the war, and most students had little or no understanding of Asia or the causes of the war with Japan. But the wartime approach to social studies wasn't any better: a 1942 poll showed that 44 percent of high schoolers didn't know what the war was about and resented the space it took up on the radio and in magazines (Ugland, 43 and 53; Blum, 46). A typical world history text of 1943 devoted 2.7 percent of its pages to China and Japan and 1.6 percent to East Asia. Militant citizens' groups forced the revision of critical parts of social studies texts, removing negative references to slavery and to the treatment of the Indians, for example, on the basis that these promoted disunity in a time of crisis (Ugland, 111–13; Wylie, 86, 95).

The war's most serious impact on the young was through prosperity and enhanced job opportunities. This, rather than the failure of parental attention, primarily created the teen culture, with its immense spending power, consumer rituals, and peer pressure to be in fashion. It also skewed the high school from a seat of learning into a social center, the fulcrum of teen life, where study competed with athletics, hair styles, clothing, pop idols, and dates. In this closed world, peer approval became of supreme importance, and adult concerns became more and more remote.

With many young adult males in the armed forces, jobs not usually available to younger teenagers, such as bowling alley attendants, were opened up. Whole new job areas, like baby-sitting needed by women workers, were created. Many employers found they liked hiring adolescents, because they were more pliable than adults and worked cheaply. The result was that teens entered the work force in larger numbers than any other group. From 1940 to 1943, the number of working teens rose 300 percent. By 1942, three million youngsters aged fourteen to seventeen had jobs (Merrill, 230–34; Ugland, 154–55, 163–66, 188).

Most of their work was not essential to the war effort, yet schools felt obliged to modify their schedules to meet the demands of students and employers. The state superintendent of public instruction for Indiana urged schools to hold student working hours to four per day, but he also told principals to allow more if employers needed it. Some schools consented to a fifty-fifty split between work and school. Many closed down altogether during peak consumer periods, like Christmas rush (Gluck, 138; Ugland, 176, 183). In a sense, schools were trapped into compliance, because if they didn't acquiesce, students would quit. One state experienced a 17 percent increase in dropouts between 1940 and 1944. Schools increasingly gave credit for outside work and yielded to student demand for vocational courses useful in the marketplace (Ugland 160, 101–2; Anderson, 93–94). The result was that much education became shallow and vocation oriented (Cohn, 7–8).

The resultant adolescent affluence was, more than any other factor, at the root of the new teen culture, which became a potent new force in America. While the Depression had extended adulthood downward, thrusting adult status and problems on children at an early age, wartime affluence extended childhood upward, creating adolescents who often lacked maturity and direction (Elder, 28). By 1944, teens were estimated to have a spending power of $750 million and, as adults bought the necessities, this was virtually all discretionary income. The media and business quickly exploited this wealth with products that were often utterly frivolous and priced too high. Magazines such as *Seventeen*, *Young America*, and *Calling All Girls* were created to mold and tap the juvenile market. Fads, such as wearing jewelry decorated with the American flag and sold to students as being a contribution to the war effort, swept the schools; epidemic buying became a feature of juvenile life (Ugland 65, 358–59, 391–93; Gilbert, 203–7).

Many adults, who felt that the Depression had robbed them of their youth, smiled on this youth culture, but the seeming immaturity of adolescent society and its disrespect for age were also bewildering and troubling. Teens' freedom seemed to symbolize, painfully, a world in flux, a world less and less subject to control by adults. Money meant freedom, since juveniles could afford the gas and the cars to get out from under their parents' supervision. Polls showed that teens thought that gas rationing was the worst restriction of the war. With their new wealth and independence, they threw drinking parties and stayed up all night smoking cigarettes and reefers (a combination of tobacco and marijuana) in cinemas and bowling alleys (Shindler, 89; Gorer, 76). Some youths joined gangs and there was a rash of vandalism, such as slashing seats on public transport and stealing cars to joyride. The delinquency rate in Detroit increased 24 percent between 1938 and 1943 (Winkler, 46). Of most concern to the white middle class, the rise in crime rate for white youth outpaced that for black youth by 250 percent (Ugland, 241).

What was happening? Studies suggested that business prosperity and juvenile delinquency moved in the same direction. Money gave young people an exhilarating sense of unrestricted freedom and power, which produced immature or wild behavior. One irate letter to the Indianapolis News said that youth had too much, was too coddled, and had too little demanded of it. "They must have thrills, speed, excitement; that's one reason why they break laws" (Ugland, 261). The visiting French aviator and writer Antoine de Saint-Exupéry, author of The Little Prince, said that being a consumer did not give life a purpose: American youth was bored and at loose ends, a recipe for problems (67–68).

The ultimate difficulty was that, prosperous and unfettered as they might be, juveniles were outside the great events taking place. They were peripheral to the war effort and often felt slighted. Adolescents were attracted to personal freedom and yet yearned to be useful in the larger world. Some teachers and civic officials understood this and enlisted young people to aid the war effort through such activities as collecting scrap metal for the arms industry or building model planes for use in military aircraft spotting exercises. But some activities were of little importance, even silly at times, as when whole schools wore the national colors to encourage the troops. The anger created by feeling small and foolish was one cause of delinquency, as frustrated teens provoked adults to get their attention.

Boys could aspire to be soldiers when they reached enlistment age, but girls had few outlets for their patriotism. Many were too young to be USO workers, who dispensed refreshments and entertainment to soldiers. They could write to a man overseas, but this was far removed from daily reality—so girls who would not have sex with a civilian willingly gave themselves to men in uniform. It was estimated that 85 percent of the girls near army camps who had frequent sex with soldiers were not prostitutes but amateurs, who didn't charge (Costello, 206–7, 214).

These adolescents trying to do their bit were called Victory Girls. Many came out of their war experience all right, but for others there were severe psychological repercussions. One Victory Girl was fourteen and playing with dolls on the day Pearl Harbor was bombed. She never played again: her father went away to do war work, and her mother was too busy watching over a large family to notice each child individually. She soon went off with uniformed men, sometimes two or three a day. This fed her young ego, but it also made her wild. She developed a local reputation for being fast and was shunned by family and neighbors. After so many brief liaisons in her formative years, she had trouble forming stable, lasting relationships. After the war, she had three marriages, all of which failed. Looking back in 1985, she felt that the war had given her too much adult freedom too quickly (Terkel, 241–43).

Young people who reached puberty in the late 1940s and early 1950s often felt little ambivalence about the teen culture they inherited. The hallmark of this culture included irresponsibility, freedom, being separate from the larger society, and antiintellectualism. An Italian-American, looking back on the war, most regretted that it led his generation to pursue the shallow excitements sold by the commercial leisure industry and to reject the cultural traditions of their ethnic community. In particular, Italian-American youth no longer knew or cared for opera, which in his youth had enriched the daily lives of many Italian-Americans and was now considered a pleasure accessible only to highbrows (Terkel, 139).

At one level, some teen behavior was not much more than an aping of adult patterns. Older people might call juveniles frivolous and irresponsible, but many of them were also enjoying a new buying power and shared little of the sacrifice of Americans overseas. Lee Oremont, a supermarket owner in Los Angeles, whose business did very well serving war workers, recalled: "I think the war was an unreal period for us here at home. Those of us who lost nobody at the front had a pretty good time. The war was not really in our consciousness as a war" (Terkel, 313–14). Those who visited the hospitals, such as the popular singing group the Andrews Sisters, saw some of the war's human cost. "We saw boys with no arms or legs, with half-faces." But they too did very well in the war, and it was hard not to enjoy it—their audiences were large, and their records were big sellers. Maxene Andrews recalled: "There was a sort of frenzy and a wonderful kind of gaiety. There was much more money around than there had ever been" (292).

Many people rationalized doing well from the war because they were involved in war work or other essential labor and could therefore say that their affluence was a fruit of patriotism. One woman who made and spent a lot of money during the war said, "It had been an enjoyable experience." "I was glad I did it, that I'd done my part" (Gluck, 113). Her correlation between fun and duty was not cynical. For many civilians on the "production front," the war allowed a correlation between victory and self-interest. A lot of people did do their best to conserve, living frugally, and putting their spare earnings into war bonds. But it was also true that corporations, organized labor, and many individuals equated their own interests with the national good and rationalized self-indulgence as patriotism: victory would come substantially through Americans making and spending on the home front.

Business attacked labor organizers, suggesting that worker agitation caused loss of productivity and led to the deaths of soldiers. But business, too, exploited the conflict. As Theodore S. Repplier, executive director of the Advertising Council, put it: "Business and advertising have a continuing social responsibility, *which brings rich returns to those who act on it*" (Fox, 55). Business got immense tax incentives because, as Secretary of War Henry L. Stimson said, the corporations wouldn't fully cooperate otherwise. In return for being on the team, big business also insisted that New Deal efforts to help labor through Social Security and other social welfare programs be curtailed (Winkler, 10, 87).

Companies used the war to sell their brands. General Electric touted a Mazda light bulb "that survived Pearl Harbor." Radio commercials for funeral homes and burial plots were always aired when the casualty lists were read. One ad suggested that to the Four Freedoms should be added a fifth: freedom from ruptured hernia by using their trusses. "You're unpatriotic, That's what!" was the cry of a husband whose shrunken shirt proved that his wife had failed to buy a Sanforized brand (Fox, 34, 37).

Business vulgarized the ideological meaning of the struggle between totalitarianism and democracy by equating the latter with consumer choice. Prevented after 1942 from making such items as cars, refrigerators, and toasters, business identified the Axis as enemies primarily of free enterprise and equated victory with the renewal of consumer choice. "WHAT THIS WAR IS ALL ABOUT," said one Royal typewriter ad, was the right to "once more walk into any store in the land and buy anything you want" (Fox, 34). The New York *Daily News* said the war was being fought to get back to baseball and a full tank of gas (Sevareid, 215).

Organized labor sometimes showed the same narrowness of vision. Industrial strikes doubled between 1942 and 1943 and jumped again in 1944 and 1945. In 1944 alone, nearly nine million workdays were lost to strikes (Winkler, 41). That same year, as Allied victory seemed assured, absenteeism became chronic, and voluntary labor turnover (workers quitting) reached 61 percent in the manufacturing industries (Nelson, 99). Much of this was due to stress on the worker, such as pressure on women to return home and raise the kids. But much came sheerly from the search for higher wages and better positions at the expense of war production.

People in the 1940s were no more and no less dedicated and selfless than other generations. John Kenneth Galbraith, an economist who was put in charge of price controls in 1942, recalled that in the war years domestic consumption doubled. "Never in the history of human conflict has there been so much talk of sacrifice and so little sacrifice," he thought (Terkel, 320). Many businessmen and consumers had come to equate democracy less with the right to vote than with the right to shop. Military victory was the means, but consumption was the end. Perhaps after the deprivation of the Depression, this was to be expected.

The taste for goods was sharpened by a combination of shortages and high wages. In addition to the ban on mechanical items such as radios, record players, and vacuum cleaners, there was rationing of staples like butter, sugar, and gas. Even women's stockings were in short supply. As items became scarce in 1942, there was panic buying; customers stampeded meat markets, and the hoarding of essentials added to the general scarcity. A black market developed, patronized by people who saw themselves as 100 percent American; middle-class customers and their regular merchants colluded to cheat fair rationing. One-third of those questioned by pollsters admitted that they would buy anything they needed on the black market (Blum, 94–97).

Many Americans, for the first time in history, had more money than they knew what to do with. The gap between the top fifth and bottom fifth in income actually narrowed for the only time in the century (Perret, 440). The middle class made the greatest proportionate gain. A lot of people had discretionary income, and business shaped new spending habits to tap this wealth. Some consumers would buy anything. Tiffany's sold a five-thousand-dollar V for Victory brooch (Shindler, 19). One store manager said: "People want to spend money, and if they don't spend it on textiles they'll spend it on furniture; or ... we'll find something else for them." The average department store purchase rose from two dollars to ten dollars during the war (Winkler, 34).

With many families enjoying two incomes, there was a reassessment of what constituted need, and the trend began whereby many luxuries have come to be perceived as necessities. The war created a new and materialistic middle class. In 1944 the shops were stripped of goods long before Christmas, and on December 7, the anniversary of Pearl Harbor, Macy's had its best sales day ever (Blum, 98).

However, if there was prosperity on the home front, an air of anxiety remained—and may have actually intensified as the war neared its end. One major fear was that there would be a new and worse depression when millions of men in uniform were demobilized, flooding the job market at the very time when war industries would be retooling for peacetime production.

Just as disturbing for America's stability was a perceived decline in family values. "Are we facing a moral breakdown?" was by 1945 a favorite radio talk show topic. Delinquency continued to rise, as did divorce, with half a million breakups in 1945. Many of these failed relationships came out of unique wartime circumstances: young women had felt moral pressure to marry a GI and send him overseas happy. Often, such whirlwind romances, fuelled by the adrenaline flow of war, could not survive sustained separation or the reality of daily contact in the flatter atmosphere of peace. Where couples were clearly incompatible, these war marriages were best ended. But critics also saw in the statistics a decline in American values and identified as the major culprit women working outside the home during the war. A 1945 State Farm Insurance ad showed a hysterical girl being carted away to a foster home because her mother was out working (Honey, 54). Women were urged to leave their jobs, which would then be available for returning veterans, and to focus on restoring a healthy home life.

There was gratitude to women for their contribution to the war effort, but this stopped short of according them full legal equality. In 1945 the Equal Rights Amendment failed in the U.S. Senate. As the war ended, a disproportionate number of women workers were laid off. Many accepted this cheerfully, but others felt betrayed by the turnaround. A fired woman worker at the Tacoma Navy Yard said, "Many women in here are plenty unhappy though. The taste of independence has spoiled 'em" (Anderson, 163).

The exodus of women from the work force is intelligible when we understand that the bulk of Americans had seen women's war work as temporary and not a permanent change in labor patterns. Most wartime advertising and government propaganda had emphasized that women's work was only for the duration of hostilities, and it was as-

Fig. 7. Advertisement in the *Saturday Evening Post*, May 1944

133

sumed that women would make a smooth transition back to the home—just as it was taken for granted that veterans would get back to work without too much emotional difficulty. There was limited patience for members of either group who evidenced long-term adjustment problems.

Throughout the war, ads reminded women that, though they might work, their first priority was to be attractive to men. The *Detroit News*, for example, suggested that the ideal female riveter was "like a cross between a campus queen and a Hollywood starlet" (Winkler, 53). A Tangee lipstick promotion said that one reason America was fighting was "the precious right of women to be feminine and lovely" (Hartmann, 199). The continuing accent on sex appeal suggests how little real change in the female persona the war had inaugurated. For many women, preserving the "feminine mystique" was a more important concern than opening career paths.

Despite the showcasing of the working woman during the war, women did not really break through the major barriers that kept the professional world a white male preserve. Men abandoned certain areas of work as women began joining the work force in 1942. Clerical, typing and secretarial jobs, which had been fifty-fifty between the genders in 1940, were in the female domain by 1945. Bank tellers and store clerks also came to be female positions. More women were employed in traditionally female occupations, such as nursing and teaching, but women in advanced technical work, like chemical or electrical engineering, remained few. They gained little ground in law or medicine and were kept out of most supervisory positions in business and industry; the assumptions being both that their careers were temporary and that they were temperamentally best suited to low-level, repetitive work. Further, they earned 60 percent of the male rate for the same work (Costello, 265). In short, the war did not radically change employment patterns, and most women were in the kind of low-echelon positions that were easily terminated.

A majority of middle-class women, who could afford to quit working after the war, wanted to. This is primarily why there was not a revolution in women's roles because of the war. Women often refused to join unions, rejecting a permanent commitment to a trade. One postwar poll showed that 76 percent of returning homemakers felt they had made no sacrifice in quitting. In 1946, seven of eight adults polled felt that homemaking was a full-time job (Campbell, 87, 232).

The revolution many women of this generation wanted was not in the marketplace but in the home. They wished to return to the kitchen, but in doing so, they did not want to recreate the world of their mothers; they wanted to reinterpret it. A dominant memory was of the Great Depression and of extended families: parents, siblings, grandparent, aunts, and unemployed uncles living on top of each other in cramped old houses, with little privacy or room for individuality. Parents had controlled the behavior and the finances of unmarried daughters, whose wages went into the family kitty. These daughters, now grown, dreamed of new, clean, well-lit, one-family homes in the suburbs, where they would have the latest labor-saving devices and could raise a nuclear family with the privileges and luxuries they had lacked in their youth. This was their dream of independence. A working woman who in 1944 rejected her daughter's wish for a WAC uniform as her Christmas gift and instead gave her a doll to cultivate her "feminine interest" was articulating the prevalent view of the modern woman (Campbell, 234).

For many women, war work interrupted their dreams, albeit the prosperity of wartime meant that the dream could be fully realized after the war. The Rosie the Riveter image shouldn't obscure the fact that the major enhancement of woman's role in the war was not as producer but as consumer of goods. Women, along with juveniles, were the major buyers, particularly as traditionally male items, such as cars and lawn mowers, were off the market. And the role of consumer fit perfectly with middle-class aspirations for suburbia. From 1944 on, women's magazines, powerful organs of consumerism, shaped and supported this vision with major articles on the new "victory home" and the wonderful world of appliances that would shortly be available to the homemaker. The war did not inaugurate or even set the stage for the later feminist campaign: that came in the 1970s, and it was a reaction by the daughters of the women who had marched to suburbia in 1945 and 1946.

In all, the war brought great prosperity to the United States, and many Americans—though not all—shared in it. But it also brought great geographic and social changes. The strain in the cultural fabric elicited a conservative reaction by 1944 and left America rich but somewhat anxious as it faced the postwar world.

seven

A New World

THROUGHOUT World War II both sides spoke of a new world order coming about through the triumph of their values. Promises of a finer day are part of the compensation governments offer for the suffering and sacrifice of war. In August 1941, the United States and Britain declared that the fight was for the right of national self-determination and for the Four Freedoms: freedom of speech and religion, freedom from want and fear. On January 1, 1942, twenty-six Allied nations endorsed these goals. America spoke out as a powerful champion of these freedoms. The spirit of optimism was captured by Secretary of War Stimson when, in 1942, he said in the screen introduction to *Prelude to War*, a film in the *Why We Fight* series, "We are determined that before the sun sets on this terrible struggle our flag will be recognized throughout the world, as a symbol of freedom on the one hand ... and of overwhelming power on the other."

In 1945, when it became clear that the Soviets would not support the principle of national self-determination in their sphere, the United States, because of its economic and political power, was recognized as the one clear leader of the free world. America responded to the challenge. To encourage the building and preservation of free institutions, the United States shared its bounty with the world. Under the Marshall Plan alone (named after Secretary of State George C. Marshall, who proposed the idea in 1947), over $12 billion in aid was used to spark European economic recovery. By 1951, European industrial production had risen 64 percent.

At home, despite a short-lived depression immediately after the war, there was unprecedented prosperity. About 64 percent of Americans were homeowners after the war, versus 44 percent on the eve of war. Many new products enhanced the quality of life, from antibiotics in medicine to home aids like automatic washers and dryers, first marketed in 1946 (Hess, 142). These were good times, and Americans could take pride in their achievements, both at home and abroad.

Yet no military crusade can sustain the expectations placed upon it to produce a perfect world. The world that emerged in 1945 was better than that of 1939, but it was not without its problems and blemishes. Ironically, the very greatness of the evil that had been overcome and the completeness of the Axis defeat obscured the fact that the victory was not perfect and that not everyone shared equally in its fruits. The point has troubled English professor and combat veteran Paul Fussell. "If for years you fancy that you are engaged in fighting utter evil, if every element and impulse of society is busy eradicating wickedness, before long you will come to believe that therefore you yourself must incarnate pure goodness." The West's sense of virtue, says Fussell, obscured the fact that it was "defending something pretty defective against something even more loathsome" (*Bomb* 78). For many of the world's population, including Americans, the Four Freedoms were not realized: the poor still suffered want, and minorities and women still did not have full freedom.

There was something of a moral smugness about the Western Allies in 1945. They sat in judgment on others and condemned them, often correctly, for cruel and wantonly brutal acts, but the West rarely asked itself if some of the crimes the enemy committed were not usual in total war, rather than the result of a unique perversity. Hence, the West didn't analyze its own actions late in the war as the intensity of killing increased. Japanese generals Yamashita and Homma were executed for using excessive force and failing to protect "the weak and unarmed." Yet the United States had destroyed hundreds of thousands of defenseless civilians in the bombing of Japanese cities. And U.S. soldiers had sometimes refused to let Japanese soldiers surrender, killing them instead. This was really inevitable in a war fought between totally committed peoples, but it didn't justify MacArthur's saying during the Homma trial that "no escutcheon is more unsullied of revenge and passion than that of the United States" (295, 298).

The destruction inherent in a long global war must to some degree brutalize all involved. This is understandable. The error is in adopting a posture of moral innocence that refuses to recognize this. For example, the Canadian writer James Bacque contended that the U.S. and French armies deliberately kept German prisoners short of food, water, and shelter in 1944–45 and that up to one million of them died of neglect. He also charged that many were handed over to the French to do forced labor or to fight against the Vietnamese (xix–xxi, 35–44, 62–75, 102, 144–45). Bacque's credibility has been assailed by Stephen Ambrose, a biographer of Dwight Eisenhower, the man who would bear ultimate responsibility for these crimes. Ambrose pointed out that Bacque at times relied on slender or circumstantial evidence and that it would have been hard to keep so great a scandal quiet for so long (*New York Times Book Review*, February 24, 1991). On the other hand, American guards have come forward to support Bacque. One wrote: "I witnessed the atrocities Stephen E. Ambrose tries to deny or gloss over" (*New York Times Book Review*, April 14, 1991).

The truth is probably somewhere in the middle. Much of what Bacque decried as deliberate cruelty was surely unintended neglect brought about by the chaos of war and the difficult task of trying to feed enormous numbers of refugee civilians and prisoners of war. But there was also undoubtedly significant deliberate cruelty. Allied soldiers late in the war were angry at the Germans for the destruction and suffering they had caused. As the death camps were opened and the extent of Nazi mass murder revealed, it is not surprising that retaliation took place. As another American guard admitted: "we sometimes slipped over the boundary of civilized behavior and resembled to some extent what we were fighting against" (*New York Times Book Review*, April 14, 1991).

War-torn countries under Anglo-American control were generally well administered, but there was also a lack of advance planning, some ineptitude, and corruption, with a thriving black market involving soldiers and civilians. The journalist Frank Gervasi reported from Italy that civilians could not find food: Allied soldiers stole from the populace and the government, and once GIs stole a trainload of sugar, complete with the engine (502, 561–68, 582, 584). John Horne Burns in *The Gallery* (1947) and Joseph Heller in *Catch-22* (1961) later endorsed this picture of misery and corruption, while Graham Greene in his 1949 novel *The Third Man* exposed the illicit drug trade in occupied Austria.

America came out of the war the one country not damaged by the fighting, making some people believe that a special providence watched over America. "The Big Guy is on our side," Ernie Pyle said during the fighting (Fussell, *Wartime*, 165). This, together with America's role as the foremost democracy, gave some leaders a unique sense of mission that blinded them to the dangers inherent in trying too hard to impose their world view on others. John F. Kennedy, a war veteran, said in 1963, "We in this generation are—by destiny rather than choice—the watchmen on the walls of freedom." His view led to deep

American involvement in Vietnam. When asked how American intervention in that country differed from French involvement, he replied: "They were fighting for a colony, for an ignoble cause. We're fighting for freedom, to free them from the Communists" (Tuchman, 287).

Until World War II, most covert operations were considered to be morally questionable, even reprehensible. Assassination, for example, was seen as a tool of anarchists and revolutionaries, not of legitimate states. Secretary Stimson for years objected to all intelligence work, saying, "gentlemen don't read other people's mail" (Casey, 6). But the Axis appeared so evil that covert operations became part of the game. Thus, Allied special operations assassinated the ruthless Nazi official Reinhard Heydrich, whose crimes included the massacre of the citizens of Lidice, Czechoslovakia, and who was credibly depicted as a werewolf by American poet Edna St. Vincent Millay. But we now forget that it was the uniqueness of the evil that justified such methods.

Since the war, covert operations, including sabotage, the destabilization of foreign governments, even collusion in assassination, have become routine in peacetime. Undeclared war and surprise attack, ironically, have become acceptable. Many Americans believe they have the right to remove a foreign head of state by direct military action: at the time of the 1989 Panama invasion, 88 percent felt this way (*Newsweek*, October 16, 1989). In Vietnam, murder squads, reprisals on villages, and the destruction of agriculture by both sides reproduced crimes for which the Nazis had been tried (Taylor, 144–45, 152).

World War II could not create a world free from fear, because there was never a realistic possibility that the democracies and the Soviets could form a lasting partnership or that the Communists would move after the war to a more representative form of government. For most of Communist Russia's existence there had been hostility with the Western democracies. When America and Russia became allies in December 1941 there was some hope that this forced alliance would be a window of opportunity for better understanding and cooperation for world peace. To encourage acceptance of Russia as an ally, wartime propaganda, particularly films, played down Soviet authoritarianism, picturing the Russians as hard-working, down-to-earth people, basically like midwesterners. In a world divided by the media into Axis slave powers and Allied free nations, the Russians had to be portrayed this way. The power of the media quickly changed their image, as polls showed that a majority of Americans in 1942–44 saw the Russians as more like themselves than even the British were. Stalin was *Time* magazine's 1943 "man of the year."

At the command level, FDR developed a viable working relationship with Stalin, as he did with Winston Churchill. Both FDR and Stalin believed in the crucial role of great powers, and neither intended their nation's policies to be dictated after the war by smaller states. Roosevelt framed his concept of a United Nations so that the major powers—America, Russia, Britain, and China—would dominate through the Security Council and, through individual veto power, would retain complete autonomy. Each power would have a regional sphere of influence and would act as the world's policeman within it, thus guaranteeing the peace. FDR hoped that bringing Russia into a leadership role in the family of nations would develop a greater sense of security among the Soviet leadership and, consequently, a liberalization of the Communist system.

Realistically, such a scenario was unlikely. The success of FDR's plan rested on his personal relations with other world leaders, but since Stalin did not respect the principle of national self-determination or the Four Freedoms, the ultimate scenario could not be realized. With Russian brutality in Eastern Europe as peace neared, the media stopped its positive portrayal of Russia. "Do you know what it was like to be a woman when the Russians came in?" asked Marlene Dietrich in *A Foreign Affair* (1948), playing a Berliner who has been raped by the Russians. Now the rape symbol seemed a fitting one for Russia.

During the war U.S.-Soviet relations were soured at the top level by differences in perception of the load each was carrying. The Russians, who bore the brunt of the German ground onslaught from 1941 on, argued that the Western Allies weren't doing their share before the D-Day invasion, of June 1944. While the Anglo-Americans faced 12 Axis divisions in Italy, the Soviets were fighting 180 divisions on the eastern front. But the democracies could respond that they had also to fight the Japanese and that they could not realistically invade Hitler's Fortress Europe until their navies had won the battle of the Atlantic.

The Russians also expressed some distrust of the British-American demand for unconditional surrender. They suspected that this was designed to rob the Nazis of hope and make them fight to the last ditch, thus butchering more Russians. In fact, the major concern was to avoid a repeat of 1918, when Germany had been allowed to surrender before the complete defeat of its armies, a fact that led Hitler to argue that Germany had not been defeated but had been betrayed by its liberal politicians. This time the Nazis would be clearly, thoroughly defeated.

The United States sent lend-lease to Russia, which helped relations, but according to insiders like Charles Bohlen of the State Department, the United States sometimes promised more than could be delivered (Bennett, 101). Also, late in the war, said Joe Marcus, an administration official, the United States reneged on shipments of war materials for fear they would be used against them in a future confrontation. The worry had some basis (Terkel, 326–27).

Two issues were ultimately crucial to the estrangement between Russia and the United States. The first was spheres of influence. By 1939, Stalin believed that a great nation's security lay in having friendly smaller states along its borders as a buffer zone against invasion. The war furthered this belief. Twice in thirty years Germany had attacked Russia through eastern Europe, and over four million Russians died as Nazi prisoners. The Soviets craved territorial security at any price. But Russia's preoccupation with a buffer zone of subject states meant the blighting of democratic hopes for countries caught in the Russian sphere at the end of war, and it alienated America and Britain.

The Russians felt that the English and Americans didn't allow free choice in their spheres, either. FDR and Churchill distrusted European leftist groups and sometimes refused to work with them in forging the peace. During the conquest of North Africa in November 1942, the Allies made a deal with Admiral Jean-François Darlan, the Vichy governor and Nazi collaborator, snubbing the Free French forces under General Charles De Gaulle, who were seen as too leftist. And the United States never officially denounced Vichy or endorsed the radical antifascist Comité National de la Résistance.

In Italy, after Mussolini's overthrow, America and Britain excluded Russia from the settlement. The resistance, who were suspected communists, were disarmed and sent home, and the administration of pro-Fascist Marshal Pietro Badoglio was installed. In Greece the Royalists, who had not been anti-Fascist, were similarly installed in power. Yet U.S. and British manipulations cannot be compared to Soviet repression. In their spheres, free elections and free-market economies were normally encouraged.

The second major area of contention was over nuclear weapons: the democracies did not trust the Russians sufficiently to share this powerful new secret with them. The resultant mistrust and concomitant arms race molded American-Soviet relations for the next forty-five years. Some scholars have charged that the United States used the A-bombs on Japan partly to end the Pacific war before the Russians could come in and get a share in the peace settlement there, partly to intimidate Russia with a display of America's military might. The weight of scholarly opinion is against this position. At the time that the bombs were dropped, the Soviets were still potential allies in the Pacific. The bombs were dropped to end the war quickly and unconditionally by any means available. At the same time, the A-bomb monopoly, and the U.S. refusal to give it up despite advice from its own scientists, fueled the cold war and Russia's determination to have a nuclear capability.

In the United Nations the Russians tried to get the United States to surrender its monopoly, but failed. Between VJ Day and July 1946, the United States spent $13 billion on defense, partly for A-bomb tests and for superbombers (B-29s and B-36s) to deliver the weapon. The United States also acquired airfields around the world, which threatened the Soviet Union.

In response to Soviet pressure to end nuclear weapons entirely, on June 14, 1946, America proposed a plan (developed largely by Bernard Baruch) calling for an international body to control the world's uranium supply and to license nuclear facilities. But the agency would be dominated by the United States, which would also keep its monopoly of nuclear weapons until some unspecified future date. To underline the point, seventeen days later the United States exploded test bombs at Bikini atoll. Despite warnings from scientists that the Soviets would have the bomb in three to five years, the American military believed their monopoly would last up to two decades. In 1949 the Russians successfully carried out a nuclear test.

The cold war forced America to compromise its wartime commitment to self-determination in Asia. During the war American leaders repudiated European imperialism and pledged that they were not fighting to restore Western colonies. Secretary of State Sumner Welles declared, "Our victory must bring in its train the liberation of all peoples.... The age of imperialism is ended" (Hess, 122–25). This was of momentous potential significance, because Japanese victories early in the war had robbed Westerners of their aura of military invincibility, and now independence movements were alive all over the region. Within two years of VJ Day, Britain withdrew from India, dooming French involvement in Indochina (Vietnam) and Dutch involvement in Indonesia. Ho Chi Minh, the Vietnamese nationalist leader, looked to the United States for help in resisting a French return, and he read the American Declaration of Independence at the celebrations marking the Japanese defeat in 1945. Yet in 1950, following several shocks, the United States felt obliged to back the French: in 1949 Russia exploded an atom bomb and China went communist, and in 1950 North Korean Communists invaded South Korea.

The worst shock to the American system was when China fell to the Communist forces of Mao Tse-tung. That this huge nation could succumb convinced Americans that communism was a disease so powerful that it could penetrate the whole globe, and it intensified their commitment to the cold war. Their wartime propaganda had misled them into believing that Chiang Kai-shek was a Western-style political leader bent on making China a democracy, whereas he was in fact a feudal warlord with semidictatorial powers. He led a government that was authoritarian, corrupt, and hated by many of the peasants.

The cold war undermined progressive forces in the United States. Even before the war ended, there was a growing conservative sentiment in the nation. Partly this was a reaction against the relatively lax moral and social standards of wartime. Partly it represented a determination on the part of business, now that prosperity had returned, to curtail the social progressivism of the New Deal. The reactionary swing was symbolized by the dropping of liberal Vice President Henry Wallace as Roosevelt's running mate in the 1944 election in favor of the more moderate Harry S. Truman. FDR recognized the conservative trend and trimmed his policies accordingly.

Freedom of speech, one of the Four Freedoms, suffered in the aftermath of war. To have been a New Dealer, to have worked closely with the Russians during the war, or to oppose America's nuclear monopoly in the postwar world might make you subject to investigation by the House Un-American Activities Committee. In 1947, federal employees became subject to loyalty checks, which led to many firings on little evidence. Communism became the scapegoat for some domestic problems, including juvenile delinquency.

Red scares went back to the nineteenth century, but the intense paranoia of the 1940s and 1950s owed much to the war. Propaganda had depicted the Axis powers as a monolithic world conspiracy of slave states, without individual character or humanity. Ads talked of "an enemy who never sleeps," who was "right here in America," "always close, sneaking in the shadows." In 1943 John Roy Carlson published *Under Cover*, a book exposing over thirty-two Nazi or Fascist organizations in America. When, after the war, communism replaced fascism as the West's primary opponent, it was easy to believe that the country faced a monolithic conspiracy, with agents throughout America.

The failure of World War II to bring a genuine peace had major consequences. The arms race ultimately ruined the Soviet economy and severely damaged the U.S. economy. Each country has massive stockpiles of weapons, which will be expensive to dispose of. In 1988 the United States possessed 37,657 nuclear weapons, the USSR had 17,656. There is also dangerous waste at abandoned arms plants, such as a decaying site in Fernald, Ohio, and at overseas bases in Europe and Asia, all of which will cost billions of dollars to clean up. The army estimates that it has 309 polluted sites in Germany alone, and the bill for restoration there could run to over three billion dollars (*U.S. News & World Report*, November 30, 1992, 28–31).

The end of the war brought problems for some American women. Those who wanted to continue working at the kind of jobs that had opened to them during the war faced widespread difficulty. A majority of whites of both sexes felt that women should be full-time homemakers. Literature on child welfare argued that absentee parents and group child-care had damaged war babies and had produced juvenile delinquency. Federal day-care funds were cut in March 1946. Dr. Benjamin Spock, an influential pediatrician, argued that the healthy child's development required full-time mothering (Anderson, 176–77). Women's magazines popularized this view, while films showed the independent woman as socially dangerous. For example, in *Double Indemnity* (1944) and *The Postman Always Rings Twice* (1946), men who hooked up with the "new woman," bereft of traditional values, ended up ruined, even committing murder for these unnatural females. The marriage rate, a reflection of the urge to "settle down and have kids," jumped 50 percent in 1946 and remained 20 percent above the prewar rate for the rest of the decade (Costello, 272).

The period saw setbacks for women who didn't want this dream. Between 1945 and early 1947, females lost 1 million factory jobs, .5 million clerical jobs, and 400,000 sales positions. Women's share of paid work fell from 36 percent to 28 percent (Hartmann, *Home Front*, 90–92). Some shrinkage was inevitable, as industry cut back to prevent an economic depression after the end of the war boom, but when the economy recovered and workers were recalled, women were left out. Detroit car makers now claimed that the work women had done in the war was too heavy or too technical for them. By April 1946, women's share of auto work was 7.5 percent, down from 25 percent during the war (Anderson, 165–71). These cuts hurt lower class families most, because only by both spouses working could these families afford the luxuries America had become used to during the war. Furthermore, the professions also reasserted male dominance: although 12 percent of the 1945 entering medical students were women, only 5 percent of the 1955 entering medical students were (Hartmann, *Home Front*, 109).

The military also saw little role for women in its bailiwick after the war. After demobilization, female personnel fell from 266,000 to 14,000; in 1948 women were officially restricted to 2 percent of enlisted strength (Segal, 118). Women found that promotion was difficult and that many specializations were barred to them. Unlike men, women veterans didn't always find that war service was a help in civilian life. Although nurses could easily get the same type of job they had in the military, female mechanics, managers, and pilots were ignored by employers. Some men actually thought that a woman with war service was, ipso facto, too independent or morally loose. Certain federal agencies denied women veterans' benefits, and women were barred from the Veterans of Foreign Wars.

Homosexuals, like the independent woman depicted in films, became a target of the postwar reaction to the freer atmosphere of wartime. From about 1947 into the 1950s, homosexuals were a major subject of investigation. They were denounced as perverts, child molesters, and Communists. One congressman claimed that the Kremlin had a list of American homosexuals that it used to blackmail them into spying. In 1950 homosexuals in federal service were targeted, and over sixty per month were dismissed (Bérubé, 265–68). Homosexual veterans were frequently denied benefits under the GI Bill, such as college tuition, home loans, job training, and hospital care. Marty Klausner's homosexual discharge cost him his educational allowance. Then he couldn't get a job because his service record followed him around. "Why they don't round us all up and kill us I don't know," he said. Some homosexual veterans finally got benefits with the help of the American Legion, the CIO, the NAACP, and the army surgeon general's office (230–32).

Ethnic minorities found that the Four Freedoms didn't always apply to them. Mississippi Senator Theodore Bilbo said in 1947 that blacks shouldn't be misled by wartime rhetoric into expecting equality or the end of segregation (Tyler, 102). African-Americans faced discrimination in jobs, housing, and educational opportunities. Lowell Steward, a veteran pilot, couldn't get work in civil aviation; at Long Beach Municipal Airport he was told, "they didn't have no niggers at this base" (Terkel, 346–47). States like Alabama printed separate civics texts for minorities, which omitted all reference to civil rights. By 1952, 87 percent of southern black women and 65 percent of southern black men had never voted. In 1948, fifteen states still had miscegenation laws (Hartmann, *Home Front*, 124), so that black veterans who had married whites overseas or whites who had married Asians couldn't return to these states. In 1967 the Supreme Court struck down such laws (Shukert and Scibetta, 241).

Discrimination galled ethnic veterans who found their services ignored and their rights withheld. Only 7.5 percent of veterans in the

South who received job training through the GI Bill were black, even though they represented 33 percent of southern servicemen (Foner, 176). Blacks who reacted against such discrimination were labeled Communist, and the Ku Klux Klan was revived to oppose these "militants." On July 20, 1946, Macio Snipes, a veteran and the only black to vote in his Georgia district primary, was gunned down in one of several racial murders (Foner, 178–79).

The violation of the Four Freedoms produced a growing black demand for civil rights. Membership in the National Association for the Advancement of Colored People (NAACP) grew from 50,556 in 1940 to 450,000 by 1946 (Dalfiume, 90–106). James Baldwin, the distinguished African-American writer, believed that the postwar betrayal of equality brought on the clashes of the 1960s. Picture, he said, a soldier coming home: "search, in his shoes, for a job, for a place to live; ride in his skin, on segregated buses; see, with his eyes, the signs saying 'White' and 'Colored.'" Such experiences would produce "the fire next time." White Americans, said Baldwin, pretended to be innocent, both of the war service of blacks and what was done to them on their return. "It is the innocence which constitutes the crime," he concluded (76–77 and 16).

We may ask how racism could have continued when we had just fought the most costly war in history to destroy the racist Nazi regime. But we must understand that Nazi racism per se was not the cause of hostilities: it was Hitler's aggression against other sovereign states, beginning with Poland. No state went to war to prevent his maltreatment of "undesirables" within his own population. And saving concentration camp victims was not our primary aim. There was in fact a degree of callousness toward Hitler's victims shown by all the Allies, although the myth of total Allied moral nobility in the war has obscured this.

Most particularly in Russia, but also in Britain and America, anti-Semitism was quite apparent in the 1930s and 1940s. Jews were excluded from the best clubs and hotels. Employers could practice subtle discrimination because it was legal to ask an applicant's religion. Jews were attacked in the media by right-wing commentators who shared many views with the Nazis. The influential media personality Father Charles E. Coughlin accused families like the Rothschilds of using their wealth to dominate the media, business, and banking in a conspiracy to control America. His views were echoed on the street by people like Sheril Cunning's grandfather: when he saw a big Jewish party in a restaurant, he would say, "the kikes are taking over" (Terkel 233).

Neither Britain nor America did much during the Nazi years to help

Jews fleeing Germany. The Immigration Act of 1924 restricted the number of applicants who could annually enter the United States from any given country. Despite pleas from Jewish and humane groups, the quota was not liberalized to help fugitives. As a result, only 120,000 Jews entered the United States from 1933 to 1941; many thousands more were turned away. Only in January 1944 were some thousands beyond the quota admitted. This insensitivity affected other wartime policies. At the 1943 Moscow Conference, although Hitler's crimes were listed, his treatment of Jews went unmentioned. America and Britain refused to break open the concentration camps by commando raid and, even in late 1944, when there were few aerial targets left in Germany, declined to bomb the rail lines to the camps.

In defeated Germany, some American military personnel began to feel closer to the Germans than to the camp inmates. They took the filth and torpor of the victims as indicative of their character rather than of the degradation that had been forced on them. In March 1946 the *Reader's Digest* decided that the reason "so many GIs like the Germans best" was that they were cleaner and friendlier than most Europeans. As early as September 1945, an army survey showed that 22 percent of GIs thought the Nazi treatment of Jews was justified and that another 10 percent weren't sure. At home, Jews were accused of avoiding the draft; and Jewish soldiers were harassed by Gentiles (Abzug, 154, see also Stouffer 2:564, 571). Many of Arno Mayer's fellow officers were anti-Semitic; once he was handed a paper with the lines, "When we finish with the Germans and the Japs / We'll come back and kill the Jews and the blacks" (Terkel, 470).

During the war, the U.S. government sometimes worked with anti-Semites abroad when the alternative was to support radical left-wingers. General George Patton and his staff took this philosophy of expediency to its logical extreme in Germany. Although Patton was sickened by the death camps, he failed to understand the plight of the survivors, whom he came to see as "a sub-human species without any of the cultural or social refinements of our time." His wartime hatred of the Nazis quickly dissipated, and he publicly advocated the employment of notorious Nazis in the struggle against communism in Europe. Patton was fired for his views, but some of what he advocated became policy (Farago, 515–20; Engelman, 334; Abzug, 27, 156–57, 103). The United States did shelter and employ Nazi war criminals who could be useful in, say, the nuclear rocket program. In 1983, the United States admitted it had employed Klaus Barbie, a notorious Nazi butcher, and had helped him escape to Bolivia to avoid trial for war crimes committed in France (Terkel, 474–77).

At Nuremberg, senior German officials were tried for war crimes, an important step in asserting the right of the international community to protect itself against aggression. But these Germans were tried primarily for crimes against other peoples; for liquidating millions of their own people, they were never made fully accountable before the bar of international justice.

As the Nuremberg trials dragged on, American public interest in them waned. Many people were concerned with the trial of Japanese officials, who were hated more than the Germans by many Americans because of their treatment of U.S. prisoners. More Japanese than Germans were executed following trials, which lasted until 1951. As a final irony, the pictures of concentration camp victims released during Nuremberg actually may have stiffened American hostility to lowering immigration restrictions because the immigrants were seen as helpless dependents. Support for the expanding state of Israel offered a safer alternative (Abzug, 171).

The myth of national unity in World War II has blinded Americans to the continuing racism in U.S. culture and to its consequent racial strife. This is labeled a problem of the 1960s, when a society that had apparently been happy and united came suddenly and mysteriously unglued because of a bad war, Vietnam. Another myth of good wars versus bad wars is that only the combat veterans from Vietnam suffered lasting adjustment problems; the 1945 vet came home to enjoy prosperity, satisfied with a job well done, and with few qualms about the war. This was in fact true for many veterans, but not all. Many veterans, particularly the majority who never saw combat, adjusted quickly. But some suffered an anguish that damaged their lives and those of their families. For some, the stress continues even today.

Veterans with physical wounds sometimes took years to recover or to die. Stan Baker, a GI from Washington State, had severe leg wounds, from a machine gun burst, that wouldn't heal. They kept forming blood clots. Seven years after the war, a clot broke away and moved to the heart, killing him (Hilsman, 99–100). Some had disfigurements to cope with. A nurse recalled one hospitalized pilot during 1945 who was so badly burned that he was unrecognizable. Beside his bed he kept a photo of himself before the injuries and swore he would never get up until he looked like that again (Terkel, 129). Civilians tried to be sympathetic but sometimes couldn't stomach it. A man in the same hospital had lost one side of his face, including the nose; his wife planned to divorce him (127–28).

There was some hypocrisy among civilians who didn't want to be

reminded that the war hadn't been all fun for the boys. One woman recalled that when a cousin became engaged to a GI with a missing leg,
the family made a fuss over him at dinner but then, after the couple
left, said "wouldn't you think she'd know better than to marry a crip-
ple?" (Terkel, 235). We are now more sophisticated in understanding
that a handicap does not render you unfit to lead a full life; in the
1940s such an injury could condemn you to be treated as a burden,
without a function.

Some veterans had mental wounds that could not be cured. Eugene
Sledge said that some marines on Okinawa were so stunned by the
concussion of shells that the rest of their lives would be spent in mental limbo (264). Eric Sevareid thought that many combat soldiers
emerged only half alive mentally (501). Other survivors could function
normally but had to overcome nervous reactions to specific traumatic
stimuli. Men who had faced land mines couldn't walk on grass for
years afterward. One pilot had to pull off the road when the thwacking
of his car tires on the concrete joints reminded him of the sound of
flak over Germany (Jones, *WWII*, 84). Another man dived under his in-
laws' dining table when a plane buzzed low overhead (Blum, 334–35).

Many overcame these difficulties in a comparatively short period.
Others continued to suffer. In 1967, a paratrooper who had nearly
drowned on a drop in Normandy would still "wake up in a cold sweat
and nearly jump out of bed" (Keegan, 89). William Manchester, who
fought in the Pacific, in the 1980s still chose seats in restaurants that
would give maximum protection from hostile fire (12). John Garcia,
who in the dark killed a woman and child he mistook for enemy
troops, said in 1985: "That hounds me. I still feel I committed murder" (Terkel, 21).

Why, if posttraumatic stress disorder affected WWII veterans, do we
have the myth that this only began with Vietnam? For one thing, in
the 1940s open expression of feelings by men was considered a weakness. The John Wayne buttoned lip prevailed. Charles Taylor warned
his wife before demobilization that he would not talk about the war
but would just try to be a regular guy. Most vets, he said, "would
rather have the years they were away from home in a war a complete
blank" (Litoff, 256–57; see also Terkel, 142). Other soldiers wanted to
talk but feared they would be seen as monsters by a public unfamiliar
with real war. To protect his old buddies, one sergeant gave rookie replacements the most dangerous assignments, such as walking point.
They got killed. Afterward, he felt bad and would have liked to talk to
his wife about it but feared "she'd think it was horrible" (Jones, *WWII*,
255).

Psychologists reinforced the reticence, seeing guilt feelings as retro-gressive, a hindrance to a life-affirming philosophy. "Even the simplest soldier," said veteran J. Glenn Gray, "suspects that it is unpopular to-day to be burdened with guilt" (174; 23-24). Between October 1945 and June 1946, nearly three million personnel were demobilized. Given the pace, people had to believe readjustment was routine. The easiest thing was to assume that "our boys" were coming back just as they left. A combat veteran recalled Red Cross workers giving out candy and comic books to returning troops: "They were still treating us as children" (Fussell, *Wartime*, 288). And magazines popularized a quick fix, *Good Housekeeping* telling wives that their husbands should stop "oppressive remembering" in two to three weeks (Jones, *WWII*, 255). The army, more conservative, thought most men should be doing well in eight to ten weeks (*Let There Be Light*).

This was naive. As veteran James Jones put it, men had "once seen something animal within themselves that terrified them," and it would take years to get over the shock (Jones, *Red Line*, 339). Some veterans fled human society. A GI in Italy said, "I want live so far back in the hills that I'll never see another human being" (Murphy, 188). Others made family life miserable. Trying to repress feelings, they drank, gambled, suffered paralyzing depression, and became inarticu-lately violent. A paratrooper's wife would "sit for hours and hold him while he just shook." Afterward, he started beating her and the chil-dren: "He became a brute." And they divorced (Terkel, 108).

In 1992, a woman said of her brother who fought in the Pacific: "We never understood him when he came back from the war. He left as this bright, energetic eighteen-year-old and returned languid and somewhat of an alcoholic. He got married, then quickly divorced, and died of cir-rhosis of the liver at thirty-four. I never knew what happened to him over there to make him so sad" (Hennessey, 1). We have been slow to document much of this damage done by the war, partly because fami-lies hushed it up and partly because, for years, alcoholism and wife beating were tolerated, even material for comedians. Only recently have we begun to acknowledge and catalog what we were seeing.

Some marriages suffered great stress. Soldiers overseas often kept going because of an idealized image of home, frozen in time. "Expect a Rip van Winkle," wrote John M. Wright to his wife (175). But America and the spouse had changed. She was older; she was less perfect than the dream image. "Somehow I didn't quite get the thrill I thought I would get," one veteran admitted (Stouffer, 2:634). Women had enor-mous adjustments to make, too. Many had acquired independence in the war, a new earning power, and self-confidence. Psychologists told them to put aside these competencies to assuage the bruised male ego. Remember, said *House Beautiful*, "he's head man again.... Your part in the remaking of this man is to fit his home to him, understanding why he wants it this way, forgetting your own preferences" (27). This was a tall order, particularly as the woman's role was paradoxical: she was to be meek and attentive, but if the man didn't get to work, she was to push him forward. In such confused circumstances, marriages floundered. By late 1945, the divorce rate for veterans under forty-five years old was one in twenty-nine, compared to one in sixty for civilians (Hartmann, *Home Front*, 165).

Over a million Americans married while overseas, and these marriages faced special strains. The foreign bride of a GI could face tremendous difficulties in adjusting to America and hostility if she was German or Japanese. Some women, expecting the America of Hollywood films, were shocked by the reality, especially of rural life. One French girl expected *Gone With the Wind* but got a Georgia sharecropper's cabin without toilet or running water (Shukert and Scibetta, 120). Interracial couples were often denied immigration papers and had to live abroad. Many of these marriages broke up. A further special strain on veterans and their dependents was that immediately after the war they were three times as likely as civilians to be unemployed. Massachusetts reported 67,000 unemployed former servicemen by March 1946 (226). This meant that many couples who could not be together during the war now had to live with in-laws under trying conditions. In January 1946, 60 percent of married veterans in the Northeast lacked their own homes (221).

But society showed its gratitude to veterans by giving a helping hand through the GI Bill. This aided a great many veterans and gave them a middle-class status they might never have had otherwise. Officially labeled the Serviceman's Readjustment Act, and passed in June 1944, the bill guaranteed veterans fifty-two weeks of unemployment benefits, cheap housing loans, other loans, medical assistance, and up to four years of education or job training. Under the bill, over eight million veterans got further education or training, easing the pressure on the job market and ultimately helping their career potential (Severo and Milford, 288–89). Veterans achieved higher educational levels than their civilian peers. By 1946 1.5 million were in college (Severo and Milford, 290). The vice president of a Chicago publishing firm believed that "the GI Bill made all the difference in the world" to him and that he "could never have afforded college" (Terkel, 55, also 135–37).

Most Americans agreed that the bill was warranted and did great good, but some worried that this extensive entitlement for a special segment of society was the thin wedge of socialism. Dixon Wecter, a historian, warned of this in a 1944 essay on America's approach to returning veterans. In the same year, Robert J. Watt, head of the American Federation of Labor, warned that the special status given veterans would encourage all minorities to claim special entitlements (Severo and Milford, 295).

Such views are debatable. But it is true that veterans' benefits became the most expensive single social welfare legislation in the national budget. They increased the original cost of the war by over 125 percent (Clayton, 661ff). By 1950 veterans' benefits represented 30 percent of public social welfare spending, and costs have continued to grow (Segal, 90). In 1990 more than half the men over age sixty-five were veterans, amounting to 7.2 million recipients of special medical and pension benefits, which added to the growing strain of the elderly on the American worker (Segal, 88).

The GI Bill impacted education and made higher education a normal part of the American dream. On the positive side, it allowed far more people to get a college education. But it may also have furthered the decline in university standards and curriculum content. Veterans often wanted strictly vocational courses, continuing the wartime trend away from the liberal arts. And colleges speeded up programs for veterans, who already felt left behind by the war. George Bush finished Yale in two and a half years. Professors were sometimes reluctant to flunk veterans, and administrators needed their federal funds, so grade inflation increased. Universities became increasingly dependent on the GI Bill and other military-related grants, diminishing their academic independence and drawing them into the growing military-industrial-government complex. In the early 1950s, 99.5 percent of federal aid to higher education was military related (Segal, 90).

At its best, the GI Bill helped massively to create a new, aspiring middle class, with educational and income attainments inconceivable a generation before. At its worst, critics said, the bill created the new middle class too quickly for it to be truly sophisticated: it was dull, antiintellectual, and obsessed with buying right and looking right. It lived in mass suburbs with repetitious architecture (little boxes made of ticky-tacky) and an artificial culture based on aggressive Americanism and distrust of eccentrics and outsiders. It was insecure in its newfound comfort, uptight, and hostile to nonconformists. Obsession with the flag as a precious symbol of Americanism, playing the national anthem at ball games, and other overt manifestations of patriotism dated from the war period and became the settled traditions of white middle-class life thereafter.

Whatever the role of the GI Bill, certainly the war encouraged what William H. Whyte called organization culture: a trend toward bureaucracy, conformity, and standardization in everything from clothing to values to political candidates. Uniformity began to increase when millions of Americans underwent military discipline in the country's largest organization, the armed forces. Later, big government interfered in the lives of citizens through such agencies as the Internal Revenue Service to a degree that would have been inconceivable a generation earlier. Big business, too, imposed standardization through its products and its personnel procedures. After a successful war, the military became a success model, and corporations adopted military-style hierarchical management. James Jones, a veteran, writer, and social critic, maintained that the war produced a demand for "team players" with a related loss of respect for individualism (*Red Line*, 474).

The sociologist David Riesman thought that by 1950 the pressure to conform to mass opinion was producing not leadership but management, whose aim was to preserve the status quo and to discourage unpopular decisions or new courses unsanctioned by opinion polls. He noted that before the war ended even generals had ceased to be leaders: they wouldn't tell unpopular truths or advocate tough positions, and they courted, and deferred to, the media (Riesman et al., 130–31). In this atmosphere, America would produce a generation of young people who would be "other-directed," thinking and acting not according to the dictates of an inner voice but according to peer pressure. Signs of such a pattern were there in the war. Riesman called this "the lonely crowd" (21).

The most famous exposition of conformity to authority as a primary value was Herman Wouk's *The Caine Mutiny* (1951), a fictional story of an American minesweeper whose captain, Queeg, was exhausted and mentally unstable after prolonged war service. During a storm that threatened to capsize the boat, he became paralyzed and was relieved by his first officer, Maryk, who saved the ship. Maryk was tried for mutiny and acquitted, but Wouk made it clear that Maryk should not have challenged the captain. The ethic of an organization demands that we serve even the incompetent, because they represent authority.

William H. Whyte, an editor of *Fortune* magazine, feared that such views would rob America of needed personal initiative, self-reliance, and a willingness to take business risks. He commented angrily, "Here, certainly, is an outstanding denial of individual responsibility.

The system is presented as having such a mystique that apparent evil becomes a kind of good." Whyte also noted that Wouk's villain was not the mad captain but the intellectual officer, Keefer, who first pointed out that the captain was insane, and encouraged others to question the system. He was thus "too clever to be wise." The message is that it is better to be an average team player who fits into the organization than a smart critic or a whistle-blower (Whyte, 245–46).

Implicit in *The Caine Mutiny* is approval for suppression of dissent, which characterized the early cold war period, with its witch-hunts and censorship of material deemed Communist or subversive of morals. One book often removed from school libraries was Anne Frank's *The Diary of a Young Girl*. It was censored because of Frank's references to her developing sexuality and her occasional defiance of her parents. Frank was a European Jew who wrote her book in hiding. The Nazis killed her in 1944. The suppression of her story is an ironic comment on freedom of speech as a war aim.

The manipulation of news during the war created a permanent trend. Today, as much as 70 percent of daily news may be PR put out by politicians, business, or the media itself. This means that we are often fed a very incomplete and misleading version of reality. This was clear in the 1991 Gulf War, when the military censored the war news not only to protect military security but to present a cosmetic version of the fighting that would not upset the public (Jonathan Alter et al., "Will We See the Real War?" *Newsweek*, January 14, 1991).

The secrecy surrounding the atom bomb project was a major step on the road now taken. Necessarily, the Manhattan Project was conducted under the tightest security, but this meant that the decision to inaugurate the nuclear age was taken by a handful of officials, some of whom were not elected. No legislative body in the democracies deliberated this momentous issue. H. Bruce Franklin, a student of superweapons, maintained that the bomb destroyed the core of democracy: there can be no free flow of knowledge or opinion on the crucial issue of a nuclear strike, and the life of the planet has been placed in the hands of a few all-powerful leaders (145–46).

The war that brought prosperity and a burgeoning middle class also nurtured conformity and an intolerant Americanism. More people became educated, but materialism and a contempt for the intellectual as irrelevant also increased. Ironically, this paradoxical mix helped to propel members of another generation into another war. Philip Caputo grew up in the comfortable white suburbs of 1960s Chicago. He went to the University of Chicago. He had it made. But the sheltered, secure existence his war-generation parents wanted for him was both too much and too little: he felt smothered by comfort and wanted more from life than the suburbs could provide. He responded to the inspiring words of a WWII veteran, President Kennedy, who beckoned him to a cause, the containment of communism in Southeast Asia (4–6). He volunteered for Vietnam, where he became steadily disillusioned and an opponent of the war (320, 325, 328).

He and other volunteers at first believed they were following in the footsteps of their fathers, as portrayed in the film *Sands of Iwo Jima* (1949), starring John Wayne as the tough marine leader, Sergeant Stryker. But Stryker is a celluloid image—and he is killed at the end of the film, frozen in time as the perfect American hero. He doesn't come home to put on weight, settle down, and buy a home in the cozy suburbs. Some of the real fathers did try to say what the war was really like, men like Norman Mailer and James Jones. They wanted to tell the next generation about what happens in a war between Asian and Caucasian people. But society largely rejected their testimony, and the John Wayne image became the mainstream version of reality.

Caputo ended up being tried for the murder of civilians in a theater of war not much more dirty or confused than the fathers had fought in. What he did was try to recreate a myth, a myth that the previous generation had fought in the best war ever.

Afterword

THE OPENING CHAPTER of this work suggests that the popular image of World War II is incomplete. It is distorted by oversimplification and glamorization. Each succeeding chapter attempts to illustrate this theme in detail through analysis of a major facet of the war experience. In closing, let us briefly summarize some of the major points of this argument and say a few words about the problem of mythologizing the past.

It has frequently been said that World War II proves you cannot appease potential aggressors. This is seen as the key lesson learned by the war generation. Had the democracies stood up to the European dictators in 1937 or 1938, it is argued, the war either would not have happened or it would have been more easily won. In fact, the history of the 1930s gives no such clear lesson. We now see that Hitler's territorial ambitions could not be curbed by diplomatic means, but this was not so clear at the time. Nor does it follow that every world leader who opposes America is a Hitler who cannot be brought to reason short of war. Moreover, even though war with Hitler was finally inevitable, it is debatable that this war would have been any shorter or less difficult one or two years prior to 1939. By waiting, Britain built up the air defenses that saved it in the 1940 Battle of Britain, while on the other hand, Italy's military resources waned.

The only possible chance the major powers had of saving Czechoslovakia was if the Soviets and the democracies could have worked together, because Russia was the only major land power that could have placed significant ground forces in the way of a German thrust eastward. When cooperation failed, the debacle was almost certain. Perhaps, then, a potential lesson might be that world peace depends on major powers working together despite their philosophical antagonisms. Finally, although it is rarely noted, in the Pacific the United States and Britain did not try to appease Japan's ambitions but used deterrence instead, and this more confrontational policy also failed. It may even have helped to provoke war.

World War II was in many ways a battle of technology, as combatants struggled to produce more and better weapons—which has given

Afterword

the conflict a reputation as a war of superweapons, of tanks and planes making lighting thrusts and surgical strikes on highly fluid battlefronts. But while it is true that at times the war was one of swift conquest and mobile maneuver, particularly in the opening phases, as Axis forces overwhelmed ineptly led and poorly equipped opponents, much of the war was characterized by grinding attrition, in which hammer blows were traded in a wasteland not very different from the battlefield of World War I. When the Allies took back ground from their wily foes in their skillfully prepared defensive positions, they had to use immense firepower, producing a brute force push with ponderous destruction. Total war has a momentum that leads to total destruction. Many Americans were spared knowledge of the immense carnage because they never left the States or never saw a battlefront. Censorship sanitized their image of combat.

Combat was not glamorous for those engaged in it. Men suffered enormous mental and physical stress from the exposure to unexpected and shocking violence. American armed forces were not happy warriors; many combat soldiers felt they did more than their share of suffering and dying. Some resented those who were home enjoying prosperity, and some have continued to suffer psychological or physical pain as a result of their wartime experience. Dealing with the experience of combat takes more than a parade. Death was normally not romantic, particularly when the victim was blown apart: many Americans fail to understand that most MIAs simply ceased to exist. William R. Cubbins, a bomber pilot, said of such a death, "To me, death in the lonesomeness of night-blackened skies is so impersonal it violates the rules of dying. Death should never be without meaning or purpose, or dignity. To disappear suddenly in the faceless void of night is to lose one's very existence, to become as an incomplete sentence" (Cubbins, *The War of the Cottontails: A Bomber Pilot with the Fifteenth Air Force* [1989], 189–90).

American ethnic minorities, although they had fought against the Nazi superman ideology, faced pervasive discrimination in military as well as civilian life. Discrimination also affected underprivileged white males, who were disproportionately represented in combat infantry companies.

At home, there was overwhelming support for the war, but this entailed few sacrifices or tough choices for the many who prospered as the war economy grew. While there was great patriotism, there was also selfishness on the part of corporations, organized labor, and individuals. The black market was active. Despite the myth, it was not the war per se that ended the Depression or that brought prosperity to

American life; it was government spending in an underutilized economy. Had the same amount been spent during the New Deal, the effects would have been largely the same. Consequently, the United States makes a significant error when it assumes that any time it is in the economic doldrums a war will prime the economic pump.

To the degree that America has simplified the complex experience of World War II, it is left with an incomplete and therefore misleading legacy. Some Americans have been led to overvalue force as a tool of policy and to consider diplomatic initiatives appeasement. As political commentator Robert J. Samuelson pointed out, (*Newsweek*, March 2, 1992), the war so dominated the American imagination that war has become a pseudonym for life itself: we have had the cold war as well as wars on drugs, crime, poverty, and illiteracy. We have price wars and ratings wars and even a war between the sexes. America has never quite recovered emotionally from the sense of vulnerability brought about by Pearl Harbor. With the end of the cold war, many Americans cherish being the world's only military superpower.

The ultimate problem of powerful myths about an idealized past is that they postulate a golden age, when things were better than they are now, a peak of efficiency from which the country has declined and which it must refoster if it is to prosper. In short, America's future lies in reclaiming its past. It is understandable that Americans should see the 1940s as this golden age. As a result of the war, America became prosperous and powerful. But no magic formula produced this scenario; it was a unique situation, produced largely by the fact that America alone of the great world powers was not a battleground. These circumstances cannot be recreated.

This is just as well, for the image of this golden age is highly selective. It leaves out the fact that America of the 1940s was wracked by change and troubled by many of the same problems that vex it now. It faced a rising divorce rate, juvenile delinquency, declining educational standards, and a loss of the traditional verities. And it did not always manage to resolve these difficulties. Americans do themselves a disservice when they assume that their predecessors did everything better than they do. Usually, those who want to return to the past are those who know too little about it. The war created problems that are even now not fully resolved, such as what to do about nuclear weapons and their threat to the future of humanity. The war highlighted racism in the culture and guaranteed that the issue of civil rights would be on the national agenda in the decades following 1945.

The past and its legacies are complex. We should consider all the ramifications of the war, not just the glorious and dramatic moments captured for us in Hollywood movies. The war was not a discrete event that ended when the last enemy surrendered unconditionally, leaving America the most powerful superpower in the world. The war was a profoundly disturbing moment in the flow of history, the after effects of which, like waves radiating out from a pebble dropped in water, continue now.

Bibliographical Essay

T HIS ESSAY does not attempt an exhaustive discussion of all the
books on World War II. Instead, it seeks to provide the reader with
a guide to those sources I found most useful in writing the text
and to give students and general readers a list of volumes for further
study that are well written, entertaining, and provocative, as well as
sheerly informative. At times, there are too few authorities on a subject to allow for this kind of selectivity.

one
Mythmaking and the War

In putting together the popular portrait of the best war ever, I used a
variety of sources in common currency, such as local newspapers,
magazines, even television programs. The reader would easily be able
to compile a similar picture by looking through the files of such magazines as *Time* and *Newsweek*, particularly for the period 1989–92,
when fear peaked that the war generation was leaving public life.

To understand the variety and complexity of wartime experiences,
the best place to start is with the fine oral history by Studs Terkel,
"The Good War": An Oral History of World War Two (1985). Terkel
has an almost unique talent as an oral historian for eliciting the candid
memories of interviewees. I have used his book extensively throughout the text to give the views of frank and perceptive participants in
the war. Although it deals with many more conflicts than that of
1939–45, Richard Holmes's *Acts of War: The Behavior of Men in Battle* (1986) is extremely useful for obtaining a grasp of the whole military experience.

The variety of statistics that I draw upon in this and other chapters
are readily available in standard textbooks on the war. Two that are
particularly useful in this regard are Gerald D. Nash, *The Great Depression and World War II: Organizing America, 1933–1945* (1979);
and Allan M. Winkler, *Home Front U.S.A.: America During World
War II* (1986).

Paul Fussell challenges the romantic view of the war in two

provocative works: *Thank God for the Atom Bomb and Other Essays* (1988); and *Wartime: Understanding and Behavior in the Second World War* (1989). Fussell, a combat veteran and literary critic, may go too far in stating his case, but he offers a much-needed counterbalance to the mainstream. I have drawn considerably upon his ideas to suggest the underside of the war. For example, Fussell deals on page 24 of *Wartime* with the swimming tanks that sunk. Fussell is also good at revealing the image-making in the public perception of men like George Patton (e.g., *Wartime* 152–64).

Andrew A. Rooney's thoughts on the war are in his "An Essay on War," in *A Few Minutes with Andy Rooney* (1981), 168–75. Russell Baker's views on the Great Depression are expressed in *Growing Up* (1982). Philip Wylie's strictures on wartime America are in *Generation of Vipers* (1942; repr. 1955). Roger Hilsman's view of the war is in *American Guerilla: My War Behind Japanese Lines* (1990).

Two seminal postwar works of fiction that try to tell the truth about combat are James Jones, *The Thin Red Line* (1962); and Norman Mailer, *The Naked and the Dead* (1948). Illustrating the point that serious drama cannot compete with the less-taxing film version, Jones's book has been checked out of the Northern Kentucky University library only twice since it was purchased. A fine candid nonfictional memoir of combat is William Manchester, *Goodbye, Darkness: A Memoir of the Pacific War* (1980). See also James Jones, *WWII* (1975). An excellent scholarly introduction to the reality of warfare in the era is by British military historian John Ellis, *Brute Force: Allied Strategy and Tactics in the Second World War* (1990). Mutual racism and ferocity in the Pacific are described by John W. Dower in *War Without Mercy: Race and Power in the Pacific War* (1986).

The best overview of press coverage and censorship is Phillip Knightley, *The First Casualty: From the Crimea to Vietnam; the War Correspondent as Hero, Propagandist, and Myth Maker* (1975). My approach owes much to him. John Steinbeck is remarkably honest about how the war was reported in his introduction to his war reports, *Once There Was a War* (1958; repr. 1981). Two memoirs by major journalists offer many insights into the politics and public relations of war. They are Frank Gervasi, *The Violent Decade: A Foreign Correspondent in Europe, Asia, and the Middle East, 1935–1945* (1989); and Eric Sevareid, *Not So Wild a Dream* (1969). Three good volumes of actual war reports are Ernie Pyle, *Here Is Your War* (1943; repr. 1974); his *Brave Men* (1944); and A. J. Liebling, *Mollie and Other War Pieces* (1964). Biographies that deal with the public relations efforts of two leading publicity seekers are Ladislas Farago, *Patton: Ordeal and Triumph* (1966); and Michael Schaller, *Douglas MacArthur: The Far Eastern General* (1989).

On the significance of the rise of mass circulation publications like *Reader's Digest* and superhero comic books, see Ariel Dorfman, *The Emperor's Old Clothes: What the Lone Ranger, Babar, and Other Innocent Heroes Do to Our Minds* (1983). Ian I. Mitroff and Warren Bennis offer stimulating insights into twentieth-century media manipulation of reality in *The Unreality Industry: The Deliberate Manufacturing of Falsehood and What It Is Doing to Our Lives* (1989). The importance of commercials in molding the dominant view of the war is well demonstrated in Frank W. Fox, *Madison Avenue Goes to War: The Strange Military Career of American Advertising, 1941–45* (1975).

There are many studies of the movie industry during the era. Three sound surveys are Bernard F. Dick, *The Star-Spangled Screen: The American World War II Film* (1985); Clayton R. Koppes and Gregory D. Black, *Hollywood Goes to War: How Politics, Profits, and Propaganda Shaped World War II Movies* (1987); and Colin Shindler, *Hollywood Goes to War: Films and American Society, 1939–1952* (1979). Jeanine Basinger pursues the formulas that came to dominate the themes of war films in *The World War II Combat Film: Anatomy of a Genre* (1986). Also useful are Clyde Jeavons, *A Pictorial History of War Films* (1974); and Lawrence H. Suid, *Guts and Glory: Great American War Movies* (1978). Video and discount stores carry many examples of WWII movies. In addition to the combat films mentioned in the text, *Wake Island* (1942) and *Guadalcanal Diary* (1943) are good examples of the genre. *South Pacific* (1958) was based loosely on James A. Michener's *Tales of the South Pacific* (1947).

The Good War myth played an important role in the public images of Presidents Bush and Reagan. See, for example, Joe Hyams's biography, *Flight of the Avenger: George Bush at War* (1991). The importance of film in the self-concept and historical perception of Ronald Reagan is pointed out in Michael Paul Rogin, *Ronald Reagan, the Movie* (1987); and Garry Wills, *Reagan's America: Innocents at Home* (1987). For Wills on Reagan's ability to mythologize the past, see, for example, pages 52, 76, 119, and 168. Reagan's appeal for young people is cataloged in Wanda Urbanska, *The Singular Generation* (1986). Spielberg's "The Mission" is available in VHS format under the title *Amazing Stories: Book One*. John Costello talks about the reality of 1940s mores in *Virtue Under Fire: How World War II Changed Our Social and Sexual Attitudes* (1985).

To compare how America's "worst war," Vietnam, has been treated in popular culture, see Albert Auster and Leonard Quart, *How the War Was Remembered: Hollywood and Vietnam* (1988); and John Hellman, *American Myth and the Legacy of Vietnam* (1986). Veterans' comments on how the movie version of World War II inspired them to go to Vietnam as young men are found in Ron Kovic, *Born on the Fourth of July* (1976); and Bill McCloud, *What Should We Tell Our Children About Vietnam?* (1989). Poet and social critic Robert Bly charges directly that the WWII generation of veterans misled the young men coming after them about the nature of war, in *Iron John: A Book About Men* (1990), 95.

two
No Easy Answers

To understand the interaction of global events between the wars, see the survey by Daniel R. Brower, *The World in the Twentieth Century: The Age of Global War and Revolution* (1988). Also see Raymond J. Sontag, *A Broken World, 1919–1939* (1971); and William W. MacDonald and John M. Carroll, eds., *European Traditions in the Twentieth Century* (1979). The importance of the right to bear arms in a civic context is explained by John Keegan in the opening sections of *The Second World War* (1990). I examine nineteenth-century Western male involvement with war in Adams, *The Great Adventure: Male Desire and the Coming of World War One* (1990).

The idea that monolithic dictatorships were in a worldwide conspiracy was stated clearly in a series of films called *Why We Fight*, made for the U.S. War Department by Frank Capra. The first episode, *Prelude to War* (1943), makes graphic use of the Tanaka memorandum. It is widely available on videotape. The arguments for and against appeasement are laid out in Peter Calvocoressi, Guy Wint, and John Pritchard, *Total War: The Causes and Courses of the Second World War* (rev. 2d. ed., 1989). This is particularly helpful in showing the impact of Japanese actions on British policy. Good companion studies are P. M. H. Bell, *The Origins of the Second World War in Europe* (1986); and Akira Iriye, *The Origins of the Second World War in Asia and the Pacific* (1987). Defense problems facing the British Empire are analyzed comprehensively in Correlli Barnett, *The Collapse of British Power* (1972).

Books that deal broadly with totalitarianism include Hannah Arendt, *The Origins of Totalitarianism* (1966); and Carl J. Friedrich and Zbigniew Brzezinski, *Totalitarian Dictatorship and Autocracy* (1965).

Bibliographical Essay

Robert V. Daniels, *The Nature of Communism* (1962), provides a useful introduction to Soviet Russia. *Stalin: The Man and His Era* (1973), by Adam Ulam, is a good biography. Alan Bullock's *Hitler and Stalin: Parallel Lives* (1991) compares the two dictators. Soviet foreign policy is discussed in Jonathan Haslam, *The Soviet Union and the Struggle for Collective Security in Europe, 1933–39* (1984); and in Jiri Hochman, *The Soviet Union and the Failure of Collective Security* (1984).

Alan Cassel's *Fascism* (1975) explores the nature of fascism in different countries. Denis Mack Smith studies the Italian dictator in *Mussolini* (1981). See also his examination of Fascist imperial designs in *Mussolini's Roman Empire* (1976). Other biographies include Ivone Kirkpatrick, *Mussolini: A Study in Power* (1964); and Elizabeth Wiskemann, *Fascism in Italy: Its Development and Influence* (1969). American journalist Frank Gervasi makes many excellent observations on Fascist Italy. See *The Violent Decade: A Foreign Correspondent in Europe, Asia, and the Middle East, 1935–1945* (1989).

Ernst Junger was one of the German veterans who refused to accept the decisions of 1918 as final. See his powerful memoir, *The Storm of Steel* (Eng. trans., 1929). A difficult but rewarding analysis of the Freikorps mentality is Klaus Theweleit, *Male Fantasies*, vol. I, *Women, Floods, Bodies, History* (1987). Hannah Vogt's *The Burden of Guilt: A Short History of Germany, 1914–1945* (1964) takes the discussion of Germany's situation beyond the simple black and white. A. J. P. Taylor, *The Origins of the Second World War* (1972), tries to argue that Germany under Hitler had meaningful objectives that went beyond simple aggression. This thesis sparked a debate that is synthesized in William Roger Louis, ed., *The Origins of the Second World War: A. J. P. Taylor and his Critics* (1972).

John Toland's two-volume *Adolf Hitler* (1976) is a well-balanced biography. Toland avoids demonizing Hitler and makes the Nazi era intelligible. Other useful biographies include Alan Bullock, *Hitler: A Study in Tyranny* (1964); and Joachim Fest, *Hitler* (1973). Fest profiles top Nazi leaders in *The Face of the Third Reich* (1970). Albert Speer's *Inside the Third Reich* (1970), the memoir of an official close to Hitler, also provides views of the Nazi inner circle. Hitler's own book, *Mein Kampf* (My Struggle) (1925; Eng. trans., 1943), is often characterized as dense and muddled; yet it is quite easy to grasp Hitler's fundamental viewpoint by browsing in the text. Good examples of the many attempts to see Hitler from a psychological standpoint are the pioneering work by Dr. Walter C. Langer, written in 1943 for American intelligence and called *The Mind of Adolf Hitler: The Secret Wartime Report* (repr. 1972); and Robert L. Waite, *Hitler: The Psychopathic God* (1977).

Bibliographical Essay

Erich Maria Remarque's antiwar novel, *All Quiet on the Western Front* (Eng. trans., 1928), was one of the many books banned in Nazi Germany. The excellent American film version (1930) was also prohibited in Germany for a time. Remarque's later novel, *A Time to Love and a Time to Die* (Eng. trans., 1954), is a first-rate love story as well as a graphic picture of existence under Hitler. Bernt Englemann's *In Hitler's Germany: Daily Life in the Third Reich* (1986) is a good oral history that gives a variety of German reactions to nazism. Robert E. Herzstein, *The War That Hitler Won: Goebbels and the Nazi Media Campaign* (1986), analyzes propaganda. In 1934, Leni Riefenstahl filmed the annual Nazi party rally at Nuremberg. Her movie *Triumph of the Will* (1935) is a tour de force of media-staged pageantry and is excellent for understanding the role of symbols and imagery in nazism's appeal. H. W. Koch, *The Hitler Youth: Origins and Development, 1922–1945* (1976), examines the party's attraction for young people. It dispels the myth that German children in the Reich were brainwashed.

On American responses to Europe, see Robert A. Divine, *The Illusion of Neutrality* (1969); Selig Adler, *The Isolationist Impulse* (1957); and Manfred Jonas, *Isolationism in America, 1935–1941* (1966). Wayne S. Cole's *Roosevelt and the Isolationists, 1932–1945* (1983) is recommended for insight into this aspect. The uneasy relations between America and Britain are sketched in Daniel Reynolds, *The Creation of the Anglo-American Alliance, 1937–1941* (1982); and in James R. Leutze, *Bargaining for Supremacy: Anglo-American Naval Collaboration, 1937–1941* (1977). Leutze argues that FDR was determined to supplant Britain as the world's dominant naval power. A more flattering portrait of British-American relations is contained in Joseph P. Lash, *Roosevelt and Churchill, 1939–1941: The Partnership That Saved the West* (1976).

American attitudes to Hitler are treated in Arnold A. Offner, *American Appeasement: United States Foreign Policy and Germany, 1933–1938* (1969). Charles A. Lindbergh, as an American visitor, was impressed by the progressive aspects of fascism and nazism. Viewing Germany as a barrier to the spread of communism, he overlooked the brutality at the heart of nazism. See his *Autobiography of Values* (1978); and *The Wartime Journals of Charles A. Lindbergh* (1970). Two fine writers observed life in the Reich and left critical accounts. One is by American reporter William L. Shirer and is titled *Berlin Diary: The Journal of a Foreign Correspondent 1939–1941* (1941). The other is *Goodbye to Berlin* (1939) by English novelist Christopher Isherwood. His writings were the basis for Bob Fosse's film *Cabaret* (1972).

Shirer's two-volume history, *The Rise and Fall of the Third Reich* (1959), though somewhat dated in perspective, still has useful insights.

Martha Gellhorn, in *The Face of War* (1967), indicts the democracies for not fighting until 1939. This book contains some good reporting on the major wars of the era. *The Spanish Civil War* (1961) by Hugh Thomas is the classic account. But Paul Preston's *The Spanish Civil War 1936–39* (1986) provides a more recent, brief account. A. L. Rowse, a British professor of history who knew most of the leading policymakers, felt that obsession with communism, allied to sheer ignorance of the nature of nazism, helped to frame the appeasement policy. See his *Appeasement: A Study in Political Decline, 1933–1939* (1961).

James B. Crowley, *Japan's Quest for Autonomy: National Security and Foreign Policy, 1930–1938* (1966), sets out Japan's basic dilemma. A very readable account that notes the increasing dominance of the military in Japanese policies is John Toland, *Rising Sun: The Decline and Fall of the Japanese Empire* (2 vols., 1970). M. Harries and S. Harries, *Soldiers of the Sun* (1992), is a recent popular history of the Japanese army, its structure and campaigns. See also Haruko Cook, *Japan at War* (1990); and Sabura Ienaga, *The Pacific War: World War II and the Japanese, 1931–1945* (1978), especially chapter 3. The brutality that marred Japan's claim to represent a liberating and enlightened force in Asia is documented in H. J. Timperley, *Japanese Terror in China* (1958); and in Lord Russell of Liverpool, *The Knights of Bushido: The Shocking Story of Japanese War Atrocities* (1958), which is more even-handed than its title suggests.

On American attitudes to Japan, see Dorothy Borg, *The United States and the Far Eastern Crisis of 1933–38* (1964); and John E. Wiltz, *From Isolation to War, 1931–1941* (1968). Japanese-American relations are charted in Akira Iriye, *Across the Pacific: An Inner History of American–East Asian Relations* (1967); and Charles E. Neu, *The Troubled Encounter: The United States and Japan* (1975). Homer Lea, an American soldier of fortune, was an early exponent of the "yellow peril" approach to Japan's growing power in the Pacific. See his *The Valor of Ignorance* (1909); and *The Day of the Saxon* (1912).

three
The Patterns of War, 1939–1945

In framing my perspective, the most formative general military history was John Ellis, *Brute Force: Allied Strategy and Tactics in the Second World War* (1990). Michael J. Lyons, *World War II* (1989), is a solid short survey. Robert Leckie's *Delivered from Evil* (1987) is longer and opinionated but worth browsing in. Also see B. H. Liddell Hart, *History of the Second World War* (1970). M. K. Dziewanowski's *War at Any Price* (1991) details the war in Europe.

Students of the American military must read Russell F. Weigley. Begin with *The American Way of War* (1973). Maurice Matloff, ed., *American Military History* (1969), one of the Army Historical Series, is still very reliable. James M. Morris, *America's Armed Forces* (1991); and Gary R. Hess, *The United States at War, 1941–1945* (1986), are up-to-date general histories. Edward K. Eckert, *In War and Peace: An American Military History Anthology* (1990), provides useful document excerpts. See also Geoffrey Perrett, *There's a War to Be Won: The United States Army in World War II* (1991). Samuel Eliot Morison's *The Two Ocean War* (1963) remains the classic account of naval operations. Also valuable is John Creswell, *Sea Warfare, 1939–1945* (rev. ed., 1967).

General Heinz Guderian gives an eyewitness account of the blitzkrieg in *Panzer Leader* (1952). Nicholas Harman's *Dunkirk: The Patriotic Myth* (1980) is a good revisionist account of the Allied debacle in 1940, which stresses British lack of enthusiasm prior to Dunkirk. Walter Lord's *The Miracle of Dunkirk* (1982) is a more traditional account. Roger Parkinson's *Summer 1940: The Battle of Britain* (1977) puts that encounter in a balanced perspective. Hitler's military leadership, including Operation Barbarossa, receives provocative analysis in John Keegan, *The Mask of Command* (1987). I am impressed by the German performance in North Africa, but readers might want to consult the different view in Charles Douglas-Home, *Rommel* (1973).

A standard work on British-American strategic planning is Maurice Matloff and Edwin M. Snell, *Strategic Planning for Coalition Warfare* (1953). Mark Stoler, *The Politics of the Second Front: American Military Planning and Diplomacy in Coalition Warfare, 1941–1943* (1977), delineates the basic differences in U.S. and British strategy. Forrest C. Pogue's *George C. Marshall* is the acknowledged biography of the U.S. chief of staff. See especially volume 2, *Ordeal and Hope, 1939–1942* (1966); and volume 3, *Organizer of Victory, 1943–44* (1973). There are good biographical materials on the key American commanders in Europe. I suggest Stephen E. Ambrose, *Eisenhower* (1983); Ladislas Farago, *Patton: Ordeal and Triumph* (1966); George S. Patton, Jr., *War as I Knew It* (1947); Omar Bradley and Clay Blair, *A General's Life* (1983); and Russell F. Weigley, *Eisenhower's Lieutenants* (1981).

Michael Howard's *Mediterranean Strategy in the Second World War* (1968) is a useful brief account. M. Garland, *Sicily and the Surrender*

Bibliographical Essay

of Italy (1965); and W. G. F. Jackson, *The Battle for Italy* (1967), cover those campaigns. On Normandy, see Max Hastings, *Overlord: D-Day, June 6, 1944* (1984); Martin Blumerson's *Breakthrough and Pursuit* (1961); and Blumerson's *The Duel for France* (1963). John Keegan's *Six Armies in Normandy* (1983) is a unique attempt to see northern European operations from the perspectives of all the major combatants. Cornelius Ryan describes Market Garden in *A Bridge Too Far* (1974). On the Battle of the Bulge, see Hugh M. Cole, *The Ardennes: The Battle of the Bulge* (1965); and Charles B. MacDonald, *The Last Offensive* (1973).

The air war has received copious coverage. Anthony Verrier's *The Bomber Offensive* (1968) is a thorough basic study. On the British, see John Terraine, *A Time for Courage: The Royal Air Force in the European War, 1939–1945* (1985). Old but still useful is David Divine, *The Broken Wing: A Study in the British Exercise of Air Power* (1966). H. Bruce Franklin traces the historical American search for a war-winning wonder weapon (such as the Norden bombsight or the atom bomb) in *War Stars: The Superweapon and the American Imagination* (1988). Ronald Schaffer's *Wings of Judgment: American Bombing in World War II* (1985) argues convincingly that Americans, despite their disapproval of British area bombing, came to use the same basic strategy. See also Michael Sherry, *The Rise of American Air Power: The Creation of Armageddon* (1987); and his "The Slide to Total Air War," *New Republic*, December 16, 1981. Martin Middlebrook's *The Schweinfurt-Regensburg Mission* (1983) recreates one seminal air operation. David Irving describes Dresden in *The Destruction of Dresden* (1963); and Kurt Vonnegut, Jr., in *Slaughterhouse-Five* (1969), evokes the emotional trauma.

Ronald H. Spector's *Eagle Against the Sun* (1985) is a basic general history of the Pacific war. Other good overviews are Basil Collier, *The War in the Far East* (1969); and John Costello, *The Pacific War* (1981). Pearl Harbor receives thorough treatment in Gordon W. Prange's *At Dawn We Slept* (1981). John Toland deals well with the Japanese conquests in *But Not in Shame: The Six Months after Pearl Harbor* (1962). In addition to work on the Japanese military cited in chapter 2, see S. L. Mayer, ed., *The Japanese War Machine* (1976). Edwin Palmer Hoyt, *Blue Skies and Blood: The Battle of the Coral Sea* (1975); and Gordon W. Prange, *Miracle at Midway* (1982), are well-written accounts. Robert Leckie details Guadalcanal in *Guadalcanal: The Turning Point of the War* (1965). The standard biographies of the Pacific commanders are E. B. Potter, *Nimitz* (1976); and William Manchester, *American Caesar: Douglas MacArthur* (1978). MacArthur's *Reminiscences* (1964) are self-serving but interesting. Michael Schaller's *Douglas Mac-Arthur: The Far Eastern General* (1989) is very critical of the general.

Basic accounts of the subsidiary Japanese theaters are Don Moser, *China, Burma, India* (1978); and Brian Garfield, *The Thousand-Mile War: World War II in Alaska and the Aleutians* (1969; repr. 1982). The destruction of Japanese commerce is described in Clay Blair, Jr., *Silent Victory: The Submarine War Against Japan* (1975); and W. J. Holmes, *Undersea Victory: The Influence of Submarine Operations in the Pacific* (1966). Richard F. Newcomb, *Iwo Jima* (1965); and William Belote, *Typhoon of Steel: The Battle for Okinawa* (1970), describe those actions.

Russell Spurr's *A Glorious Way to Die: The Kamikaze Mission of the Battleship Yamato* (1981) puts kamikaze tactics in an intelligible material and cultural context. Rikihei Inoguchi, Tadashi Nakajima, and Roger Pineau, *The Divine Wind* (1958), sees the attacks from the Japanese point of view. Barton J. Bernstein, *The Atomic Bomb: The Critical Issues* (1976), summarizes some fundamental arguments pro and con. See also the additional discussion in the chapter 7 essay below. John Hersey vividly describes the aftermath of the bombings in *Hiroshima* (1946). The standard study of Japan's submission is J. C. Butow, *Japan's Decision to Surrender* (1954). The failure of cultural understanding between the Allies and the Japanese is analyzed in John W. Dower, *War Without Mercy: Race and Power in the Pacific War* (1986).

four
The American War Machine

Surveys useful for giving a general picture of the American war machine include Gerald D. Nash, *The Great Depression and World War II: Organizing America, 1933–1945* (1979); and A. Russell Buchanan, *The United States and World War II*, 2 volumes (1964). Allan M. Winkler's *The Politics of Propaganda: The Office of War Information, 1942–1945* (1978) suggests how the war was portrayed to the home audience. Walter Mills, *Arms and Men: A Study in American Military History* (1958), places the managerial and technical changes of the era in a context of historical evolution. Geoffrey Perret, *A Country Made by War* (1989); and John Keegan, essay, "Britain and America," [London] *Times Literary Supplement*, May 17, 1985, delineate the enormous growth in America's military and economic power during the war at a relatively low financial and human cost. The relative importance of lend-lease to the Allied war effort is analyzed in Peter Calvocoressi, Guy Wint, and John Pritchard, *Total War: The Causes and*

Courses of the Second World War (rev. 2d. ed., 1989). Russell F. Weigley's provocative ideas are in "Shaping the American Army of World War II: Mobility versus Power," in Lloyd J. Matthews and Dale E. Brown, eds., *The Parameters of War* (1987).

In charting the effects of wartime mobilization on American culture, the following are particularly useful: Keith L. Nelson, ed., *The Impact of War on American Life: The Twentieth-Century Experience* (1971); John Morton Blum, *V Was for Victory: Politics and American Culture During World War II* (1976); John Costello, *Virtue Under Fire: How World War II Changed Our Social and Sexual Attitudes* (1985); and Allan M. Winkler, *Home Front U.S.A.: America During World War II* (1986). Acute contemporary observations are in Geoffrey Gorer, *The Americans: A Study in National Character* (1948); Eric Sevareid, *Not So Wild a Dream* (1969); Frank Gervasi, *The Violent Decade: A Foreign Correspondent in Europe, Asia, and the Middle East, 1935–1945* (1989); and John Steinbeck, *Once There Was a War* (1958; repr. 1961).

Paul A. C. Koistenen ably assesses the growth of government-business ties in *The Military-Industrial Complex: A Historical Perspective* (1980). Also see Gregory Hooks, *Forging The Military-Industrial Complex: World War II's Battle of the Potomac* (1991); and Joe R. Feagin and Kelly Riddell, "The State, Capitalism, and World War II: The U.S. Case," *Armed Forces and Society* 17 (Fall 1990). On the commercial selling of the war, see Frank W. Fox, *Madison Avenue Goes to War: The Strange Military Career of American Advertising, 1941–45* (1975). Bruce Catton, journalist and popular historian, criticizes the growth of organization society in *The War Lords of Washington* (1948). Merle Curti expresses his concerns about the failure of critical thinking in *The Growth of American Thought* (1943). The coming of academe into the government orbit is described in Robin Winks, *Cloak and Gown: Scholars in the Secret War, 1939–1961* (1987). Most histories of strategic bombing comment on civilians' lack of sensitivity to enemy suffering. A specific discussion is in George E. Hopkins, "Bombing and the American Conscience During World War II," *Historian* 27 (May 1966).

A good history of selective service is David R. Segal, *Recruiting for Uncle Sam: Citizenship and Military Manpower Policy* (1989). On dissent, see James Burk, "Debating the Draft in America," *Armed Forces and Society* 15 (Spring 1989). George Q. Flynn's *Lewis B. Hershey: Mr. Selective Service* (1985) looks at the modern draft in the context of its founding father. James Jones's novel *From Here to Eternity* (1951) captures the idiom of the prewar regular army. His portrait of the long-service noncom is particularly good and helps to explain why the first draftees would have had trouble adjusting to their situation. Irwin Shaw's 1948 novel and the subsequent 1958 film, *The Young Lions*, gives a good view of basic training, including the harassment of a Jewish recruit. Neil Simon's play and 1988 film, *Biloxi Blues*, pursues a similar theme. Both are available on videocassette.

The best collection of primary-source data—interviews and surveys—for analyzing GI life is the mine of information put together by the research team headed by Samuel A. Stouffer and published under his name as *The American Soldier*, volume 1, *Adjustment During Army Life*, and volume 2, *Combat and Its Aftermath*, both published in 1949 and reprinted in 1965. Studs Terkel's *"The Good War": An Oral History of World War Two* (1985) has some revealing memoirs of life in the war machine. Two very helpful studies of the military experience are S. L. A. Marshall, *Men Against Fire* (1947); and John Ellis, *The Sharp End: The Fighting Man in World War II* (1980). For accusations that momism was ruining the fiber of American manhood, see Edward A. Strecker, *Their Mothers' Sons: The Psychiatrist Examines an American Problem* (1946; repr. 1951); and Philip Wylie, *Generation of Vipers* (1942; repr. 1955). The failure of the troops to understand the issues at stake in the war is detailed in David L. Cohn, "Should Fighting Men Think?" *Saturday Review of Literature*, January 18, 1947.

T. N. Dupuy studies army performance in *A Genius for War* (1977). Martin Van Creveld's analysis of organizational behavior is contained in *Fighting Power: German and U.S. Army Performance, 1939–1945* (1982). See also his *The Training of Officers: From Military Professionalism to Irrelevance* (1990). An example of the traditional view of Prussian top-down control, even into schooling, is Gregor Ziemer, *Education for Death: The Making of the Nazi* (1941). The German army's performance late in the war is remarkable because, by this stage, its personnel were considerably inferior to the elite of 1939 and now drew upon foreign or physically second-rate material. See Charles W. Sydnor, Jr., *Soldiers of Destruction: The SS Death's Head Division, 1933–1945* (1977).

Examples of American discipline and leadership faltering during captivity are found in John M. Wright, Jr., *Captured on Corregidor: Diary of an American P.O.W. in World War II* (1988); William R. Cubbins, *The War of the Cottontails: A Bomber Pilot with the Fifteenth Air Force Against Nazi Germany* (1989); and Kurt Vonnegut, Jr., *Slaughterhouse-Five or the Children's Crusade* (1969), which has a scathingly funny critique of the different American and British behavior patterns under the pressure of captivity. Military "chickenshit" is described in Paul Fussell, *Wartime: Understanding and Behavior in the Second*

World War (1989). Chickenshit destroys an enlisted man in Robert Lowry's novel *Casualty* (1946), where the protagonist deserts and is killed after being busted for standing a drunken man's guard duty. "What had happened to him was just some more of the meaningless discipline that was a thing to be endured" (132).

Other sources on the army experience cited in the text are from John Colby, *War from the Ground Up: The Ninetieth Division in WWII* (1991); Ladislas Farago, *Patton: Ordeal and Triumph* (1966); J. Glenn Gray, *The Warriors: Reflections on Men in Battle* (1959; repr. 1970); John Hersey, *Into the Valley: A Skirmish of the Marines* (1943; repr. 1970); James Jones, *The Thin Red Line* (1962); and *WWII* (1975); Philip Kaplan and Rex Alan Smith, *One Last Look: A Sentimental Journey to the Eighth Air Force Heavy Bomber Bases of World War II in England* (1983); Barbara Klaw, *Camp Follower: The Story of a Soldier's Wife* (1944); John Keegan, *The Second World War* (1990); John Keegan and Richard Holmes, *Soldiers: A History of Men in Battle* (1986); Judy Barrett Litoff, David C. Smith, Barbara Woodall Taylor, Charles E. Taylor, *Miss You: The World War II Letters of Barbara Woodall Taylor and Charles E. Taylor* (1990); Norman Mailer, *The Naked and the Dead* (1948; repr. 1968); William Manchester, *Goodbye, Darkness: A Memoir of the Pacific War* (1980); Bill Mauldin, *Up Front* (1945; repr. 1968); Audie Murphy, *To Hell and Back* (1949); Ernie Pyle, *Here Is Your War* (1943); and E. B. Sledge, *With the Old Breed: At Peleliu and Okinawa* (1981).

There are no thorough studies of Mexican Americans in the war. Stanley Steiner, *La Raza: The Mexican Americans* (1970); and Robert C. Jones, *Mexican War Workers in the United States* (1945), offer starting points in Hispanic history. The best study of native Americans is Alison R. Bernstein, *American Indians and World War II* (1991). Also, see John Collier, "The Indian in a Wartime Nation," *Annals of the American Academy of Political and Social Sciences*, 223 (1942); and Alvin M. Josephy, Jr., *Now That the Buffalo's Gone: A Study of Today's Indians* (1982). Good starting points for blacks and the military include Neil A. Wynn, *The Afro-American and the Second World War* (1976); together with Jack D. Foner, *Blacks and the Military in American History* (1974). See also Robert W. Mullen, *Blacks in America's Wars* (1973); and Ulysses Lee, *The Employment of Negro Troops* (1966). Students should try to see the War Department's film, *The Negro Soldier*, released in 1943 as part of Frank Capra's *Why We Fight* series and available on VHS videocassette. Aimed at encouraging black support for the war, the film avoids the problem of race in American society. Racial hostility as a factor adding ferocity to the war is dealt with in John W. Dower, *War Without Mercy: Race and Power in the Pacific War* (1986).

The history of homosexuals receives thorough treatment in Allan Bérubé, *Coming Out Under Fire: The History of Gay Men and Women in World War Two* (1990). Charles Jackson, *The Fall of Valor* (1946), gives a feel for how the mainstream saw homosexuals. In this novel, a male professor (in the humanities, suspect as effeminate) is ruined after making a sexual advance toward a marine officer on leave.

Histories of American women that discuss their role in the war machine include Karen Anderson, *Wartime Women: Sex Roles, Family Relations, and the Status of Women During World War II* (1981); D'Ann Campbell, *Women at War with America; Private Lives in a Patriotic Era* (1984); Sherna Berger Gluck, *Rosie the Riveter Revisited: Women, the War, and Social Change* (1988); and Susan M. Hartmann, *The Home Front and Beyond: American Women in the 1940s* (1982). Particularly relevant here is Maureen Honey, "The 'Womanpower' Campaign: Advertising and Recruitment Propaganda During World War II," *Frontiers: A Journal of Women Studies* 6 (Spring–Summer 1981). A typical view of Nazi efficiency in herding women together for work and breeding is contained in the 1937 novel by Katharine Burdekin, *Swastika Night* (repr. 1985). A more realistic assessment of relative efficiency in utilizing female resources is Leila J. Rupp, *Mobilizing Women for War: German and American Propaganda, 1939–1945* (1978).

five
Overseas

John Costello, *Virtue under Fire: How World War II Changed Our Social and Sexual Attitudes* (1985), is excellent on GI mores abroad. Graham Smith, *When Jim Crow Met John Bull* (1987), examines the racial clash in Britain. James Michener's *Tales of the South Pacific* (1947) is useful for the Asian theater. Frank Gervasi, *The Violent Decade: A Foreign Correspondent in Europe, Asia, and the Middle East, 1935–1945* (1989); and Eric Sevareid, *Not So Wild a Dream* (1969), were shrewd observers of the American impact overseas. Studs Terkel's *"The Good War": An Oral History of World War Two* (1985) has interviews with MPs and others who had an inside view of military life abroad. The War Department pamphlets giving direction to GIs going abroad are revealing, e.g., *A Short Guide to Great Britain* (1942). Elfrieda Berthiaume Shukert and Barbara Smith Scibetta, *War*

Brides of World War II (1989), look at how the GI appeared to foreign civilians. Two recent movies deal dramatically with GIs overstepping the bounds of social restraint while overseas. *Death of a Soldier* (1986) follows a sex offender in Australia. *Chicago Joe and the Showgirl* (1990) is about a GI gangster and his female accomplice in wartime London.

The two seminal contemporary studies of Americans in combat are Samuel A. Stouffer, *The American Soldier*, volume 1, *Adjustment During Army Life*; volume 2, *Combat and Its Aftermath* (1949; repr. 1965); and S. L. A. Marshall, *Men Against Fire* (1947). Their findings are endorsed in two fine later studies: Richard Holmes, *Acts of War: The Behavior of Men in Battle* (1986); and John Ellis, *The Sharp End: The Fighting Man in World War II* (1980). Students should also know John Keegan's pioneering work on the nature of combat in general, called *The Face of Battle* (1976). Also see Keegan and Richard Holmes with John Gau, *Soldiers: A History of Men in Battle* (1986); and Martin Van Creveld, *Fighting Power: German and U.S. Army Performance, 1939–1945* (1982).

There are numerous personal accounts of combat. Anthologies include Annette Tapert, ed., *Lines of Battle: Letters of American Servicemen, 1941–1945* (1987); and Paul Fussell, ed., *The Norton Book of Modern War* (1991). Other useful general sources include Edward K. Eckert, *In War and Peace: An American Military History Anthology* (1990); Paul Fussell, *Wartime: Understanding and Behavior in the Second World War* (1989); James Jones, *WWII* (1975); and Geoffrey Perret, *A Country Made by War* (1989). Accounts by outstanding war reporters include Martha Gellhorn, *The Face of War* (1967); Bill Mauldin, *Up Front* (1945; repr. 1968); John Steinbeck, *Once There Was a War* (1958; repr. 1961); and Ernie Pyle, *Brave Men* (1944; repr. 1974); and Pyle's *Here Is Your War* (1943). Harry Brown's *A Walk in the Sun* (1944; repr. 1985) gives the best description of a day in the life of a combat infantryman. Charles A. Lindbergh carefully describes the war on all fronts in *The Wartime Journals* (1970). One of the best GI poets is Louis Simpson; he wrote *A Dream of Governors* (1959) and *Selected Poems* (1965). J. Glenn Gray's *The Warriors: Reflections on Men in Battle* (1959; repr. 1970), the memoir of an intelligence officer, is unusual for its philosophical framework.

The mistaken belief that psychological casualties were weaklings is expounded in Edward A. Strecker, *Their Mothers' Sons: The Psychiatrist Examines an American Problem* (1946; repr. 1951); and George S. Patton, Jr., *War as I Knew It* (1947). Ladislas Farago comments on Patton's attitude in *Patton: Ordeal and Triumph* (1966). Dixon Wecter talked to emotionally damaged veterans and gives us an account in *When Johnny Comes Marching Home* (1944; repr. 1970).

Audie Murphy was honest and informative in describing fighting in southern Europe in *To Hell and Back* (1949). Mitchell Goodman's novel *The End of It* (1961) also gives an excellent feel for ground fighting in Italy. Two recent works built on first-person accounts of fighting in northern Europe are Cecil B. Currey, *Follow Me and Die: The Destruction of an American Division in World War II* (1984); and John Colby, *War from the Ground Up: The Ninetieth Division in WWII* (1991). I also found very useful Judy Barnett Litoff, David C. Smith, Barbara Woodall Taylor, and Charles E. Taylor, *Miss You: The World War II Letters of Barbara Woodall Taylor and Charles E. Taylor* (1990). Minor sources for the European war include H. Lew Wallace and William R. Burns, "From the 'Bulge' to Dresden: A Soldier's Odyssey," *Perspectives in History* 1 (Spring 1986); and Dan Decker, "Transcript of an interview with Bob Calahan and Art Crosswait, Veterans of the Seventy-Eighth Artillery Battalion of the Second Armored Division, December 8, 1989," Oral History Archive, Northern Kentucky University.

The classic memoirs of Pacific theater combat are William Manchester, *Goodbye, Darkness: A Memoir of the Pacific War* (1980); and E. B. Sledge, *With the Old Breed: At Pelelui and Okinawa* (1981). I also found Roger Hilsman, *My War Behind Japanese Lines* (1990), very good on jungle warfare. Important autobiographical novels include James Jones, *The Thin Red Line* (1962); and Norman Mailer, *The Naked and the Dead* (1948; repr. 1968). John Hersey, *Into the Valley: A Skirmish of the Marines* (1943; repr. 1970); and Richard Tregaskis, *Guadalcanal Diary* (1943), reflect the immediate reaction of GIs to the Japanese enemy.

Philip Kaplan and Rex Alan Smith, *One Last Look: A Sentimental Journey to the Eighth Air Force Heavy Bomber Bases of World War II* (1983), has a wealth of useful reminiscence by survivors of the air war. William R. Cubbins, *The War of the Cottontails: A Bomber Pilot with the Fifteenth Air Force* (1989), is also very informative. Students should take seriously John Heller's fictionalized account of air warfare *Catch-22* (1961) and not treat it simply as black comedy. On the air war in the Pacific, see *Goodbye to Some* (1961) by Gordon Forbes, a naval pilot. Brian Garfield, *The Thousand-Mile War: World War II in Alaska and the Aleutians* (1969; repr. 1982), deals with the difficulties of flying in an inhospitable region. *The Memphis Belle*, a 1943 color documentary shot by a film crew that went on the Belle's last mission over Fortress Europe, has good combat footage and is available on videocassette. I do not recommend the 1990 fictionalized *Memphis Belle*.

James J. Weingartner, "Massacre at Biscari: Patton and an American War Crime," *Historian* 52 (November 1989), deals with an incident of prisoner execution. Paul Fussell talks candidly about abuse of the enemy dead in *Thank God for the Atom Bomb and Other Essays* (1988). The mutual racial antipathy in the Pacific is analyzed in John W. Dower, *War Without Mercy: Race and Power in the Pacific War* (1986). The Japanese brutality that provoked Allied retaliation is described in, for example, M. L. Lawton, *Some Survived* (1984); and in S. L. Falk, *Bataan: The March of Death* (1962). James J. Fahey's memoir of sea warfare, *Pacific War Diary, 1942–1945* (1974), graphically describes the kamikaze attacks and the resulting Allied conviction that the Japanese did not think about death in a normal way.

Other sources are Russell Baker, *Growing Up* (1982; repr. 1984); D'Ann Campbell, *Women at War with America: Private Lives in a Patriotic Era* (1984); Walter White, *A Rising Wind* (1945; repr. 1971); and Herman Wouk, *The Caine Mutiny* (1951; repr. 1973).

six
Home Front Change

The histories of the domestic scene that I found most valuable are Allan M. Winkler, *Home Front U.S.A.: America During World War II* (1986); Gerald D. Nash, *The Great Depression and World War II: Organizing America, 1933–1945* (1979); and John Morton Blum, *V Was for Victory: Politics and American Culture During World War II* (1976). Other general studies include Richard Polenberg, *War and Society: The United States, 1941–1945* (1972); Richard Polenberg, ed., *America at War: The Home Front, 1941–1945* (1968); Richard R. Lingeman, *Don't You Know There's a War On? The American Home Front, 1941–1945* (1970); Geoffrey Perrett, *Days of Sadness, Years of Triumph: The American People, 1939–1945* (1973); and James L. Abrahamson, *The American Home Front* (1983). For the retrospections of participants, Studs Terkel's *"The Good War": An Oral History of World War Two* (1985) is again indispensable.

In developing my views on why World War II provided no magic formula for economic success, I used the materials on the costs of wars in Keith L. Nelson, ed., *The Impact of War on American Life: The Twentieth-Century Experience* (1971); Henry C. Murphy, *The National Debt in War and Transition* (1950); and James L. Clayton, "Vietnam:

The 200 Year Mortgage," *Nation* 208 (May 1969). During the Gulf War, many popular journals carried good economic analyses. See, for instance, Jane Bryant Quinn in *Newsweek*, January 28, 1991, and February 4, 1991.

The dislocation caused by wartime change is analyzed in John Costello, *Virtue Under Fire: How World War II Changed Our Social and Sexual Attitudes* (1985); and Francis Merrill, *The War and Social Problems on the Home Front* (1948). On population movement, see Henry S. Shyrock, Jr., and Hope T. Eldridge, "Internal Migration in Peace and War," *American Sociological Review* 12 (1947). One of the best intimate accounts of migrant life is Harriette Arnow's fictionalized treatment, *The Dollmaker* (1954), about an Appalachian family in Detroit.

On racial problems and the start of the civil rights movement, see Richard Dalfiume, "The Forgotten Years of the Negro Revolution," *Journal of American History* 55 (June 1968); Bruce Tyler, "The Black Double V Campaign for Racial Democracy During World War II," *Journal of Kentucky Studies* 8 (Sept. 1991); and Walter White, *A Rising Wind* (1945; repr. 1971). On the Detroit riot, see Robert Shogan and Tom Craig, *The Detroit Race Riot: A Study in Violence* (1964); Dominic J. Capeci, Jr., and Martha Wilkerson, *Layered Violence: The Detroit Rioters of 1943* (1991); and Alfred McClung Lee and Norman D. Humphrey, *Race Riot* (1943).

On the treatment of Japanese Americans, good accounts include Roger Daniels, *Concentration Camps U.S.A.: Japanese Americans and World War II* (1971); Michi Weglyn, *Years of Infamy: The Untold Story of America's Concentration Camps* (1976); and Bill Hosokawa, *Nisei: The Quiet Americans* (1969). Students should also see the recent evocative movie interpretation, *Come See the Paradise* (1990), available on videocassette.

The plight of army wives was described graphically during the war by Barbara Klaw in *Camp Follower: The Story of a Soldier's Wife* (1944). Also see the excellent oral histories in Elfrieda Berthiaume Shukert and Barbara Smith Scibetta, *War Brides of World War II* (1989). On the drive to get women into the labor force, see Maureen Honey, "The 'Womanpower' Campaign: Advertising and Recruitment Propaganda During World War II," *Frontiers: A Journal of Women Studies* 6 (Spring–Summer 1981). Edward A. Strecker criticizes women for smothering their children in *Their Mothers' Sons: The Psychiatrist Examines an American Problem* (1946; repr. 1951). Excellent recent histories of women in the war include Karen Anderson, *Wartime*

Bibliographical Essay

Women: Family Relations and the Status of Women During World War II (1981); D'Ann Campbell, *Women at War with America: Private Lives in a Patriotic Era* (1984); Sherna Berger Gluck, *Rosie the Riveter Revisited: Women, the War, and Social Change* (1988); Susan M. Hartman, *The Home Front and Beyond: American Women in the 1940s* (1982); and Leila J. Rupp, *Mobilizing Women for War: German and American Propaganda, 1939–1945* (1978).

Two foreign visitors who made acute observations on the tenor of American life in the period were Geoffrey Gorer, *The Americans: A Study in National Character* (1948); and Antoine de Saint-Exupéry, *Wartime Writings, 1939–1944* (1986). For the Depression's impact on family life and the war generation, see Glen H. Elder, Jr., *Children of the Great Depression: Social Change in Life Experience* (1974). Tennessee Williams treated imaginatively the loss of male role models and the sense of adolescent drifting in *The Glass Menagerie* (1944).

Fear of rising delinquency during the war is traced in the first chapters of James Gilbert, *A Cycle of Outrage: America's Reaction to the Juvenile Delinquent in the 1950s* (1986). Unfortunately, the best study of teen life during the war is not widely available. It is an unpublished Ph.D. thesis by Richard M. Ugland, "The Adolescent Experience During World War II: Indianapolis as a Case Study," Indiana University, 1977. Adolescent behavior and educational failure were scathingly attacked in Philip Wylie, *Generation of Vipers* (1942; repr. 1955). Colin Shindler looks at the movie theater and cultural change in *Hollywood Goes to War: Films and American Society, 1939–1952* (1979).

Sharp criticisms of secondary and higher education are leveled in David L. Cohn, "Should Fighting Men Think?" *Saturday Review of Literature*, January 18, 1947. The military's impact on the universities is documented in "Report of Committee A on 'Academic Freedom and Tenure' for 1943," *Bulletin of the American Association of University Professors* 30 (1944).

Frank W. Fox analyzes business use of the war to sell products and the direct link between freedom and consumerism in *Madison Avenue Goes to War: The Strange Military Career of American Advertising, 1941–45* (1975). On labor and the war, see Martin Glaberman, *Wartime Strikes* (1980); and Nelson Lichtenstein, *Labor's War at Home: The CIO in World War II* (1982).

Other sources are John Ellis, *The Sharp End: The Fighting Man in World War II* (1980); Frank Gervasi, *The Violent Decade: A Foreign Correspondent in Europe, Asia, and The Middle East, 1935–1945* (1989); Judy Barrett Litoff, David S. Smith, Barbara Woodall Taylor, and

Charles E. Taylor, *Miss You: The World War II Letters of Barbara Woodall Taylor and Charles E. Taylor* (1990); and Eric Sevareid, *Not So Wild a Dream* (1969).

seven

A New World

Paul Fussell's thoughts on the war are contained in *Thank God for the Atom Bomb and Other Essays* (1988); and *Wartime: Understanding and Behavior in the Second World War* (1989). On Japanese war crimes trials, see R. H. Minear, *Victor's Justice* (1971); A. Brackman, *The Other Nuremberg* (1987); and A. F. Reel, *The Case of General Yamashita* (1949). Also see Douglas MacArthur, *Reminiscences* (1964). James Bacque's accusations are in *Other Losses: An Investigation into the Mass Deaths of German Prisoners at the Hands of the French and Americans After World War II* (1989). Stephen E. Ambrose replies in the *New York Times Book Review*, "Ike and the Disappearing Atrocities," February 24, 1991. The controversy continues in the "Letters" section of the April 14, 1991, edition. John Horne Burnes, *The Gallery* (1947), gives excellent sketches of soldiers and civilians in occupied Naples. Graham Greene's novel *The Third Man* (1949) was made into a fine film starring Orson Welles.

A typical example of a WWII assassination is described in Callum MacDonald, *The Killing of SS Obergruppenfuhrer Reinhard Heydrich* (1989). Edna St. Vincent Millay's poem, *The Murder of Lidice* (1942), describes Heydrich as a werewolf who "howls in his tomb...And scratches the earth from his grave away." The American killing of Admiral Isoroku Yamamoto in 1943, though controversial at the time, similarly pointed the way to postwar covert operations. William Casey is a good example of an OSS officer who continued a career in covert operations after the war. He became head of the CIA and was involved in Iran-contra, dying just as that episode became public; see his *The Secret War Against Hitler* (1988). On possible war crimes in Vietnam, see Telford Taylor, *Nuremberg and Vietnam: An American Tragedy* (1970).

On American-Soviet relations and the coming of the cold war, see Daniel Yergin, *The Shattered Peace: The Origins of the Cold War and the National Security State* (1977); John L. Gaddis, *The United States and the Origins of the Cold War, 1941–1947* (1972); Louis J. Halle, *The Cold War as History* (1967); and Lynn Etheridge Davis, *The Cold War Begins: Soviet-American Conflict over Eastern Europe* (1974). FDR's relationship with the Russians is deftly covered in Edward M. Bennett,

Franklin D. Roosevelt and the Search for Victory: American-Soviet Relations, 1939–1945 (1990). On American distrust of European liberationists, see Milton Viorst, *Hostile Allies: FDR and Charles DeGaulle* (1965); and Dorothy S. White, *Seeds of Discord: DeGaulle, Free France, and the Allies* (1964). There are some provocative ideas on the nature of the postwar world in Carl N. Degler, *Out of Our Past: The Forces That Shaped Modern America* (rev. ed. 1970), 414–65.

On the A-bomb and diplomatic relations, see Barton J. Bernstein, *The Atomic Bomb: The Critical Issues* (1976); Michael S. Sherry, *Preparing for the Next War: American Plans for Postwar Defense, 1941–45* (1977); Sherry, *The Rise of American Air Power: The Creation of Armageddon* (1987); H. Bruce Franklin, *War Stars: The Superweapon and the American Imagination* (1988); Ronald Schaffer, *Wings of Judgment: American Bombing in World War II* (1985); and Martin J. Sherwin, *A World Destroyed: The Atomic Bomb and the Grand Alliance* (1975; repr. 1977).

On the conservative reaction in American politics, see John Morton Blum, *V Was for Victory: Politics and American Culture During World War II* (1976). John Roy Carlson's book, *Under Cover* (1943), has not been reprinted but can be obtained in major libraries or through interlibrary loan. On the costs of the arms race and superpower status, see Paul Kennedy, *The Rise and Fall of the Great Powers* (1987).

On the movement to suburbia, see Elaine Tyler May, *Homeward Bound: American Families in the Cold War Era* (1988). The powerful postwar image of the full-time mother contrasted with wartime attacks on "momism" in works like Edward A. Strecker, *Their Mothers' Sons: The Psychiatrist Examines an American Problem* (1946; repr. 1951). See also John Costello, *Virtue Under Fire: How World War II Changed Our Social and Sexual Attitudes* (1985). Works dealing with the problems faced by working women include D'Ann Campbell, *Women at War with America: Private Lives in a Patriotic Era* (1984); Karen Anderson, *Wartime Women: Sex Roles, Family Relations, and the Status of Women During World War II* (1981); and Susan M. Hartmann, *The Home Front and Beyond: American Women in the 1940s* (1982).

On African-Americans and the pursuit of equality, see James Baldwin, *The Fire Next Time* (1962; repr. 1964); Richard M. Dalfiume, *Desegregation of the United States Armed Forces: Fighting on Two Fronts, 1939–1953* (1969); Jack D. Foner, *Blacks and the Military in American History: A New Perspective* (1974); and Bruce Tyler, "The Black Double V Campaign for Racial Democracy During World War II," *Journal of Kentucky Studies* 8 (Sept. 1991). On homosexuals and civil rights, see Allan Bérubé, *Coming Out Under Fire: The History of Gay Men and Women in World War Two* (1990).

On anti-Semitism and American policy toward Hitler's victims, see David S. Wyman, *The Abandonment of the Jews: America and the Holocaust, 1941–1945* (1984); Haskel Lookstein, *Were We Our Brothers' Keepers? The Public Response of American Jews to the Holocaust, 1938–1944* (1985); Arthur D. Morse, *While Six Million Died: A Chronicle of American Apathy* (1968); and Richard L. Rubenstein, *The Cunning of History: The Holocaust and the American Future* (1987). Varied American reactions to the Holocaust appear in Robert H. Abzug, *Inside the Vicious Heart: Americans and the Liberation of Nazi Concentration Camps* (1987). A good example of how Americans became sympathetic toward the Germans is Raymond F. Toliver and Trevor J. Constable, *The Blond Knight of Germany* (1985). The subject of this adulatory biography, German air ace Erich Hartmann, fought on Germany's eastern front. Also see Ladislas Farago, *Patton: Ordeal and Triumph* (1966), on Patton's attitude; and comments on the American occupation of Germany in Bernt Englemann, *In Hitler's Germany: Daily Life in the Third Reich* (1986).

On the G.I. Bill, see Richard Severo and Lewis Milford, *The Wages of War: When America's Soldiers Came Home* (1990); and Dixon Wecter, *When Johnny Comes Marching Home* (1944; repr. 1970). Other sources cited in the text are David R. Segal, *Recruiting for Uncle Sam: Citizenship and Military Manpower Policy* (1989); and James L. Clayton, "Vietnam: The 200 Year Mortgage," *Nation*, May 26, 1969. Two fine 1946 films address the GI's adjustment problems: John Huston's documentary about psychologically damaged men, *Let There Be Light*; and *The Best Years of Our Lives*, a fictional treatment of three veterans' situations. *Maria's Lovers* (1984) brilliantly portrays the damage to a veteran's marriage brought on by his experience as a prisoner of war. The difficulties for veterans' wives is dealt with in Susan M. Hartmann, "Prescriptions for Penelope: Literature on Women's Obligations to Returning World War II Veterans," *Women's Studies* 5 (1978). On overseas marriages, see Elfrieda Berthiaume Shukert and Barbara Smith Scibetta, *War Brides of World War II* (1989).

Among the minor sources on veterans are Sean Hennessey, "Oral History Interview with his mother, May 1991," transcript in possession of the author; and John P. DeMarcus, Jr., "World War II Experiences of W. Frank Steely," *Perspectives in History* 2 (Spring 1986). Steely, a professor and university president, says that the G.I. Bill "was an opportunity to expand one's horizons and to become exposed to various academic and scholarly pursuits." If it were not for the war, "he probably would not have left the fairly isolated Kentucky environment in which he was raised" (20). Other sources on veterans' adjustment problems are Studs Terkel, *"The Good War": An Oral History of World War Two* (1985); Samuel Stouffer, *The American Soldier*, 2 volumes (1949; repr. 1965); J. Glen Gray, *The Warriors: Reflections on Men in Battle* (1959; repr. 1970); Roger Hilsman, *American Guerrilla: My War Behind Japanese Lines* (1990); James Jones, *The Thin Red Line* (1962); Jones, *WWII* (1975); John Keegan, *Six Armies in Normandy* (1983); Judy Barrett Litoff, David C. Smith, Barbara Woodall Taylor, and Charles E. Taylor, *Miss You: The World War II Letters of Barbara Woodall Taylor and Charles E. Taylor* (1990); William Manchester, *Goodbye, Darkness: A Memoir of the Pacific War* (1980); Audie Murphy, *To Hell and Back* (1949); E. B. Sledge, *With The Old Breed: At Peleliu and Okinawa* (1981); and John M. Wright, Jr., *Captured on Corregidor: Diary of an American P.O.W. in World War II* (1988).

On how the war narrowed individual freedom and enhanced illiberal tendencies in America, see Richard Polenberg, "The Good War? A Reappraisal of How World War II Affected American Society." *Virginia Magazine of History and Biography* 100:3 (July 1992). In 1954 Herman Wouk's *The Caine Mutiny* (1951; repr. 1973) was made into a fine movie, starring Humphrey Bogart as Captain Queeg. William H. Whyte's strictures are in *The Organization Man* (1956; repr. 1972). David Riesman, et al., *The Lonely Crowd: A Study of Changing American Character* (1950; repr. 1961), describes the "other-directed" personality. Anne Frank's *The Diary of a Young Girl* (1947) became the basis for a 1959 play and a moving 1980 film titled *The Diary of Anne Frank*. *Sands of Iwo Jima* (1949) is available in most video stores. Philip Caputo's experiences are described in his *A Rumor of War* (1977).

Other sources are Frank Gervasi, *The Violent Decade: A Foreign Correspondent in Europe, Asia, and the Middle East, 1935–1945* (1989); Gary R. Hess, *The United States at War, 1941–1945* (1986); Eric Sevareid, *Not So Wild a Dream* (1969); and Barbara W. Tuchman, *The March of Folly: From Troy to Vietnam* (1984).

Index

Abyssinia, 35, 36
Adolescents, impact of war on, 125–29
Advertising, 73–75, 130
African-Americans. *See* Black soldiers
Airmen: combat experience of, 109–10; superstitions of, 108–9
Alcohol consumption, 94
Allied forces: bombing by, 53–55; D-Day invasion, 55–57
Amazing Stories, 9
Ambrose, Stephen E., 138
America. *See* United States
American Way of War, The (Weigley), 55
Andrews, Maxene, 129
Andrews Sisters, 129
Appeasement, 2, 5, 21
Arcadia Conference, 48
Asia, British interests in, 35
Atomic bomb, 66–67
Austro-Hungarian empire, 23
Axis forces, defeat of, 47–53, 55–57

Bacque, James, 137–38
Badoglio, Pietro, 141
Baker, Russell, 6
Baker, Stan, 148
Baldwin, James, 146
Barbie, Klaus, 147
Bataan, 12
Berlin, Irving, 12
Bilbo, Theodore, 145
Black, Timuel, 101
Black soldiers, 9, 77–78, 83–84, 93, 122
Bohlen, Charles, 140–41
Bolsheviks, 23
Bombing attacks, 53–55, 65–67
Born on the Fourth of July (Kovic), 15
Bradley, Omar, 57, 97
Britain: Asian interests of, 35; Battle of, 46–47; after World War I, 25. *See also* Royal Air Force

Brown, Harry, 92
Bureaucracy, 75–79, 153
Burns, John Horne, 138
Bush, George, 4, 16, 114, 115, 152

Caine Mutiny, The (Wouk), 153–54
Caputo, Philip, 154–55
Carlson, John, 16–17
Carlson, John Roy, 143
Catch-22 (Heller), 138
Censorship, 9–10
Chamberlain, Neville, 38, 39
Chiang Kai-shek, 40, 62, 143
China, Japanese expansion into, 28–29, 30, 35, 40–41
Churchill, Winston, 5, 35, 51, 141
Clark, Mark, 10, 102
Coca-Cola, 118
Cohn, David L., 88
Combat: for airmen, 108–10; mental breakdowns in, 53, 95–97, 112–13; reality of, 94–113
Concentration camps, 33
Conroy, John J., 113
Conscientious objectors, 77–78
Costello, Eddie, 113
Costello, John, 73
Coughlin, Charles E., 146
Cronkite, Walter, 9
Crosby, Bing, 12
Cubbins, William R., 157
Cunning, Sheril, 146
Curti, Merle, 75–76
Czechoslovakia 24, 37, 39, 156

Darlan, Jean-François, 141
Dawes, Charles G., 24
Dawes Plan, 24, 25, 26
Dawson, Geoffrey, 34
D-Day invasion, 49, 55–57
"Death of the Ball Turret Gunner, The" (Jarrell), 17

Index

DeChick, Joe, 8
De Gaulle, Charles, 141
Denmark, 45
Depression, The, 29–30
Diary of a Young Girl, The (Frank), 154
Dietrich, Marlene, 140
Divine, David, 68
Dönitz, Karl, 54
Double Indemnity, 144
Draft, military, 76–79
Drug use, 94
Dunkirk, France, 45–46
Dupuy, Trevor N., 79

Eakin, Ira, 110
Eden, Anthony, 41
Eisenhower, Dwight D., 10, 49, 138
Ellis, John, 7
England. *See* Britain
Enigma coding system, 46
Equal Rights Amendment, 132
Estonia, 45
Exclusion Act, 29

Fair Employment Practices Committee, 119–20
Fall of Valor, The (Jackson), 77
Farewell to Arms, A (Hemingway), 27, 36
Fascism, 28, 32
Fighting Power (Van Creveld), 79–81
Films. *See* Movies
Finland, 44–45
Firestone Corporation, 36
Flamethrowers, 74
Foreign Affair, A, 140
For Whom the Bell Tolls (Hemingway), 36
Four Freedoms, 136
France: relationship with Germany, 36–37; after World War I, 25, 35
Franco, Francisco, 20, 36
Frank, Anne, 154
Franklin, H. Bruce, 154
Fraser, Evelyn, 86
Freikorps, 24
Fussell, Paul, 94, 137

Galbraith, John Kenneth, 131
Gallery, The (Burns), 138
Garcia, John, 149

Garson, Greer, 70
Gellhorn, Martha, 36, 105
Generation of Vipers (Wylie), 8
Germany: air force, 38; defeat of, 55–58; depression in, 30; invasion of Poland, 43–44; Nazi movement, 30–35; relationship with France, 36–37; relationship with Italy, 36; reparations extracted from, 23–24, 26; after World War I, 24–25
Gervasi, Frank, 138
GI Bill, 145, 151–53
Goebbels, Joseph, 33
Gorer, Geoffrey, 124, 125
Gray, J. Glenn, 101, 150
Great Britain. *See* Britain
Greene, Graham, 138
Gulf War, 4–5, 154; compared with World War II, 115–17

Hanley, Joe, 87
Hearst, William Randolph, 34
Heller, Joseph, 107, 138
Hemingway, Ernest, 27, 36
Hersey, John, 66
Heydrich, Reinhard, 139
Hilsman, Roger, 6
Hirohito, Emperor, 20
Hiroshima, Japan, 66, 67
Hiroshima (Hersey), 66
Hispanic workers, 120
Hitler, Adolf, 1, 4, 5, 20, 21, 25; aggression of, 39–40, 58, 146; as evil, 6; as German leader, 30–35, 37
Ho Chi Minh, 142
Holland, 45
Homosexuals, 8, 123, 145; in military, 78–79, 84–85, 145
Horne, Lena, 122
Housing shortages, 119
Hyams, Joe, 4

Immigration Act of 1924, 147
Infantrymen, 86–87, 104
Isolationism, 26
Italy: air force, 38; relationship with Germany, 36; after World War I, 27–28; in World War II, 49–51
Iwo Jima, 65

Index

Jackson, Charles, 77
Japan: aggression of, 59–61; atrocities of, 111–12; attack on Pearl Harbor, 47, 60; defeat of, 62–68; expansion into China, 28–29, 30, 35, 40–41; foreign policy of, 40–42; racial stereotyping of, 61; rise to world power, 28–30; soldiers as victims, 112
Japanese-Americans, 120–21
Jarrell, Randall, 17
Jews, 146–47, 154
Jim Crow laws, 122
Johnson, Lyndon B., 3
Jones, James, 7, 15, 105, 150, 153
Juvenile delinquency, 125–29, 132

Kamikaze attacks, 65
Kaye, Danny, 12
Kennedy, John F., 138–39, 155
Klausner, Marty, 145
Kovic, Ron, 15

LaRocque, Gene, 4, 100
Latvia, 45
Laws, Victor, 5
Leacock, Richard, 88
League of Nations, 25, 26, 35–36
Le May, Curtis, 65
Lend-lease Act, 46–47, 71, 140–41
Lesbians, 84. See also Homosexuals
Let There Be Light, 14
Lifeboat, 12
Lindbergh, Charles A., 38
Lithuania, 45
Longest Day, The, 14
Lynch, Charles, 9

MacArthur, Douglas, 8, 10, 60, 63–64, 137
McEnroe, Tim, 4
McFadden, Don, 120
McKeown, Bob, 5
McMurray, Mike, 5
McNair, Leslie, 102
Mailer, Norman, 14, 107
Manchester, William, 89, 96–97, 107, 149
Manchuria, 28, 30, 35
Manhattan Project, 154
Mao Tse-tung, 142
Marcus, Joe, 141

Marshall, George C., 84, 136
Marshall Plan, 136
Mayer, Arno, 147
Medical care, 107
Mein Kampf (Hitler), 31
Memphis Belle, 3
Mental problems, related to war, 7, 53, 95–97, 112–13, 149–50
Messina, Italy, 51
Michener, James, A., 13
Military, U.S., 81–86, 91–94; alcohol consumption of, 94; blacks in, 82–84, 93; drug use, 94; homosexuals in, 84–85; ideological commitment of, 88–90; inefficiency of, 79–81, 98; infantry, 86–87; minorities in, 82–84; morale in, 86–89; psychiatric casualties, 95–97, 112–13, 149–50; sex in, 12, 93–94, 123; women in, 12, 85–86, 144–45
Millay, Edna St. Vincent, 139
Mitchell, Billy, 38
Modine, Matthew, 3
Montgomery, Bernard, 57
Moon Is Down, The, 12
Morris, James M., 54
Moscow Conference, 147
Movies, 11–12, 13–15
Murder in the Air, 16
Murphy, Audie, 14, 96, 111
Mussolini, Benito, 20, 27–28, 35, 36, 49
Myrdal, Gunnar, 120
Mythologizing of past, 1–2, 156–59

Nagasaki, Japan, 66, 67
Naked and the Dead, The, 14
Nazi movement, 30–35
Nazi-Soviet Nonaggression Pact, 40
Nimitz, Chester, 64, 65
Normandy Invasion, 10
North, Oliver L., 69
Norway, 45
Novak, William, 69
Nuclear weapons, 66–67, 141–42, 143–44, 154
Nuremberg trials, 148
Nye, Gerald P., 38

Okinawa, 63, 65
Omaha Beach, 55
Operation Barbarossa, 47

Index

Operation Torch, 49
Oremont, Lee, 129
Organized labor, 131
Ottoman empire, 22

Patton, George, 10, 14, 51, 58, 77, 81, 95–96, 111, 147
Pearl Harbor, 47, 60
Penicillin, 107
Persian Gulf crisis. *See* Gulf War
Philippines, MacArthur in, 64–65
Pius XI, Pope, 28
Poland, 39; German invasion of, 43–44
Postman Always Rings Twice, The, 144
Posttraumatic stress disorder, 7, 149
Propaganda, 73–75, 130
Pyle, Ernie, 12–13, 86, 88, 91, 101, 110, 138

Racial tensions, 82–83, 119–20, 122, 145–46. *See also* Black soldiers
Reader's Digest, 11, 147
Reagan, Ronald, 15–16
Remarque, Erich Maria, 32
Repplier, Theodore S., 130
Riesman, David, 153
Roehm, Ernst, 32
Rommel, Erwin, 49
Rooney, Andy, 4
Roosevelt, Franklin D., 36, 38, 140, 141, 143
Royal Air Force, 46, 53
Russia, revolution in, 22–23. *See also* Soviet Union

Saint-Exupéry, Antoine de, 128
Samuelson, Robert J., 158
Sands of Iwo Jima, 14, 15, 155
Schwarzkopf, Norman, 5
Scott, George C., 14
Segregation, 16. *See also* Racial tensions
Selective service. *See* Draft, military
Serviceman's Readjustment Act. *See* GI Bill
Sevareid, Eric, 9, 92, 125, 149
Sex in military, 12, 93–94. *See also* Homosexuals
Shirer, William L., 32
Sicily, 49–51
Simpson, Louis, 101
Sledge, Eugene B., 105, 149

Smoot-Hawley tariff, 30
Snaith, William, 110
Snipes, Macio, 146
Social Darwinism, 22
Solomon islands, 63
Somervell, Brehon B., 70
South Pacific, 13–14
Soviet Union: as ally of Britain and France, 39; contribution to war effort, 71–72; Hitler's invasion of, 40, 47; relationship with U.S., 139–43
Spain, 36
Spielberg, Steven, 19
Spock, Benjamin, 144
Stalin, Josef, 23, 39–40, 47, 139–40
Stein, Lisa, 5
Steinbeck, John, 9–10, 12, 82
Steward, Lowell, 145
Stewart, Kermit, 113
Stiles, Bert, 109
Stimson, Henry L., 84, 130, 139
Stouffer, Samuel A., 87
Sudetenland, 37

Tales of the South Pacific (Michener), 13
Talmadge, Eugene, 122
Taylor, Charles, 149
Taylor, Paul, 114
Taylor, Robert, 11
Thin Red Line, The, 14
Third Man, The (Greene), 138
Third Reich. *See* Germany; Hitler, Adolf
Thomas, Evan, 114, 115
Truman, Harry, 16, 66, 76, 143

U-boats, 49
Under Cover (Carlson), 143
Under Fire: An American Story (North), 69
Union of Soviet Socialist Republics. *See* Soviet Union
United Kingdom. *See* Britain
United States: industrial production, 70–73, 117–19; isolationism of, 26; neutrality of, 45; policy toward Japan, 41–42; relationship with Soviet Union, 138–43; role of, in World War II, 69–70; stock market crash, 26–27, 29–30. *See also* Military, U.S.

Index

Van Creveld, Martin, 79–81
Venereal disease, 94, 107, 124–25
Versailles Treaty, 23, 24
Veterans: benefits for, 151–53; emotional problems of, 7, 149–50
Victor Emmanuel III, 28
Victory Girls, 129
Vietnam war, 15, 148

Walk in the Sun, A, 14, 92
Wallace, Henry, 143
War criminals, 147–48
War Manpower Commission, 123
Watt, Robert J., 152
Wayne, John, 5, 14–15, 155
Weaponry, 71–72
Wecter, Dixon, 152
Weigley, Russell F., 55, 72
Welles, Sumner, 8, 142
Whyte, William H., 153–54
Wilhelm II, Kaiser, 23
Wills, Garry, 16
Wilson, Woodrow, 25
Women: in military, 12, 85–86, 144–45; in work force, 70, 123–24, 132–35, 144
World War I, aftermath of, 25–28
World War II: aftermath of, 137–39; Allied losses in, 53–54; American contribution to, 69-70, 90; Axis defeat in, 47–53; black soldiers in, 9, 77–78, 83–84, 93, 122; bombing in, 53–55; bureaucracy generated by, 75–79; causes of, 20–21; as compared with Gulf War, 115–17; D-Day invasion, 55–57; death rate, 6; delinquency during, 125–29; divorce rate, 123, 132, 151; economic impact, 6, 71, 115–19; as era of prosperity, 114–15, 136–37, 157–58; German offensive in, 43–47; historical roots of, 21–25; housing shortages, 119; impact on industry, 70–73; 117–20; Japanese defeat in, 63–68; medical advances during, 107; memorabilia, 2–3, 15; in the movies, 11–12, 13–15; mythologizing of, 2–19; Pacific campaigns, 6, 58–63; propaganda, 73–75, 130; psychiatric casualties, 7, 53, 95–97, 112–13, 149–50; public spending during, 117; reality of combat, 94–113; reporting of, 9–11, 12–13; Royal Air Force in, 46, 53; segregation in, 16, 119–20; social impact of, 8–9, 121–129; veterans of, 148–53; women in, 13, 85–86
Wouk, Herman, 92, 153
Wrigley's, 118
Write, John M., 150
Wylie, Philip, 8, 9, 125

Yamamoto, Isoroku, 61
Yamato (battleship), 65, 67

The American Moment
Stanley I. Kutler, Series Editor

The Twentieth-Century American City, 2d ed. by Jon C. Teaford

American Workers, American Unions, 1920–1985, 2d ed. by Robert H. Zieger

A House Divided: Sectionalism and Civil War, 1848–1865 by Richard H. Sewell

Liberty under Law: The Supreme Court in American Life by William M. Wiecek

Winning Is the Only Thing: Sports in America since 1945 by Randy Roberts and James Olson

America's Half Century: United States Foreign Policy in the Cold War, 2d ed. by Thomas J. McCormick

American Anti-Communism: Combating the Enemy Within, 1830–1970 by Michael J. Heale

The Culture of the Cold War by Stephen J. Whitfield

America's Welfare State: From Roosevelt to Reagan by Edward D. Berkowitz

The Debate over Vietnam, 2d ed. by David W. Levy

And the Crooked Places Made Straight: The Struggle for Social Change in the 1960s by David Chalmers

Medicine in America: A Short History by James H. Cassedy

The Republic of Mass Culture: Journalism, Filmmaking, and Broadcasting in America since 1941 by James L. Baughman

The Best War Ever: America and World War II by Michael C. C. Adams

Uneasy Partners: Big Business in American Politics, 1945–1990 by Kim McQuaid

America's Right Turn: From Nixon to Bush by William C. Berman

Industrializing America: The Nineteenth Century by Walter Licht

Moralists and Modernizers: America's Pre-Civil War Reformers by Steven Mintz

The Jacksonian Promise: American Society from 1815 to 1840 by Daniel Feller

Domestic Factors in the History of American Foreign Relations by Melvin Small